LOVELOCITY

Tales of Travel & Tropical Island Life

RACHEL LOVELOCK

2023

Cover Artwork by Hari Prast
Cover Graphic Design by Phil Stoodley

CONTENTS

For my late brother Jeremy
When I was twenty, you told me I should become a writer.
Thank you for believing in me, Jez, you are forever in my heart.

FOREWORD

Travel is in my blood…

My father began his working life as a merchant seaman. Later, he joined the RAF and flew Sunderland flying boats during World War II, before becoming a civil airline pilot. Naturally, he travelled all over the world. Outside of his work, my dad was an avid sailor, a navigator, and a writer. To me, his general knowledge appeared infinite, and if he didn't know the answer to any of my many questions, he would always look it up, very often in the Encyclopaedia Britannica.

My mother grew up in Gibraltar, Spain, Bermuda, and Malta. During the 1950s, she was occasionally, and casually, employed as an air hostess on some of my dad's flying trips. My mum was also an artist, an accomplished dressmaker, a superb swimmer, and a wonderful role model.

When I was young, my favourite storybook was a gorgeously-illustrated junior edition of the Arabian Nights; whose tales of desert kingdoms held a mysterious attraction for me. I viewed these chronicles through a hazy romanticised lens, which allowed my imagination to run wild. I also loved my parents' real life travel stories. For as long as I can remember, my mum and dad encouraged me to be a free spirit, and to travel.

I was blessed to have three gentle, caring, adventurous brothers, all a fair bit older than me. The eldest, Christopher, lived in the US for forty years. As a Harvard professor and a leading authority on service management, he would present seminars all over the world, and never missed an opportunity to extend his business trips so that he could visit family and friends in faraway places. He always made time for me, and his advice was invaluable; he was a wise and generous man. Initially, he spent two years in Montreal; and he set sail to his new home by ship. I remember when I was eight years old, my parents obtained special permission for me to take the day off school so that we could all go down to the Southampton docks to see him off. We then drove to a prominent vantage point from where we could watch the *cockpit-green* liner cruising out through the English Channel, and we could clearly see the white handkerchief that Christopher was waving from the top deck.

My father was so proud of him; to this day I remember his comment, 'Thank God, at least one of our children has found the spirit of adventure.'

My second brother, Roger, became a naval officer and also toured the world, voyaging to the exotic Far East and bringing me treasured gifts including a Chinese lantern and a paper parasol from Singapore, and a pair of wooden bobblehead nodding dolls from Hong Kong. Overseas postings took him and his family away to live in Sydney and then Oslo for a few years. Roger is multi-skilled at anything he turns his hand to, from engineering to carpentry, building and plumbing to gardening, and a whole lot more besides. He showed me how to change the oil and the sparkplugs in my car; he taught me to ski, and because he was a daredevil, he inspired me to be brave.

My youngest brother, Jeremy, was a bonafide hippie. He had long hair and wore a full beard and an Afghan coat; he lived on a commune in Switzerland and followed the hippie trail through Turkey, Iran, Afghanistan and Pakistan to India with a beautiful older woman. I idolised him, wanting to be a barefoot hippie too, yearning to wear a sarong and flowers in my hair. Jeremy was a musician and a songwriter, with a deep love for nature, photography and the arts. He had a special bond, a gift, with wild birds and animals. When he emigrated to Australia in 1974, a country that was to become his forever home, I remember feeling abandoned. All three of my brothers were now living overseas, and I missed them terribly.

My childhood dream was to live on a tropical island and become a travel writer. Instead, I followed the careers advice I'd been given at school and spent far too many years working for a corporate company in the UK, before jumping for joy at the fortuitous offer of a golden handshake.

Since 1998, I have been living my barefoot dream in Bali, wearing frangipani blossoms in my hair and writing about my island-home for international guidebooks, coffee table books and magazines, while exploring the far-flung reaches of the Indonesian archipelago to find inspiration for my travel writings.

Woven loosely around my life story, this book is a compilation of anecdotes and travel tales from heaven and from hell, as well as a narrative of the challenges, hurdles, friendships and love that I encountered and found on my journey to my new life. Despite this being a difficult and at times risky transition, I believe that anyone who is truly passionate about travelling or pursuing a bohemian overseas lifestyle will understand that we must take the rough with the smooth. Our bad experiences, our raw stupidity, the detrimental choices, and the mistakes that we make are all part of the learning process, teaching us to really appreciate the highs. And hey, it is those highpoints of our travel adventures, those magical chance encounters in exotic locations, serendipitous opportunities, out of the ordinary transformative experiences, and retrospectively hilarious disasters, which not only make the best dinner party stories but also prove to be the truly cherished moments that we never forget.

1
MINT TEA & MISTAKES IN MOROCCO
1979

Until I left school, all of my overseas holidays were, of course, dependent upon the whims and finances of my parents. Each trip served to fuel my passion for adventure, but my first non-family-influenced holiday abroad was like a virgin voyage of self-discovery. At the time, it was the most thrilling and dangerous journey of my life.

My flat-mate, Fiona, and I were students with overdrafts, but lack of money was not going to stop us from going interrailing around Europe during our summer holidays. The 'Interrail', all-you-can-ride, train travel pass offered an opportunity to notch up as many countries as possible in the four weeks we had available. It would be our first taste of backpacking abroad. We planned it carefully. Hours were spent poring over maps, guidebooks, and Cook's International Train Timetable, on the nylon carpet in front of the electric fire in our cold flat in Exeter. Train journeys, we decided, should be undertaken at night; this way we could save on travel time and also on the cost of accommodation. To our delight, Morocco was included in the list of countries that we were entitled to visit, despite not being part of Europe. I also wanted to catch up with a friend in France and my cousin in Italy; Fiona had a friend in Denmark and had re-established contact with a good-looking male pen pal in Switzerland. Our upcoming trip was full of promise and possibility.

I extended my overdraft and bought a rucksack but had to make do with my bulky padded sleeping bag, which took up too much precious space. Fiona's sleeping bag had been purchased from an army surplus store; waterproof and warm, complete with a hood, it could be condensed to the size of a fourteen-ounce baked bean can.

We set out on a wet afternoon in early August, laden with three days' worth of homemade Marmite sandwiches and bottled water drawn from the tap, aimed at reducing our initial expenditure on food and drink. We took the train to Weymouth and the ferry across the English Channel to France. This was long before the completion of the Channel Tunnel, but we made good time and full of *joie de vivre* we arrived in Paris, our first destination, at eight o'clock the following morning.

Our heavy rucksacks weighed us down, but we still walked for miles along the banks of the River Seine and ascended to the second level of the Eiffel Tower, which was as far as our stringent budget would allow. We went to the Louvre and paid homage to the Mona Lisa behind her protective glass. Of the eight-zillion people who visit the Louvre every day, ninety-nine percent of them are there to see the Mona Lisa, but they still make you go through forty-seven rooms to reach her. Montmartre was my favourite area. Set upon a hill 130 metres above the city, looking grandly out over all of Paris, it seemed to me to be the very essence of all things French, with umbrella-shaded street cafés and quaint bistros. Here, we glimpsed some *prostituées de jour*, soliciting lunchtime favours; they looked like caricatures clad in red satin and black lace. The artists, with their easels, paint-splattered smocks and black berets were equally cartoonish in appearance.

In the evening we caught the train to Madrid. As darkness fell, we sped past Spanish families, eating, drinking, and singing by lamplight on the verandas of their little houses beside the railway track. That night was the first time we crawled into our sleeping bags on the dirty floor of a carriage crowded with other young interrailers. It was way too uncomfortable and rather too intimate, but we made some new friends.

Madrid was sweltering, so we gave up on the idea of sightseeing. Instead, we took the advice of a local and spent the day at a swimming pool in the hills, a short regional train ride away. In the late afternoon, we boarded the slow train to Algeciras, a Spanish seaport facing the coast of Africa, and the gateway to Morocco – that Islamic land so rich in mystique. Our destination was Tangier, and we were heading for adventure.

The train was composed of traditional six-seater compartments with a side corridor running the length of each car. It was crowded but not, surprisingly, with other interrailers.

Every single one of the small compartments had been taken over by Moroccan families; nylon market bags and cardboard boxes blocked the luggage racks. They had hung their clothes over the doors and windows; we were far too intimidated to enter.

We moved up to the front end of the train and sat in the corridor at the junction between the first carriage and the engine. The train utilised an innovative system of air-conditioning, and certainly didn't conform to the European standards of safety, for every inward-opening door was wide open. We welcomed the cool fresh air.

Two Moroccan guys joined us. They were students at college in France, on their way home to Casablanca. The very name, Casablanca, evoked exotic images of smoky bars and Humphrey Bogart; and these two young men were also exotic, and gorgeous. They introduced themselves as Yassin and Said and invited us to play cards on the grimy deck. I was attracted to tall, dark Yassin, with his long black hair, while Fiona was drawn to smiling Said, who looked very cool in his strange baggy white Muslim clothes and knitted prayer cap. We sat up talking and laughing with them all night, and they invited us to travel with them to Casablanca and stay with their families. It was only the third day of our trip and things were already becoming very exciting.

The dawn broke to find Yassin and I sitting on the exterior steps of the open door of the train, speeding past bountiful fields of Spanish plum tomatoes and sweet cantaloupe melons. The crops were almost ready for harvesting and we could smell the sweet scent of the fruit on the wind. I forgot about my bank overdraft in rainy old England, I was really truly travelling, pursuing my passion, and never before had I felt so blissfully carefree.

The port of Algeciras was busy and stinky, Fiona and I were tired but elated and our flowing hippy skirts were dirty.

Fuelled with the thrill of anticipation, the four of us boarded the ferry to Tangier; most of the passengers were Moroccan apart from ourselves and maybe fifty other young backpackers. During the one-hour ferry ride, Yassin told me more about Casablanca. Porpoises danced alongside the bows of the ship and for the first time I saw the monolithic limestone promontory known as the Rock of Gibraltar, my mother's birthplace. As the town of Tangier loomed closer and closer, the foot passengers got ready to disembark, but ahead of us there seemed to be a problem. None of the other foreigners were being allowed off the boat. Puzzled and anxious we waited in line, but we too were given the same story by the immigration officials. We were not welcome in their country.

'We don't want your types in our country, you're just hippies, you're dirty, you're not going to be bringing any money into Morocco.'

Yassin and Said pleaded on our behalf but every time the answer was the same. We knew nothing about the conventions of corruption and didn't dare contemplate offering a bribe. Fiona and I hastily swapped addresses with the two young men who had become our friends and had promised us so much fun in Casablanca. Holding back the tears, we said our goodbyes. Together with all of the other backpackers on the ferry, we were ushered onto the upper deck, prohibited from entering Morocco. We retraced our voyage back to Spain, our dreams of adventure – and maybe love – in the mystical land of medinas, magic carpets, mosques and minarets had been shattered.

~*~

A fiery sun was setting over the Straits of Gibraltar, it was a spectacular sight, but Fiona and I could barely focus through our tears. Just twenty years old and convinced that I was in love with a boy I had known for less than twenty hours, I was in despair.

Many of the other backpackers, who had also been subjected to the same hostile treatment, said that they had lost all enthusiasm for visiting Morocco. Others, however, claimed they knew of another route into the country. Visions of swimming ashore under the cover of darkness, or illegally crossing the border from Algeria, scaling barbed wire fences, and dodging armed guards, danced around in my imagination. The plan was considerably less complex…

There is a Spanish exclave called Ceuta, an autonomous city administered by Spain, isolated on the Moroccan coast. Our fellow-backpackers suggested that this might be an easier point for crossing the border. With our hopes miraculously restored, we enthusiastically discussed our new plans with the fourteen Austrians and one Italian who were also game to give it a try. When we got back to the port of Algeciras, the Spanish officials were expecting us. This daily charade was part of a manipulative game, boosting the takings of the ferry company. We were ushered into the ticket office, where the waiting staff obliged us with tickets to Ceuta in exchange for more of our money. They held up the ferry for us, or so they led us to believe, and once again we were sea-borne, bound for another Moroccan border.

It was quite late when we arrived in Ceuta but once again the police were familiar with the procedure. The Austrians, the Italian, Fiona and I were allowed to spend the night in the police car park. Here, we entertained each other with travel stories, and Fiona became deeply engrossed in conversation with an Austrian boy called Yurgen. The night was balmy, and the sky was clear with a billion stars. The coarse springy grass adjacent to the car park proved to be a comfortable mattress; I allowed the soft velvet sky to envelop me and I dreamed of Yassin.

The police woke us up at six o'clock and told us we had to move on. We all wished each other well and drifted off towards the border in our separate groups. Yurgen was travelling alone and also heading for Casablanca. He asked if he could travel with us, he seemed like a sincere person, and we agreed that we might feel safer in his company. Together, we breakfasted in a café, and Fiona and I changed into clean clothes, brushed our hair, and tidied ourselves up as best we could in the washroom.

The area around the border crossing was choc-a-bloc with backpackers trying to get into Morocco. Most of them seemed to be getting turned away and my heart plummeted to the depths of my stomach. We were too inexperienced to know that the totally corrupt border police just wanted money in exchange for stamping our passports. We noticed that all the vehicles were getting across, so Yurgen had a word with one of the drivers waiting in line, a lone German named Klaus in an old white Mercedes. He said we were welcome to a lift; he was also heading for Casablanca and would happily take us all the way there. I couldn't believe our luck. We hid our rucksacks in the boot of the car and tried to look cool and self-assured as the immigration officer waved us across the border. Speeding towards Casablanca, we were confident that we would be with Yassin and Said by the late afternoon. How blissfully ignorant we were of the dangers that lay ahead.

~*~

The first town we reached was Tetouan, a dense cluster of whitewashed houses rising from a narrow valley with dramatic mountains on two sides. We observed goats sleeping on doorsteps, shy curious children with dirty faces, men in long flowing robes, and women hiding behind veils. We stopped briefly to buy some water and were immediately surrounded by a group of young Moroccan boys who – despite their lack of education – could speak up to six languages each, picked up in conversations with the numerous travellers that passed through their town. I was already feeling uneasy about Klaus; he struck me as shifty and unsavoury. It was after we had been on the road for about an hour that my discomfort significantly increased, he opened up the glove compartment to reveal what must have been a half-kilo brick of hash.

I knew that Morocco's hashish production was massive, but I was also aware that although its use was widespread and fairly tolerated, this drug was banned in Morocco and was still technically illegal. In practice, penalties tended to be levied almost exclusively against foreign tourists. What I couldn't understand was why Klaus had smuggled it across the border when it was so readily available within the country. Too frightened to lift my head, I felt sick, briefly overcome by an all-engulfing bolt of terror. I was scared to travel with this man, but it was way too late to get out of the car and take the train from Tangier.

I didn't have the opportunity to discuss my fears with Fiona until Klaus decided that he wanted to stop for a rest at a deserted beach, somewhere south of Rabat. In the company of Yurgen on the back seat, my friend had been feeling slightly more relaxed than me, and that was my other fear. The affable Yurgen was clearly interested in Fiona; what if his feelings were reciprocated? I'd caught a glimpse of them sneaking a kiss in my rear-view mirror. *What if Fiona lost interest in trying to find Said in Casablanca? What if I got stuck with the loathsome Klaus?* Fiona assured me that although she liked the young Austrian, she too was determined to find Yassin and Said. We both agreed that we were glad that Yurgen was sharing the journey with us.

We then turned our attention to the magnificent sandy beach. Yurgen and I decided to go for a swim, but we underestimated the fierce and raw rip of the Atlantic Ocean. Within seconds I was out of my depth and drifting out to sea. Klaus either didn't notice or didn't care, obliviously getting stoned beside a rock. Fiona, however, paddling ankle deep at the water's edge, noticed my distress and cried out in horror. Yurgen was close to me, also in trouble, but he managed to grab my hand and with difficulty, we fought our way back to the shore. He probably saved my life.

Shaken, we returned to the car, but now we had another problem. Klaus declared he was too stoned to drive and suggested that we all sleep in the car, in the middle of nowhere. As far as I was concerned, I had no choice but to get behind the wheel of the heavy old Mercedes – on the opposite side of the road to what I was accustomed – and speed on to Casablanca. The antics of the other road users were scary, and I was convinced on more than one occasion that we were going to be forced off the road by the horn-blaring trucks coming in the opposite direction.

We arrived in Casablanca at nightfall, and after stopping and asking enough people, we managed to find our way to the crumbling district in the Old City where Yassin had told me he lived. Nonetheless, finding his house in the warren of tiny narrow streets, signposted in Arabic, seemed like an impossible task. Frustrated, I stopped the car, and once again we were blockaded by a large group of local boys. They started banging on the windows and roof, and Klaus woke up from his hazy stupor with a jump. For about the tenth time that day, I was really frightened.

Thankfully, the boys were simply curious; they meant no harm. They assured us that we were in the right part of town, and yes, amazingly, they knew Yassin and Said. They agreed to take us to Yassin's family home and get a message to our friends – who were on the other side of town – telling them that visitors from another continent had arrived. We said goodbye to dear Yurgen and the awful Klaus and allowed other strangers to escort us to a strange house in a strange town in a strange and mysterious land.

The traditional Moroccan house was old and rambling. Behind the heavy carved wooden doors was a richly tiled hallway; we were ushered through a central open-air courtyard into a large room, bare of furniture, except for rugs and three thin mattresses on the floor. The two stunning Moroccan girls spoke to us in French, fortunately we were able to communicate. They introduced themselves as Khadija and Soufraka; they were Yassin's sisters. I couldn't believe they were only sixteen and fourteen years old. A runner had been dispatched to find Yassin and Said and inform them of our arrival. While we waited, the girls talked to us and brought us a hot drink, served in glasses from a battered silver teapot. Fiona was the first to taste the unfamiliar, green-coloured liquid, I waited for her reaction.

'It's beau-ti-ful,' she exclaimed, 'it's re-ally beau-ti-ful.' Indeed, the sweet mint tea was refreshing and delicious.

Forty minutes later, Yassin and Said arrived, incredulous and delighted that we had managed to cross the border, get to Casablanca and find them. Yassin looked so handsome; I was in love. We recounted our adventures. Shortly after midnight, Said informed us that he had to go home and invited Fiona to come too and stay overnight as a guest of his family. Fiona was keen to go, I was full of encouragement, and Said agreed to bring her back to meet up with me again in the morning. We confidently said goodnight.

It was only later that we both realised we had done the unthinkable. We had willingly separated from each other in a strange, alien country, and entrusted our lives to two foreign men whom we had known for less than a day.

I slept fitfully, fully clothed on the mattress, worried that I might never see Fiona again. Yassin slept on the opposite side of the same room. I was grateful that he was respectful; maybe things would be okay after all. In the morning, he introduced me to his family; I estimated that his mother was about forty-five, she had ten children, the eldest was twenty-nine and the youngest was a baby of six months. Despite the size of the house, all of the women slept in the same room, I was glad that I hadn't been expected to sleep with them too. Eight of us shared a communal breakfast; sitting cross-legged in a circle on the floor, we ate with our hands, dipping heavy Moroccan bread into a blackened pan containing eight fried eggs. It was a beautiful experience, I felt honoured and accepted. The women then offered to wash my clothes. I gratefully handed over a pile of dirty, train-soiled garments.

Khadija obviously thought I could do with a clean-up as well, but there was no bathroom in the house. Instead, she took me to the hammam, the traditional public bathhouse a few streets away. I was already familiar with the Orientalist paintings, in which bathhouses were depicted as languid, sexualised, mysterious and elegant – the stuff of Scheherazade and the 1001 nights. But here, I was privy to a slice of daily life, warts, hairballs and all. Voices echoed across the high domed roof, and all around us were bodies in various stages of undress. I realised that I was expected to strip off as well and was soon sharing floor space in the inner chamber with dozens of naked Moroccan women. A plump lady came over to wash me, she wore a rough loofa mitt on her hand, and she began to scrub me vigorously using black olive-oil soap. Layers of grey dead skin came off in rolls, and floated away, towards a drain in the middle of the room. At first, I was shy and self-conscious, but wow! It felt so good to be clean again.

We returned to the house, and I found Yassin waiting for me in the open courtyard where flowering creepers clung to painted fretwork windows. One of his little sisters was washing my clothes. To my amazement she had laid them out on a wide flat rock and was scrubbing them with a stone and some more of the odd-looking black olive-oil soap. I cringed with embarrassment when I saw her studying the printed picture – a colourful seaside scene, complete with deckchair and iced drink – on my favourite pair of funky knickers. Another little sister was hard at work with a pestle and mortar, grinding some wheat-grain. She told me that her next chore would be to make *khobz* – flat bread – with the fine flour. Yassin suggested that we went out.

'But I must wait here for Fiona,' I said.

'It's okay,' he assured me, 'She'll catch up with us later.'

He took me to a friend's house. To get there, we walked past an aromatic spice market before reaching a wide boulevard flanked by tall white buildings in the modern part of the city.

Yassin and his friend spoke Arabic and smoked joints. We then visited three more of his mates. At each house, the women were hospitable; they brought us mint tea, meatballs and couscous. I wondered what they thought of me. I noticed that the Moroccan women all worked exceedingly hard while the men just seemed to sit around talking and getting stoned. I was feeling very uneasy, I was so worried about Fiona, how could we have been so stupid as to separate. I was also losing interest in Yassin. So much for love at first sight. I had been overwhelmed by his family's kindness, but I felt that he was now being inconsiderate; I was excluded from the conversation, and he kept asking me for cigarette money. It was already four o'clock in the afternoon, but he still hadn't made any effort to reunite me with Fiona, despite my growing concern.

Eventually, Fiona and Said walked into the house where we were sitting, my friend's relief at finding me seemed even greater than my own emotions. One look at her face revealed that all was not well. She discretely told me she'd had a dreadful time. Said's family were wealthy, the house had marble floors, plush furniture and three lavish bathrooms. His family had been unwelcoming; his mother had been plain hostile and Said had demanded sex in exchange for what he perceived to be his own hospitality and generosity. He had been so persistent that Fiona had been convinced that he was about to rape her but, mercifully, when he'd realised that she was genuinely distressed, he had backed off.

We all stayed at Yassin's house that night. Fiona and I shared a mattress. We had agreed that we were ready to leave Casablanca. My own experiences of staying with a Moroccan family and witnessing aspects of a traditional lifestyle had been truly special. However, I felt sad that Fiona's encounter with

Said's family had been risky and unpleasant, and I felt awful for having encouraged her to go to his home.

Early the next morning, Yassin and Said took us to the railway station. This time there were no tears when we said goodbye. There was still a lot of tension between Said and Fiona, but Yassin and I agreed to keep in touch. We never saw each other again, although we did exchange a few letters, and Khadija and Soufraka wrote to me as well.

'Looking at the world through the sunset in your eyes,
Travelling the train through clear Moroccan skies...
Sweeping cobwebs from the edges of my mind
Had to get away to see what we could find...
Wouldn't you know we're riding on the Marrakech Express...'

Unscathed, Fiona and I had survived our travels and challenges so far, and many lessons had already been learnt, including the fact that it helps to get to know someone before deciding it must be love. Now we were heading off on a new adventure. Attracted by the theme of the old Crosby, Stills & Nash song, we were about to ride through the desert on the Marrakech Express.

Taking time to reflect, I think that was the point when I first realised that if I wanted something badly enough, it really was possible to make it happen. Wishes and dreams were becoming reality due to a combination of determination and destiny. The ambition to travel had been with me all my life, but the dream to visit Morocco and ride the Marrakech Express had germinated from a seed that had been sown only a few months earlier. It had been Fiona's idea to incorporate a piece of North Africa into our train travels.

'We could take the Marrakech Express, just like the song.'

I knew nothing about Marrakech and couldn't even remember the song until she sang it to me, but inspired by my friend's enthusiasm, I had familiarised myself with the lyrics and had bought a guidebook to Morocco. Now we were sitting on the hard, slatted, wooden bench seats of the train, chugging through the Moroccan desert, singing the old Crosby, Stills & Nash song for all our worth; happy to be making our dream come true. We had already been through so many escapades and yet this was only our third day in Morocco. Instead of taking the safe option, our thirst for adventure combined with our naivety had exposed us to both excitement and danger, blended with a little bit of luck and Moroccan magic.

Even more magical, however, was our first sight of Marrakech. Suddenly, out of nowhere, like a mirage, a palm-fringed oasis appeared in the midst of the rocky desert, followed by the awesome manifestation of a mediaeval pink walled city.

As soon as we emerged from the train station, we were encircled – not for the first time – by young Moroccan boys offering to be our guides. We decided to go with the flow and allowed one of them to escort us to the youth hostel. Having secured our accommodation, we then set out to explore the old city and were directed towards the Medina, the eleventh century Islamic capital, which is enclosed by ramparts and gates. The streets are too narrow for cars, so the timeless character of the city has been preserved. It is a surviving, living image of an ancient world. For me it was like stepping back in time, slipping into the pages of my favourite bedtime stories, *Tales from the Arabian Nights.* Women swathed from head to toe in black tent-like apparel, broken only by a rectangle of gauze in front of their eyes, were going about their daily business. In Jemaa el-Fnaa, the famous town square in the centre of the Medina, we encountered soothsayers, storytellers, snake charmers, acrobats in baggy pants, musicians, singers, fakirs, healers, beggars and mules. The storyteller was my favourite; wearing a long, striped, hooded robe, he was captivating his predominantly Moroccan audience with tales of what I could only assume must be flying carpets, genies, wishes, magic spells and buried treasure. I didn't understand a word of his mysterious Arabic language but I, too, was enthralled by his animated eyes and wild gesticulations.

Close to forty degrees, the dry heat was comparable to a farrier's furnace, and it was only when we set off in search of a cold drink that I was transported back to the twentieth century by the offer of a bottle of coke. More appropriately, we were enticed by huge pyramids of brilliant orange fruit, and we chose to quench our thirst with some freshly squeezed juice from one of the many stalls. The covered maze of *souks* – bazaars, cafes, food stalls and workshops – is a living labyrinth with an intricate infrastructure. We soon discovered that the palm-frond canopies and the cool shade of the stone houses made the souks the perfect place for us to hide from the harsh heat of the sun, I was mesmerised by the mystique, and was lost not only in the web of crowded alleyways but also in my childhood fantasies.

Here we learnt that specific skills are practiced within each of the different quarters; and we stopped and watched the expert craftsmen perform their centuries' old professions. We bought handwoven blankets, embroidered kaftans, earrings, water jugs, dates, nuts, sweet cantaloupe melons, exotic spices, and henna for our hair. I retched at the sight of the raw meat, hanging on hooks in the sun and covered in blowflies, but under the gaze of the great Koutoubia Mosque, I stared longingly at an endless tapestry of Moroccan carpets, their complex patterns of fiery reds, ochre, amber and crimson woven into indigenous motifs. The carpets were spread underfoot and overhead, enfolding us within enchanted tunnels, creating geometrical shapes and casting bold shadows. I drank mint tea with one of the vendors, I asked him the price of a small prayer mat, but it was way beyond my means, and I felt browbeaten by his patronising manner. I attempted to haggle but only succeeded in insulting him with my ridiculously low offer. He wagged his forefinger, wrung his hands, pursed his lips, sighed, threw back his head and laughed at me, theatrically.

I decided to forget the carpet idea, it would have made a pleasing enhancement to the nylon-covered floors of my cold flat in England, but now a new plan was forming. I didn't want to spend too much money and I didn't need any more baggage. This sojourn was only a short one, but I wanted my next travel adventure to be open-ended.

Marrakech made such an impression on me that even now, writing this more than forty years later, I have no difficulty in recalling the sun-baked rosy sandstone. I can feel the grit and the frenzy of activity in the dusty streets; I can hear the cry of the imam, and I can smell the lingering aroma of the spice market. The attack on my senses was so intense that it is hard to believe we only spent two days there. We took the Marrakech Express back to Tangier and continued our journey through Europe. Memory can be very selective and now I'm wondering why I have no recollection of actually leaving that charismatic pink walled city in the desert. I have never returned, but then again, Marrakech has never left me, magic places never do.

2
WANDERLUST
1973-1982

From a young age I was passionate about writing. I kept a daily journal, achieved good grades in my English essays and exams, and regularly wrote twenty-page letters to my friends. My plan was to bum around the world as soon as I left school. I decided that I would pay my way by picking fruit and writing travel books and I would eventually settle down on a tropical island. I had it all worked out. When I was fifteen, I shared my secret dream with my careers teacher.

'I want to be a novelist and a travel writer and live on a tropical island.'

Mrs. Pengelly frowned at me over her half-rimmed spectacles; she sneered at my 'fantasies' and told me to 'get real,' and then advised me to take up a career in occupational therapy. She shattered my dreams.

I couldn't face going to college straight after leaving school, so I went to the US for a few months, got an under-the-table job as a research assistant, and lived with my brother, Christopher, and his wife, Molly, in Cambridge, Massachusetts. I found America exciting, and I enjoyed my time there, but I wasn't bumming around the world, and the apartment in Cambridge was a long way from my tropical island dream. So, I returned to England to train for a career that might bring me the income required to feed the travel bug and the opportunity to work overseas. I respectfully accepted the offer of a place at St Loye's School of Occupational Therapy.

School was the operative word. This was not what I wanted to do or where I wanted to be. I chucked in college within my first year and secured what I intended to be a *temporary* job in a bank. My objective was to save some money and pursue my original plan of travelling the world.

And then I met Nigel…

Oh, I wasn't looking for love; why does it always seem to happen when we don't want it, and yet rarely goes off when we're searching for it? Yet I loved Nigel because he was a traveller and a humanitarian. Like my brother, Jeremy, he'd also done the hippy trail across Turkey, Iran, Afghanistan and Pakistan, and had spent a year in India.

'Maybe we could bum around the world together?' I suggested.

Nigel had returned from his own travels only a few months earlier. He'd landed a good job and his priority now was to save some money. I humoured him, I cajoled him, and I even threatened to go without him, alone. The funny thing was that he actually encouraged me to go without him; and it was then that I knew he loved me because he was prepared to set me free so that I could chase my dreams. How could I run away from someone as special as this? The only alternative was a compromise.

I arranged to take two months unpaid leave from my safe job at the bank, and I decided to buy a return ticket to Sydney to visit Jeremy with a few stopovers along the way. I booked a flight to India and a sixteen-day overland trip from Delhi to Kathmandu. Bangkok also appealed for a brief stopover, and I wanted to visit Singapore on my way home because my friend Barbara had just taken up a teaching job there. The Trailfinders' travel planner recommended that I flew from Bangkok to Australia with an airline called 'Garuda', which would entitle me to stop off in Bali on my way to Sydney.

'Where was Bali?' I wondered, but I nodded my agreement and decided that I had better check the atlas when I got home.

'Oh, I'd love to go to Bali,' sighed Nigel when I told him the news.

He'd obviously heard of the place. I was still unable to tempt him to come with me, but I'd obviously made a good choice to include Bali on my itinerary.

'They say,' revealed my mother, knowingly, 'that the Balinese girls are the most beautiful in the world.'

I idly speculated on what the men would look like.

I read everything I could find on India, Nepal, Bangkok, Singapore and Bali, but my vision of living on a tropical island and writing for my living had begun to diminish. Now that I'd met Nigel, I was rather hoping that this trip might satisfy my wanderlust. Maybe when I returned I would also feel ready to settle down in a house in England adorned with exotic souvenirs from foreign countries.

3
A PASSAGE THROUGH INDIA
1982

Full of encouragement and pride, my parents saw me off at Bretonside Bus Station. As I boarded the coach to London, my dad pushed an envelope into my hands and told me to open it later. It was a short note reassuring me that he would send me money if I got into difficulties, and if necessary, he would fly out in person to bring me home. Mobile phones and emails had not yet been invented, telephone systems were inadequate, international money transfers could take weeks, and credit cards were just useless pieces of plastic.

My dad had also enclosed five pounds and written, 'Treat yourself to a night in an upmarket hotel during your stop-over in Bali.'

Heathrow airport was busy, as always.

What if I've been directed to the wrong terminal?

What will happen to my luggage when I change flights at Paris on the way to New Delhi?

What will become of me when I arrive in India?

I was alone now, but within the next twenty-four hours I would be meeting the people who would be my travel companions on the overland trip from Delhi to Kathmandu. Believe me, this wasn't going to be an upmarket tour. There would be no flashy air-conditioned bus with a toilet on board. No fancy seats, comfortable suspension, or smooth-operating tour guide spouting a slick commentary over a microphone. This journey would take place on an old Indian bus with an old Indian driver, with shared accommodation in budget hotels. *What sort of person will I have to share my space with?*

Most of my fears were allayed before I even left Heathrow because I met some of my travelling companions in the departure lounge. It was easy to identify them; we were all displaying the same travel labels on our hand luggage. They were a mixed bunch including some intrepid explorer types wearing bum-bags and hiking boots, and an intense bespectacled scientist accompanied by his glamorous girlfriend with her blow-dried hair and high-heels. My curiosity was aroused by an elderly upper-crust lady travelling with her two sons – one was overweight, pale and pasty, the other was fit, tanned and muscular. Then there was a young couple, who told me they were heading back home to New Zealand after a twelve-month sojourn around the world, a suave well-dressed Italian man, and an independent, slightly batty, woman of fifty-five who later nominated herself as my roommate. At twenty-three, I was the youngest of the group.

We arrived at New Delhi airport at six a.m., saw the sunrise, and witnessed a bus crash during our nerve-wracking taxi ride to the YMCA hotel, the start point of our Indian adventure; a journey that would cover more than fifteen hundred kilometres.

The next four days were spent exploring Delhi in the mellow sunshine, twenty degrees warmer than frosty London. At last, I was in the country that I had been longing and planning to visit ever since Jeremy had done the hippy trail twelve years earlier.

Sometimes with my travel companions and sometimes alone, I wandered the wide avenues of New Delhi. I took the comical-looking three-wheeler scooter taxis – with motors that started on the pull of a cord – to the classy Connaught Circus.

I bartered in the underground maze of subways known as the 'air-conditioned market' for cotton shirts and a quilted jacket. On the streets I saw wild monkeys, chipmunks, green parrots, mynah birds and vultures, and I got hassled by beggars and cheated by a smartly dressed woman petitioning for an 'official' children's charity. I cruised past India Gate and the Parliament Buildings, and I visited the Gandhi Memorial and Safdarjung's Tomb, known as the 'poor man's Taj Mahal' and a taster for the real thing, which was to be a later part of the itinerary.

Yet my favourite district was Old Delhi. Set within the city walls, it was chaotic, crowded, colourful and noisy. People were shouting, children were crying, horns were blaring, tinny bicycle bells were ringing, and loud Hindi music was playing on every balcony. A little girl, wearing a sari, was washing a silver teapot in a storm drain, street-side cooks were frying chapattis, and ponies were pulling carts laden with fresh fruit and alien-looking vegetables. An exceptionally well-fed, arrogant man was loafing on the seat of a pedal rickshaw that was being frantically propelled by a skinny shirtless man, his assistant was running in front, attempting to clear the way and expecting everyone to move aside and allow them to pass. Yet only the sacred cows had the real right of way, complacently holding up the traffic as they ambled down the centre of the road, seemingly content to trade green pastures for an extraordinarily high social status.

Later, in the rocky desert of Rajasthan, I explored the Amber Palace, a high fortress where turrets and towers, lookout posts, columns with elephant-head brackets, and ornate stucco walls embellished with millions of pieces of glass, drew me into another century and indulged my romantic fantasies.

Jaipur was the next destination, India's 'Pink City' and Rajasthan's capital; its historic walled centre painted almost exclusively in a diluted shade of terracotta on the orders of the Maharaja, Sawai Ram Singh II, to welcome the Prince Albert when he visited in 1876. We got stuck in a traffic jam of bicycles and rickshaws, but there was plenty to look at while we waited: shops, havelis and the long, crenellated, city walls. The streets were lined with silversmiths, gem polishers, textile shops, and tailors working in open doorways on treadle sewing machines. To jolly us along, a man climbed aboard the bus and entertained us by singing a couple of Indian love songs. That night we stayed at the pink Jaipur Inn and dined on matar paneer, rose-flavoured lassi, and mango kulfi.

The next day was even more magical. I had befriended Debbie and Graham, the couple from New Zealand. This was my first encounter with the Kiwi accent, and I called Debbie 'Dibbie' for the next two weeks because that's how *she* pronounced her name. Together we ventured into the interior of the pink city, roaming through alleyways and bazaars, not caring if we got lost. We discovered the Hawa Mahal, the Palace of the Winds, named for the gentle breezes that whisper through its corridors. This fanciful, crumbling building was in the process of being restored and the outside was covered in wonky wooden scaffolding secured with rope. Numerous passageways and arches led us around the central courtyard. Intriguing jali-screened windows overlooked the street below, forming a concealed grandstand from where the queens and princesses would have watched processions outside without fear of being observed by the common man.

We stumbled upon an unknown temple, where a barefoot, crinkly old man with a sweet face, dressed in a dirty white dhoti and turban, appointed himself as our guide and enthusiastically showed us around. We gave him three rupees. It was almost nothing. At that time, the equivalent sum would have purchased no more than a Mars Bar in England, but it must have been worth a fortune to our old man; he looked at the coins in disbelief, turned them over in his hands, and literally jumped for joy.

After watching a red sunset in the pink city, we came across a wedding procession heralded by gas lamps and mesmerising music. The groom, riding a richly decorated white horse, was wearing garlands of rupees and heady-scented jasmine flowers. We were invited to attend the reception at a nearby hotel. The bride was dressed in red and gold, and she was crying. We learnt that the couple had only met once prior to the wedding, spending just ten heavily chaperoned minutes in each other's company. *I wonder what they talked about.*

I will never forget my first glimpse of the Taj Mahal from the bastions and ramparts of the Agra Fort; it was like a sneak preview. After drifting through dilapidated grain stores and dodging swarms of bees, my Kiwi friends and I climbed up on to the battlements and gazed across the Yamuna River at the gently swelling dome of India's most famous architectural wonder. It was dreamlike, I could not quite believe I was seeing it, and experienced an urgency to get closer. In our rush to find a rickshaw, we got lost in the noisy, claustrophobic streets of the old bazaar. Eventually, we reached the Taj, but the place was crowded, it was windy, and the reflection in the water was bloated and distorted. I returned, twice, determined to get the perfect photo. It was no coincidence that we were in Agra at the time of the full moon. That night, the white marble of the famous dome and its four tapering minarets glowed like a lustrous pearl. I returned six hours later at dawn and for a few minutes it looked cold, but as the sun rose, a pink blush illuminated the jewel-encrusted walls. It looked exceptionally serene, the air was calm and the reflection was a perfect mirror.

We stopped for a night at Khajuraho, a quiet and remote village in Madhya Pradesh, which is famous for its erotically carved twelfth-century temples. The hotel staff had been friendly, and in the morning, they offered to prepare a packed lunch for everyone in our group. It was a long drive to Varanasi and when we stopped for our picnic, we were instantly hemmed in by about two hundred teenage schoolboys. I felt a bit threatened, but they weren't hostile, just very, very curious. Upon opening our lunchboxes, we discovered that the hotel had ripped us off – we had been given mouldy chapattis which, in turn, we offered to our bemused audience.

The weather had been perfect since my arrival in India; warm, dry, and sunny with clear blue skies. When we got to Varanasi, however, there was a terrific storm with thunder and forked lightning. It was also quite cold. The night porter at our hotel brought us an electric fire. It was rusty and battered, with exposed elements. He plugged it in, on the open wooden veranda, and the two coils glowed red. The heavy rain was blowing straight in, and to my disquiet I noticed that there was no plug, just a couple of loose wires jammed into a crude socket with a broken matchstick. So much for health and safety.

The sky had cleared by five o'clock the next morning, when we got up and went down to the ghats beside the River Ganges. The streets were dirty and muddy after the rain. We took a boat ride and watched all the pilgrims and local people taking a dip before sunrise. It was one of the most bizarre sights I had ever seen; so many people washing themselves, and their clothes, and rinsing their mouths out in the holy-yet-filthy river water. We also saw funeral pyres and bodies wrapped ready for cremation, but this was India. Scary, shocking, overwhelming, and confronting, yet also full of delights, surprises, and marvels.

~*~

On day twelve of our journey, we arrived at the Nepalese border. My travelling companions were no longer strangers, some of them had become my friends, others were a source of amusement. It was now time to say goodbye to Sirjad Singh, our loyal Sikh driver; the bus was not allowed to travel any further, and we would have to take public transport to Kathmandu.

Everyone in our party was heading to Kathmandu for a different reason. Some were going trekking in the Himalayas, one couple was planning to stay for six months, and the well-dressed Italian was researching business possibilities. For another man, Nepal was to be the start point of a six-month cycling tour of Asia.

At the Nepalese border, the bureaucracy was exasperating and ridiculous. We each had to go to four different posts and incredulously, the Indian officials had no pens. Meanwhile, the whole of the border area was packed with children and local people selling their black-market merchandise. It was here that we managed to negotiate a deal with a half-empty tour bus that was destined for Pokhara and Kathmandu – the two remaining places on our itinerary. The air-conditioned coach was a lot more comfortable than the old tin can that had been our transport across India. However, for me, Sirjad Singh and his bus, together with Andy, our young laid-back tour leader, was a far more preferable option to this soulless means of travel. The constant commentary over the microphone by the suave, conceited tour guide along with the company's rules was reminiscent of being on a school outing.

Our hotel was not far beyond the border, and we were told that our accommodation was 'simple' – seven to a room, on the floor. Nevertheless, the service was excellent and the Nepalese people very friendly. We had a tasty meal and were invited to join a party being held by some Australian travellers heading in the opposite direction. I had drunk almost no alcohol in India, but this Nepalese hotel was serving rum and coke – my favourite tipple.

Graham, Dibbie, and I eagerly ordered a bottle of the sweet, dark rum, but it tasted too nice; it went down too easily. I only drank two small glasses, but I knew something was wrong. That night I kept my six roommates awake for five hours while I threw up, repeatedly and wretchedly, in the partitioned bathroom. The rum had been one of the black-market commodities at the border-crossing – two hundred proof, one hundred percent industrial ethanol blended with a rum-flavoured syrup.

Fortunately, I felt better in the morning. Nepal was extraordinarily beautiful and peaceful; we drove through the mountains, past steep cascading rice terraces, and little wooden houses with grass roofs. Everyone waved to us from the side of the road. At one point, we came across an accident; a noisy crowd had gathered around a bus that had veered off the road and plunged ten metres into a ravine. The vehicle was lying on its roof and at first, we thought that everyone was either dead or trapped inside, but it turned out that the majority of the gawping crowd were actually the passengers. They assured us that everyone was okay. Later, we had to cross a river, there was no bridge, so we took the car ferry, but this was no ordinary drive-on shuttle-boat. It was composed of two long rowing boats adjoined by a large wooden platform. The raft could carry just one vehicle at a time, and it took twelve men to row it across to the opposite bank. We had to queue for over an hour, but I was perfectly content to sit in the sun, drink tea and watch the activity.

After that, the road followed the meandering river with drops of hundreds of metres into the steep gorge below. In the distance we could see snow-capped mountains. We stopped and gave a lift to a young Nepalese boy who took us to his home to meet his family; they all came to greet us on the veranda of their crowded house. They gave us hot sweet tea, and the boy and his brothers entertained us by singing and playing a *sarangi*, which is a fiddle-like mountain folk instrument. There seemed to be about twenty children of all ages.

The boy explained, 'we have two mothers and one father.' His father had two wives and a house for each of them.

We arrived at Pokhara in the late afternoon. The town lies beside the serene Phewa Lake, and beneath the resplendent Annapurna Massif, which includes the famous 7000-metre-high Machhapuchhare or Fishtail, and the inventively-named Annapurna I, the first 8000-metre peak ever to be scaled. The next morning, I got up early to watch the sunrise over the mountains and gazed enthralled as, one by one, all the peaks in the fifty-five-kilometre-long Himalayan panorama lit up and turned to gold. This touch of Midas was life enriching, I felt wealthier than ever before.

~*~

Kathmandu was wonderful, and cold. I visited all three towns in the Kathmandu Valley, travelling by trolleybus and rickshaw. Bhaktapur was my favourite place, mediaeval and unchanged by progress; I watched potters and craftsmen at work in the tiny narrow streets.

On our last evening, everyone in our group met up for a farewell meal at a restaurant called KC's. There was a power-cut, but that was normal, an everyday occurrence. The food was superb. I had already turned vegetarian, but the most popular choice proved to be buff burgers, made from buffalo meat. The occasion was also a family reunion for three members of our party. Mary, the plummy-voiced lady – who had complained a lot about 'the smell' in India – and her two sons had rendezvoused with a third son. The two younger men were now embarking on an epic cycling expedition through the Himalayas and across China, Thailand, Malaysia, Indonesia, and Australia. It was an emotional time for Mary, anxious about her adventurous sons and tired after two weeks on the rough Indian roads, she fainted at the dinner table. Maybe she was the only one who had really thought about the danger that might be lying ahead for the two brothers. I wonder how Mary reacted to the news – ten months later – that her sons had been repeatedly shot at as they cycled through Thailand and had been lucky to escape with their lives. I read the story in an English newspaper.

I kept in touch with Debbie and Graham for many years via handwritten letters. I visited them in Christchurch, New Zealand, in 1990, but we lost touch in 1998 when I moved to Bali.

In 2021, I decided to track them down in New Zealand. It wasn't too hard, and I was thrilled to learn that they were living in Auckland, only twenty minutes away from where I was staying. We hadn't seen each other for thirty-one years. It was a joyful reunion and naturally, we had three decades of news to catch up on. This renewed friendship is far too precious to lose again.

4
STUFFED IN TURKEY
1983

My dream of indefinitely travelling the world had been condensed into a two-month return trip to Australia via India, Kathmandu, Bangkok, Bali and Singapore. It had been a compromise. I had tested my feelings for Nigel, and his for me; my journey had been a triumph and the experience had opened my mind. Happily reunited with Nigel, I now felt ready to settle down and hoped that I had rid the travel bug from my system. We bought a 120-year-old cottage, shared our home with a couple of cats, grew vegetables and took overseas holidays along roads less travelled.

~*~

London's Heathrow Airport was full of businesspeople and foreigners – Arabs in long flowing robes and red & white headdress, Indian ladies in richly-coloured saris, East Africans in kofia caps. I looked at the departure board, which indicated our flight to Istanbul; I decided that this city was the most exotic destination of the day.

Nigel and I had not booked any accommodation in Turkey; our plan was to spend a few days in Istanbul, and then rent a car and drive down to the south coast, staying wherever we fancied along the way.

Upon our arrival at Istanbul Airport, I remembered the opening scenes of Midnight Express. The duty police officers were carrying machine guns, but we had nothing to fear and were solemnly waved through the green line. We asked a taxi driver to take us to a hotel in Sultanahmet in the hub of the old city. My first view of the multi-minareted mosques, silhouetted against the early evening sky above the Bosphorus Strait, was spellbinding. With three weeks ahead of us and no fixed itinerary, anything could happen, and we were ready for adventure.

Midnight Express had achieved huge box office success, but with disastrous consequences for Turkey's tourism industry, with many people citing the film as a reason not to visit Turkey. Istanbul, however, never lacked visitors. A world metropolis and a magnet for traders, it had once been the capital of three empires.

Exploring the city was exciting; Nigel had been there before, so he became my guide. It was hectic and vibrant, noisy and polluted, mysterious, intriguing, and dripping in oriental splendour. We walked the banks of the Golden Horn. We visited the Topkapi Palace – residence of the sultans from the fifteenth century to the early 1800s. I was fascinated by Hagia Sophia, built in 548 and once the greatest church in Christendom; and I was awestruck by the magnificent Blue Mosque and its astonishing tiled interior. We combed the tangled passageways of Kapaliçarşi, the Grand Bazaar, discovering silver shops and carpet emporiums. In search of a bargain, I haggled over some cobalt-blue and turquoise ceramics, and a pair of lapis lazuli earrings. We snacked on the addictive börek cheese pastries at the Pudding Shop, which was world famous long before the release of Midnight Express, and we drank strong Turkish coffee in smoky cafes.

On day four, we rented a car and arranged with the agent to leave it at Dalaman Airport in the southwest of the country. We had booked a domestic flight from Dalaman back to Istanbul, where we would spend our last couple of days. This afforded us maximum time to explore without having to retrace our route.

We then took a leisurely tour down the Aegean coast, staying wherever we fancied in hotels that were remarkably cheap by UK prices. The people were kind and friendly and we were never short of company when we ate out in the evenings. We snorkelled in beautiful bays and secluded coves around the lovely seaside town of Marmaris. At Troy, the location of the legendary Trojan War, we wandered through the ancient city of Ephesus where St Paul preached to the Ephesians.

Our final destination was a gorgeous white sand beach and blue lagoon called Ölüdeniz. We had been enticed by postcards of the place and had decided to relax there on our last day. Our plan was to spend the night at Fethiye – the nearest village – before delivering the car to Dalaman Airport and flying back to Istanbul. After a day of swimming, snorkelling and lying in the sun, Nigel decided to have one last dip in the sea before we drove to Fethiye to find a hotel for the night. I waited on the beach guarding my bag, which contained our money, passports and plane tickets. All of our luggage was locked in the back of the car.

Nigel returned from his swim looking distressed, 'Rache, I think I've lost the car keys...'

'What?'

'I...think,' he repeated slowly, 'I've…lost…the…car…keys.'

The horror didn't sink in initially. I rummaged around in the soft fine sand and checked my bag, but Nigel was convinced he had put them in the pocket of his shorts and that they must have fallen out when he was snorkelling. We took it in turns, using the mask and snorkel to search the water's edge, trying to cover the region where Nigel had been swimming. The sea was crystal clear and so calm that we hoped we might spot the keys under the water. We hunted, fruitlessly, in the area next to the car, thinking that maybe one of us had dropped them when we first arrived, longing that they might be on the ground beside the driver's door, or still in the ignition. We even tried to break into the car, but without the appropriate tools it was impossible. The absolute dreadfulness of our situation gradually began to register. It was five-thirty p.m., we were on an almost deserted beach, sixteen kilometres from the nearest village. We had a car but no keys. All of our clothes and worldly goods, apart from our money, passports and plane tickets, were locked in the boot of the car. I was covered in sun oil and sand, dressed in a bikini and a see-thru sundress. Nigel was dressed in board shorts, wet T-shirt, mask, snorkel and fins. My hair looked like a bird's nest, and we didn't even have a comb between us. We had arranged to be at the airport – an hour's drive away – the following morning at eleven-thirty, to return the rental car and fly back to Istanbul. As the car had been rented in Istanbul, this was where the spare set of car keys would be. If we missed our plane the next morning, we would have to wait three days for another flight and would therefore subsequently miss our non-refundable flight back to London.

After my initial wave of panic, my first thought was to contact the Avis rental car agent in Istanbul. Unusually, there was a public telephone office beside the beach, but it was already late in the afternoon and I feared that the Avis office might be closed. To my relief however, I got through immediately and spoke to the nice man from whom we had rented the car. I told him about our dilemma and as expected he confirmed that the spare keys were in Istanbul, and it would take two or three days to get them to us. He gave us permission to try to break into the car and retrieve our luggage. He then said that if we could somehow get to the airport the following morning, the local Avis representative would be there to meet us as planned and would sort things out from there. He gave me the name and phone number of the local rep – in case we didn't make it to the airport – and confirmed that he would contact him in the meantime to explain the situation. While I was making this phone call, Nigel had managed to attract the attention of the only remaining people on the now-deserted beach. They were taking it in turns to try to break into the car with a piece of wire, but it was useless. However, these kindly Turkish men seemed to be genuinely concerned for our welfare and offered to drive us to Fethiye. I felt very nervous about leaving the car in a remote car park with everything we owned locked up in the boot, but as we had been unable to break into the car, I could only hope that no one else would be successful in our absence.

It took us about twenty minutes to reach Fethiye and the two men who had befriended us took us to the tourist information kiosk, where they hoped we might be able to get help. We explained our sorry predicament to a young man called Salih who appeared to be in charge. Salih told us that it was too late to do anything that evening, but if we could come back at nine o'clock in the morning, he would do everything he could to help us.

Partially reassured, but nevertheless tense and on edge because nothing more could be done for nearly fifteen hours, our next mission was to find somewhere to stay for the night. First, however, I found a minimarket where I bought toothpaste, toothbrushes, shampoo, a comb and some moisturiser for my skin, which was feeling rather sensitive after a day in the hot sun. I also managed to buy a pair of flipflops for Nigel because he'd left his in the car and had been barefoot since the beach. He hadn't been amused when I'd suggested he wear his fins.

Apart from combing the sand out of our tangled hair, there was little we could do to tidy ourselves up. I was still wearing my bikini and see-thru sundress; Nigel's T-shirt and shorts were damp and stiff with saltwater. We faced the ultimate humiliation when we were refused accommodation at the first hotel. The receptionist looked us up and down and asked if we had any luggage.

'It's locked in the back of our car,' Nigel explained.

'Sorry,' replied the receptionist, curtly informing us that there was no room at the inn.

Back in those days, there weren't many hotels in Fethiye and the one that we ended up in was rough to say the least. There were no towels in our room and no soap in the shower. I washed myself as best I could under a trickle of cold water. I used our newly purchased shampoo to eliminate the sand, salt and oil from my inflamed skin. I massaged the sand out of my itching scalp and then had to pat myself dry with my grubby beach towel. It felt so good to get clean, but the pleasure was diminished by having to get dressed again in my sandy bikini and crumpled sundress.

Nigel was equally repulsed at having to slip back into his boardshorts and scruffy old T-shirt, but at least he had a new pair of flipflops. Then, still feeling troubled and anxious about our bizarre situation, we set out to find something to eat, and decided we'd have a few glasses of Turkish brandy in an attempt to alleviate our stress. We both wondered how the hell we were going to get through the next thirteen hours.

Okay, this wasn't a life and death situation but nor was it very pleasant. I wished I could have relaxed and enjoyed my meal, but I just wasn't hungry. The Turkish Keo brandy went down better than the food, and Nigel in his usual style got talking to some friendly Turks and was challenged to a game of chess by an old man with a lived-in face and a beguiling smile. Always in his element when playing chess, Nigel was able to focus totally on his game and forget about our troubles. I wished I could've found an equally distracting activity.

At midnight, comforted by too many brandies, we returned to our austere hotel room. I couldn't get to sleep for ages and then, when I finally drifted off, I had terrible nightmares. I dreamt that we managed to break into the boot of our car to be confronted not by our luggage but by a dead body. The next scene was a Turkish jail; I'd obviously been far too influenced by Midnight Express. Later I woke up with an upset stomach, I rushed to the toilet but when I tried to pull the flush, the plastic lid of the lofty cistern fell down and hit me on the head. The flush refused to work. So, in a manual attempt, I filled the waste bin with water, but it had a large crack all down one side and it leaked all over the floor.

Feeling tired, fragile and hungover the next morning, we checked out of the hotel-from-hell and walked to the tourist information kiosk to keep our nine o'clock appointment with Salih.

After that, things happened very quickly. Without telling us what was going on, Salih hailed a taxi, and we were driven through the side streets of the little town. We stopped outside a workshop and a man appeared at the door; he was carrying a metal case. Smiling, he got into the taxi with us, and by way of explanation, he opened his toolbox to reveal screwdrivers, picks, files, and a million keys.

Salih had found us a locksmith.

Relief coursed through my veins, but we still had to endure a twenty-minute journey back to the beach where we had left the car. *Would it still be there?*

Mercifully, the car was still parked, untouched, where we had left it. It took the locksmith less than a minute to find an appropriate key, file it slightly and open the driver's door. The ignition was even easier, he unscrewed a panel, united a couple of wires and the engine roared into life. Everything was going to be okay after all. We assumed that the mission had been accomplished, and asked the taxi driver, the locksmith, and Salih how much we owed each of them. However, the locksmith told us that his job wasn't finished yet and asked us to bring the car back to his workshop and leave it with him for about fifteen minutes.

We drove back to Fethiye and waited for the locksmith to complete his task. He made us two complete new sets of keys for the doors and the ignition, and also repaired the lock on the petrol cap, which had been broken before we had rented the car. His fee was minimal, but this man had been our saviour, we expressed our appreciation by giving him a large tip. Meanwhile, Salih – a boy of no more than seventeen years old – refused to take anything for his trouble.

'You are visitors to my country; it is my job to make sure you are well looked after, and that you remember the Turkish people as being friendly, helpful and hospitable.'

We said our grateful goodbyes and embarked on our drive to the airport, arriving only half an hour later than planned, and triumphantly handing the car back to the Avis rep.

It wasn't until we got back to Istanbul and checked in to a more upmarket hotel that we had the opportunity to change out of our grubby beachwear. We had another forty-eight hours in the city and celebrated with more Keo brandy and some excellent food, but there was one final little incident that occurred at Istanbul Airport just before we departed for home…

On this occasion, we had ensured that we got to the airport in plenty of time. In fact, we were in such good time that the check-in desk for our flight was not yet open. The departure terminal was almost empty. I was clutching a large wooden camel, a souvenir of our holiday, and it actually brought a smile to the lips of the police officer who was poised at the main door with a machine gun. The heavy security reminded me that this was the location of the opening scene of Midnight Express when Billy Hayes was arrested while trying to board a plane with four-and-a-half pounds of hashish strapped to his body. It was a true story, and he was subsequently sentenced to thirty years in a Turkish jail. My thoughts were interrupted when I noticed that two local men were approaching us.

One of them was clutching a pair of leather shoes and spoke to us in what was plainly a fake Cockney accent, 'S'cuse us Guv, you going to 'eathrow?'

We nodded.

He continued, 'C'dya do us a favour? I'm a shoemaker, my business is in Londun and I 'ave to, like, urgently get this pair of shoes to me client, today. Mate, could you take 'em for us?'

They were very ordinary-looking, average-sized shoes – with thick soles – and I did wonder why any client in London would need them so urgently on a Sunday.

I was about to ask, but Nigel intervened, 'I'm sorry, we don't carry anything for anybody, I'm sure you must understand why.'

The men accepted our refusal and went off in search of a more gullible London-bound passenger.

In retrospect, the scenario was almost too corny to be real; I was glad we'd watched Midnight Express.

5
GUNNED DOWN IN SICILY
1986

The spectacle was like a scene out of The Godfather…

It was the ninth of July, a feast day. The local people were honouring San Pancrazio, the patron saint of their town, and a religious procession was advancing through the cobbled streets. The Sicilians were dressed in their best clothes. There were men wearing dark suits and black sunglasses; there were family groups, children and small lapdogs. The Roman Catholic priest and his attendants were wearing white vestments, the sweet smell of church incense mingled with the hot Mediterranean air. The parade was dominated by a life size statue of the saint, carried aloft, high above the crowd so that everyone could see. A brass band started to play. Tourists, including us, gathered to watch the activities. The atmosphere was respectful but cheery, and in a strange sort of way, anticipatory.

Suddenly, the ear-splitting and terrifying ra-ta-ta-ta-ta-ta-ta-ta-ta sound of machine gun fire emanated from somewhere at the back of the procession. People started screaming and running for cover. The band stopped playing. I dived onto the ground, shielding my body behind, and partially under, a large, parked delivery van.

Nigel and I were in Piazza IX Aprile, the main square in the Sicilian town of Taormina. The panoramic views from here are some of the most celebrated in the whole of Italy. Twin bays sweep out into a tableau of sapphire blue sea; to the south are dramatic vistas of Mount Etna, Europe's highest active volcano. Often it is crowned with snow, sometimes it is forbidding and fuming. The most photographed view captures the volcano framed by the crumbling stones and marble pillars of the large Greco-Roman amphitheatre.

Films about the Mafia have always made Sicily intriguing. We had watched The Godfather, Parts I & II, countless times, and had longed to explore this dramatic landscape with the added zest of deep-rooted blood feuds, secrecy, and murder. Finally, we had made it happen. We spent three weeks touring the island in a rented car. We visited the sleepy village of Savoca, with its small, shuttered dwellings and dazzling views of the Nebrodi mountains. It was an archetypal Sicilian hill village, which was why Francis Ford Coppola had chosen it as the location for many of the scenes in the first Godfather movie. Apparently, the town of Corleone was too developed – even in the early 1970s – to be used for filming. It was in Savoca that we saw shady-looking men in dark glasses, thick suits, overcoats and heavy shoes, smoking in the sunshine between courses outside the little trattorias, while the women and children stayed inside. It was tempting to imagine that they were muttering about how a sworn enemy would soon be 'swimming with the fishes.'

We also spent time in Palermo, the capital city, where we visited the bizarre and chilling catacombs of Cappuccini. In 1599, Capuchin monks made a shocking discovery. While exhuming bodies from the catacombs of their monastery, they found that many of the bodies had naturally mummified. Following this, the monks decided to do some mummifying of their own. Throughout Italy the friars had a fascination for bones, skulls and the embalming of dead bodies, but here they seemed to excel in this morbid task and preserved more than eight thousand children and adults from all social classes, with the last one being laid to rest in 1920. Wandering through the halls of the catacombs was a spine-chilling experience, especially after the curator told us that he would be closing the doors in ten minutes so that he could take his lunchbreak.

Dressed in their Sunday best, the mummified and skeletal bodies were propped up, some standing and some seated, many of them still had their hair. Others were in caskets or crystal urns.

Suddenly, and ominously, the catacombs were plunged into darkness.

I screamed.

The lights came back on.

It was the curator signalling our cue to leave.

Ten minutes had been enough for me.

So now, with the macabre memories of the catacombs behind us, we were in the process of being gunned down by the Mafia in the streets of Taormina.

Or so I thought.

I'd obviously been watching too many movies. A local prankster had let off some firecrackers. Panic over, the band struck up again. The warm, rich, pure tones of the trombones floated through the air like a musical cloud, while the tuba lifted off like a big balloon. Once more, the statue of the saint was raised above the crowd, and a few nervy fools like me, picked themselves up off the ground, dusted themselves down and continued to enjoy the festivities.

~*~

6
THE LANDMARK
1988

The eighties decade in the UK was an era of huge growth in the travel industry, which saw the birth of mass tourism in the form of package holidays. The airlines would offer aircraft charters on long-term contracts for the purpose of inclusive tour packages put together by travel agents and large tour operating groups such as Thomson, First Choice and Thomas Cook. At the same time, there was a corresponding growth in the number of high-street travel agents. Customers would pick up a big fat colourful holiday brochure, decide when they wanted to travel, select a departure airport, a destination and a hotel, and choose between full board, half board or bed & breakfast. Prior to this time, package holiday pricing had been restricted, but when the price controls were finally abolished, discounting became rife and the demand for cheap holidays abroad became unstoppable. Package holiday sales soared during these heyday years as price wars raged between the largest operators.

Personally, I always hated the idea of package holidays. I was deterred by the thought of being herded around like a flock of sheep upon arrival at the destination airport, before being directed to one of any number of coaches, each with some halfwit rep onboard trying to be funny. I was further turned off by the expectation of having to attend a welcome meeting in the hotel, while being forced to listen to yet another rep trying to sell daytrips to boost their commission. It's so much nicer to be independent, to do your own research in advance, to hire a car and to be free to do what you want, escape from the crowds, meet the local people and authentically experience a new country. I'm not knocking the holidaymakers who choose package holidays over the do-it-yourself options. Packages are super convenient for families and for specialist tours such as skiing trips, but apart from a few exceptions, these types of holidays were not for me. On the plus side, and to my benefit, the package tour industry generated plentiful opportunity to purchase hugely discounted flight-only tickets on charter flights to the most popular tourist spots. These were the flights associated with the package tours that had not been sold. A scheduled flight was generally much more expensive, although it was often the only option if we wished to travel to a lesser known, more exciting destination.

In the 1980s, cut price last-minute seats on charter flights were displayed on white cards in every high-street travel agent's window. I worked in a busy city centre, and every year, as the weeks and days got closer to the time of my already-approved annual leave, I'd watch the prices dropping. My hope being that I could hold out long enough to get the best possible discount on a flight-only to a Greek island, or some other destination that Nigel and I hadn't already visited.

Although airlines had automated the booking process, travel agencies remained semi-manual; they would have to call a ticket agent to put a 24-hour hold on the aircraft seat availability, giving the customer a short window of time to think about it before returning with funds to pay for the flight in full. The desk-clerk would then make another phone call to secure the reservation, and the paper tickets would be issued about a week before travel, with the agent filling in the passenger info by hand to complete the process. It was clumsy and slow compared to today when we can do it all on our Smartphones in just a few minutes.

The cheapest last-minute, flight-only, return tickets I ever secured in those days were a bargain at a mere thirty-nine pounds each; a rock-bottom price for two weeks in the sun, with our departure scheduled from Bristol Airport just eight days after making the booking. This was in July, before the beginning of the school summer holidays. Our destination was The Algarve, Portugal's beautiful southern coastline – a region blessed with glorious weather, golden beaches, fishing villages and tourist hotspots.

Bristol Airport was perfect for us, it was only a two-hour drive from home and long-stay parking was way cheaper than at Gatwick Airport, which was a four-hour-drive. Heathrow, meanwhile, didn't host low-cost airlines. Nigel and I packed our bags and headed off to Bristol Airport in my eleven-year-old Renault 6.

I had never liked my Renault 6. It had been my mum's car, and when she'd bought a new one, she'd gifted me the Renault instead of offering it to the dealership garage in part exchange. I don't mean to sound ungrateful; it was a better car than the one I already had, and it served me mighty fine for my daily commute to work – a round trip of thirty miles, but it wasn't very reliable. It was often in the service garage for repair and on cold mornings, I nearly always had to push it down the hill outside our house and give it a bump start.

Happily, it was a warm, dry morning when we set out for the airport, and the engine started on the first turn of the key. We took the A38 road to Exeter, where we joined the M5 motorway. Everything was going well but we decided to re-join the A-road at Taunton instead of staying on the motorway as far as Weston-Super-Mare. I always used to feel jittery when driving to any airport to catch a flight, and I didn't want to risk getting caught up in a weekend traffic jam on the motorway. The airport is located south of Bristol on the A38, and we knew it was a much quieter road but still relatively fast as it's a dual carriageway.

So, there we were, feeling excited about flying off to sunny Portugal, singing along to a compilation tape and comfortably cruising at about sixty miles an hour until, all of a sudden, the car started losing power. A red warning light came on and we heard a horrible clunking noise coming from the engine, accompanied by smoke, the smell of fumes, and the ominous – nay, terrifying – sound of the dead knock as a piston connecting rod hit the crankshaft, and the car came to a grinding halt. We were still about forty-five minutes from the airport and mobile phones had not yet been invented.

Nigel and I looked at each other in dismay, I released the bonnet latch, we leapt out of the car, lifted the lid and peered at the smoking engine. We didn't need a mechanic to tell us this was a hopeless situation.

'What are we going to do?' My voice was croaky.

Sign your name across my heart, suggested Terence Trent D'Arby from the still-running cassette player inside the car.

'I fear we'll have to forget all about our holiday,' said Nigel.

Time, I'm sure, will bring disappointments in so many things, it seems to be the way, crooned Terence.

'I think we should hitch.' I was a member of the AA roadside & breakdown assistance, and a plan was beginning to form in my mind, 'If we can get to the airport, I can call the AA from there and they'll come out and take the car to a repair garage on a tow truck.'

And the earth rotates to our dictates, sang Terence.

Nigel wasn't convinced that hitchhiking was the best idea. 'Surely we should stay with the car. It's worth more than what we paid for our flights.'

I weighed up the value of the car, about four hundred pounds, versus the amount of money we would lose, seventy-eight pounds, if we didn't make our flight. Nigel reminded me we had travel insurance.

'It doesn't work like that,' I sighed, 'There's a one-hundred-pound excess on the insurance policy.'

'But we can't leave the car...'

'Yes, we can.' A sensation of cautious relief was drip-feeding into my veins. 'If we'd stayed on the motorway, we'd have been obliged to stay with the car. It's illegal to even walk on a motorway, let alone abandon a car and hitch. But this road is *not* a motorway.' This was the realisation I needed, it was a sign, and it was pointing me in the direction of the airport.

We silenced Terence, put the car into neutral and pushed it up onto the wide grass verge at the side of the road. We then pulled our bags out of the back, grabbed my cassette tapes in case they got stolen, and locked the doors. I figured the AA man would have some sort of a master key. I positioned myself next to the car, our luggage at my feet, and I stuck my thumb out.

I'd done my fair share of hitchhiking in the past. When I was in the sixth form, I used to skive off school on Wednesday afternoons and hitch to Yelverton to meet my boyfriend. Cousin Rosemary and I once spent ten days hitching around Cornwall and staying in youth hostels. Fiona and I hitched to Stonehenge on the Summer Solstice and got picked up by a trouser-less man. But those are all stories for another day.

This was the first time I had ever been truly desperate for a lift, and I allowed the desperation to show on my face as I mouthed a theatrical 'pleassssse' to every driver who passed by. It would not have been too hard for anyone to glean our predicament: a frantic looking couple, with a broken-down car and travel baggage, seen hitching on the road to the airport. The minutes ticked by, and the cars drove by – but only at the rate of about three per minute; the road was worryingly quiet in this rural farming district. Finally, after fifteen minutes, a small pickup truck stopped – a farmer and his collie dog with a trailer full of milk churns. We climbed up into the cab, hauled up our luggage, and my racing heart slowed. The farmer was a kindly man, but he expressed concern at our plan to leave the car.

'It'll get towed away by the police.'

I presumed the AA would be able to help us, but we still had to get to the airport and a public phone, and I sure wished the milk transporter would churn a little faster. Eventually we reached the airport, the farmer couldn't take his vehicle inside so he dropped us off at the main entrance gate, and we lugged our bags to the departure terminal – we didn't have suitcases with wheels, we didn't even have suitcases, forget the practicalities, we'd brought soft zip-up bags with shoulder straps; we were travellers, we didn't want to be perceived as package holiday tourists. We reached the check-in counter about forty minutes before our flight was due to take off, we checked in and collected our boarding passes, there was no turning back now – Nigel was still hesitant but I was determined we would get on that plane. Heading towards our departure lounge, I found a public phone, called the AA and explained our predicament. The nice man was sympathetic but explained that they couldn't help me unless I could meet them at my car.

'But we're about to get on a flight to Portugal.'

'Do you have a friend who could meet us at the car and manage the situation for you?'

'Well, my cousin John lives in Taunton, maybe he could help. Or I could just leave the car for two weeks and then arrange for you to tow it home for me?'

'You won't be able to leave it there. The police will tow it away, put it in the pound and it will cost you two hundred pounds to get it out.'

I weighed up the cost of getting it out of the police car pound versus the thirty-nine pounds each that we'd paid for our flight. Suddenly the cost of our seventy-eight-pound holiday had escalated, or at least increased by the price of a new engine, but on the other hand, we wouldn't have to pay out seventy pounds for long-term parking at the airport.

'You should at least call the police and tell them what's happened,' was the advice of the AA man.

I made a quick decision and without even conferring with Nigel, I called the police station at Bridgwater and told our story to the duty officer.

'I'm so sorry, unless you can get the AA to tow it away, we'll have to put it in the car pound and it will cost you two hundred pounds to get it out.'

'But we'll be back in two weeks, can't you just keep an eye on it until then?'

'I'll see what I can do,' he replied.

And before I had the opportunity to thank him, my money ran out, the call was terminated, and a voice on the tannoy announced that our flight to Faro was boarding. I had neither the coins nor the time to call Cousin John.

'We should hurry, we don't want to miss that plane.'

We rushed to the departure gate, relieved to have reached the point-of-no-return, and boarded the plane. For the duration of our two-and-a-half-hour flight, I was full of anxiety, fearful that we wouldn't be able to relax and enjoy our holiday.

Thankfully, all of that changed when we touched down in Portugal and busied ourselves with renting a car and finding a hotel for our first night. We had successfully put a thousand miles between ourselves and our little problem back in Bridgwater, and we barely gave it another thought for the next two weeks.

Staying no more than a couple of nights in each town: Faro, Albufeira, Portimão and Lagos, we toured all of the south coast, and then headed north up the Atlantic coast to Lisbon, where I remember being enthralled by the Santa Justa Elevator, an Eiffel Tower-like cast iron landmark, which overlooks the city, and provides the fastest way to get from the Baixa neighbourhood to the Bairro Alto district. We also sought out what was the city's only Indian restaurant at that time. Not so easy to find when you're driving in a foreign capital on the opposite side of the road to that which you're accustomed, following a not-to-scale paper tourist map to guide you through the inexplicable one-way street systems while trying to read the road signs and decipher the Portuguese language. Seventeen years before the launch of Google Maps, this was like a treasure hunt with the prize of a fiery Goan curry at the end of it.

Travelling back along the Algarve's coastline, somewhere between Portimão and Albufeira, we stopped for a walk on the Mesozoic limestone cliffs, an area typified by sea caves, and majestic rock formations sculpted by the sea. I think we were probably looking for a beach, when we chanced upon an amazing tidal ocean pool.

It was literally a hole on the clifftop, an open-topped cave, accessible only from above, although the sea had found its own way in through an arched threshold visible only at low tide. At high tide, this was the perfect natural swimming pool, measuring maybe forty feet in length by some twenty feet across. It was about fifteen feet deep, and safe, with a soft sandy floor that was revealed at low tide, when it was possible to scramble down the sides to the bottom.

It was like uncovering a secret, there was no one there, although I'm sure that now, more than three decades later, it's become an Instagram hotspot, unless it's already been eroded by the elements. We booked into a hotel about twenty minutes' drive away and this became our swimming hole for the next two days. I fantasised about buying the clifftop land, building a Portuguese villa, and having this private pool in the garden, which was flushed twice daily by the natural rhythm of the tides, and would therefore never need cleaning.

Our final two nights were spent in Faro, we wanted to be close to the airport in case our car broke down. Joking aside, I was beginning to feel nervous about returning to England, would my car still be there? Would I be greeted by a huge fine or even legal proceedings? Would I have to buy a new engine?

Or would I have to buy a new car? We shared our story with the friendly owner of a local bar and two nineteen-year-old girls who were enjoying the final night of their holiday, which had been their first overseas trip without their parents. They told us they'd been on a tight budget, but they'd had a wild time and were now spending their last remaining escudos on *aguardente de medronho*, the local firewater. We joined in their celebration, and I think we shouted them a couple of shots.

'Don't forget to set your alarm clocks,' were our final words as we bid them goodbye at midnight, they had to get a bus to the airport at six a.m. for an eight-thirty flight.

You can imagine our surprise when we found them in the same bar again the next evening, they'd slept through their alarm and their wakeup call, missed their flight home, and were now waiting for a money transfer to come through from a caring but displeased father.

Safely on board our own flight back to Bristol the following morning, our aircraft had just begun to taxi towards the runway when it stopped rather suddenly. I glanced out of the window and witnessed a right hullabaloo as a pair of British plonkers sprinted across the tarmac, shouting and carrying their suitcases on their heads. The door of the plane was opened, the airstair was lowered and, grinning broadly, the two guys were welcomed aboard to a good-natured cheer from the passengers. It was yet another reminder of the dramas that can occur when travelling.

I peered out of the window again during our descent into Bristol Airport, we were approaching from the south, so I was hoping I might spot my car still parked at the side of the road. I couldn't see it but that didn't necessarily mean it had been towed away, maybe it just wasn't on our flight path. There was still hope. Regardless of whether or not the car was still where we'd left it, we needed to get to Bridgwater to sort things out. We got a bus from the airport, and to my astonishment, relief and delight, we drove past my car, still in the same place on the far side of the dual carriageway.

At the bus station in Bridgwater, I called the AA and once again I relayed my story.

'Ah, the Landmark,' exclaimed the nice man, confirming that one of his team would meet us at the vehicle. We then had to get a taxi to drive us two miles back to the car.

'Ah, the Landmark,' said the taxi driver, with a smile.

And so, here endeth the saga.

The AA put the car on a tow truck, taking it, and us, home. The engine had seized and was deemed irreparable. Replacing the engine was unfeasible and the car was declared a write-off.

I decided I'd had enough of unreliable old cars, I needed something newer, so I rolled over a loan, and bought a red Rover.

7
A GREEK MUSE
1983

Greece has always held a very special place in my heart. There is something captivating about her blindingly bright islands. Wildflowers, rock roses and aromatic herbs line the roadsides. Steep cliff paths lead down to deserted beaches. Colourful little fishing harbours rest beneath rugged, sun-baked mountains, while almost everywhere the strains of bouzouki music can be heard on the sweet, wood-smoke-scented breeze.

During the 1980s, I visited many of the Greek islands with Nigel. We once spent three weeks touring Crete, snorkelling in limpid seas, exploring frescoed Minoan palaces, sharing meze, making friends with the local people and dancing 'til the early hours.

The Greeks were always so friendly, making us feel like their personal guests. In Crete, we met a man called Andreas, he was a fish merchant and used to drive a small delivery van, gaily painted with images of prawns, squid, octopus and red mullet. Andreas certainly knew how to enjoy himself, he was out every night, mingling with the tourists and drinking Metaxa – a brandy-like amber spirit that's blended with a secret botanical mix. One night Andreas appeared to be in exceptionally high spirits.

'Is it your birthday?' I asked.

His reply reflected his appreciation of life, despite the recklessness of his actions, 'Last night I was driving home, drunk, down a steep mountain road. I put my foot on the brakes and nothing happened…

Tonight, I am celebrating the fact that I'm still alive.'

Sadly, after living with Nigel for more than twelve years, sharing wonderful overseas trips and eventually getting married, we broke up. At the time I was devastated, I could never imagine my life being rich again without him, but in time we both moved on to pursue our distinctly different dreams. If we had stayed together, we would have sacrificed the very best of ourselves. He wanted to go to university and get an education. In fact, he went on to gain a first in his degree, followed by the achievement of an MA and a PhD, and he is now a professor of political philosophy. My dreams were more fanciful, I wanted to be a novelist and live on a tropical island; or maybe even a Greek island…

8
THE SINGLES' HOLIDAY CLUB
1994-1998

Not long into my new status of being single, the Greek islands beckoned me again. It was the end of the summer, and I had one week left of my annual leave. Abandoning my condescending attitude towards package tours, I acknowledged that this style of holiday was actually very economical, hassle free and efficient, especially as I had so little time and I wanted to go somewhere on my own. It was only when I made further enquiries that I realised I would be subjected to extortionate single occupancy surcharges. The patronising travel agent made me feel like a victim of both social judgment and unfair discrimination. I bravely and rather pompously told him I would take my business elsewhere. The Internet hadn't yet been invented so I went home to browse the ads in the travel section of The Sunday Independent.

Solos Holidays. The name jumped out at me. At the age of thirty-six, I was too old for Club 18-30, a company notorious for the bad behaviour of the party animals that it attracted. However, Solos specialised in middle-of-the-market holidays for single people aged between thirty and forty-nine, and it seemed to be exactly what I was looking for.

Solos was offering flights to enticing destinations inclusive of single occupancy accommodation in a selection of four-star hotels. I would hopefully meet some nice people and yet I would be under no obligation to spend time with them. I made a quick phone call and the following day I received the Solos brochure in the post. I immediately followed through by booking a week on the Greek Island of Kos.

When I told my friends I had booked a package holiday with a company called Solos, dedicated to fun in the sun for single people, they laughed at me.

'You're going on a singles holiday! Hahaha. It will be full of sad desperate people looking for love and marriage.'

The strange thing was that I hadn't yet considered the implications, what if I really did end up with a group of 'sad and desperate people.' I was at the lower end of the Solos age range, what if they were all forty-nine-year-old social misfits? I pushed the negative thoughts out of my head and went shopping for a new holiday wardrobe. I had read that Kos was a party island in the Dodecanese archipelago, close to the Greek island of Rhodes and the Turkish port of Bodrum. I resolved that when I got there, I would go on numerous daytrips and be a party animal at night. I was determined to have fun.

My flight ticket arrived in the post together with three big and colourful Solos' baggage labels. I had been advised that there would be twenty-eight people in the group, and we must each display one of the Solos' labels on our hand luggage so that we could all identify each other at the airport. The rep, whose name was Mike, would be wearing a name badge, he would meet and greet us in the departure lounge, and we must make ourselves known to him. It was beginning to sound like a school outing. I started to have misgivings. Were we all going to be herded around like Greek goats?

Arriving at the airport, I devised a way to hide my Solos' luggage label in the side pocket of my flight bag. I wanted to remain incognito for as long as possible so that I could discreetly observe my new travelling companions before blowing my cover. I checked-in my luggage, bought some duty-free perfume, walked into the departure lounge, found a suitable vantage point, and sat down with my book. There seemed to be a significant number of people sitting alone. Could any of them be 'Solos Anonymous' like me?

And then I saw him…

Sporting a pudding basin haircut, he was tall and thin with pasty white skin. He was wearing an acrylic polo neck sweater tucked into his brown crimplene slacks, which were secured tightly by a belt just below his chest. His trousers were way too short, exposing his white socks and plastic sandals. Lying across one of his shoulders and resting on the opposite hip was a red satchel, on which he was proudly sporting a Solos' label. Almost unable to contain his excitement, he approached a group of three people; I was disheartened to see that they were also displaying Solos' labels. One was a bearded man in his late thirties. He had the bearing of a monk and looked to be socially awkward and shy. He, too, was wearing socks with his sandals. The next was a loud brassy-looking woman flaunting a wrinkled cleavage with the promise of pendulous breasts tucked inside her pink terry-towelling jumpsuit. The third person was large and jovial; I heard him introduce himself as Patrick, but he appeared to be about sixty. It was only later that I learnt he had fraudulently slipped through the age-barrier net by declaring his age as thirty-four, when in actual fact '34 had been the year of his birth.

I double checked to make sure my Solos' label was still well hidden, and watched as a younger man, dressed in a beige safari suit, approached the group; he was accompanied by two women. The ladies were chattering animatedly; brief introductions over, they appeared to be each other's new best friends. Both wearing shorts and low-cut T-shirts, they looked as if they were already on holiday and clearly in search of romance, love and marriage with bucketsful of sex thrown in along the way. A mournful little bell tolled inside my head. They were all *years* older than me.

What had I been thinking when I booked this holiday? What could I possibly have in common with any of these middle-aged lonely hearts?

I was going to be stuck with them for the next seven days and it was already obvious that I would be expected to join in with group tours. One thing was most definitely clear, even if I did occasionally yearn for a little bit of love and romance, I wouldn't be striking a match with any of these oddballs.

I watched as 'Safari Suit' introduced the two women to Patrick, 'Pendulous Breasts' and the 'Bearded Monk.' I concluded that this must be our rep, Mike. He turned around and looked directly at me; for an awful minute I thought I'd been busted. I feared he was about to approach me and ask me outright if I was part of the Solos' group.

I realised however, that I was being unjustly critical. It's not fair to judge a book by the cover. The airline staff announced that our flight was now ready for boarding and as discreetly as possible, I stood up to join the queue. Almost simultaneously, a Prince Charles lookalike, wearing a paisley cravat, strolled over to Mike, his hands clasped behind his back.

'I say, old chap, are you with Solo Holidays? Oh, jolly good, so am I.'

My heart sank like a stone.

What had I let myself in for?

~*~

The hot September air hit me like a furnace as I walked down the steps of the plane on to the tarmac of the international airport. Mingled with the whiff of aircraft fuel, I believed I could already discern the aromas of the Greek islands – wild herbs, garlic, citrus and ouzo.

For the last three hours I had been feeling uptight and foolish, but presently, with the warmth of the sun on my face, my spirits lifted. Perhaps things would be okay after all. I made a mental note to escape and find myself a handsome Greek Adonis. Yes, things would be okay.

Nevertheless, my positivity was dampened, once again, during the bus journey from the airport to the hotel, which felt like a portent of things to come. At least half of the group had been on Solos holidays before.

'It becomes a way of life,' said one lady charismatically, 'there's a big reunion party every year in Surrey, I hope you're all going to come.'

A young woman of about my age looked at me and winced, and thankfully, I realised I had found a friend.

We arrived at the hotel and to my delight it was large and beautiful, with two swimming pools and a collection of elegant self-contained rooms that opened directly into the fragrant gardens. I worked out that I could escape from my room, with its huge double bed, without even having to walk past reception. I reminded myself I was on holiday, and a holiday is about self-indulgence and doing whatever you want to do the most. I had no intention of spending time with the desperately seeking Solos if I didn't want to, but I liked the look of my newfound friend and I hoped that we could have some fun together.

At the welcome party, she told me her name was Leonie, from Northern Ireland. We must have looked different from the other intrepid Solos, because we were joined by another girl called Carol, who also seemed out of place. Within forty minutes of our arrival, the three of us had made a pact to do our own thing, and within an hour we had invented nicknames for the remaining twenty-five, ill-assorted members of the Solo's Lonely Hearts Club Band.

Fears diminished, I examined a whole host of day-tours and activities and booked myself on a boat excursion to a neighbouring island including water sports and lunch; a shopping expedition to the port of Bodrum – a place I'd visited once before, years earlier – on the nearby Turkish coast; and a daytrip to the historic Greek island of Rhodes. Kos seemed to be pretty touristy, but that was fine, I was looking forward to some vibrant nightlife.

With our new positive outlook, Leonie, Carol and I were gracious enough to talk to some of the other Solos that evening in the hotel bar before we went out. We all agreed that we liked Patrick, the sixty-year-old Irishman who had lied about his age because he was looking for a lady under fifty. Then there was Malcolm, a Solos' veteran, he reminded us of Rod Stewart; he was a hoot. Beverley with the wrinkled cleavage was vociferous and over the top. Helen was needy yet resolute, and it showed; she acted fast and by the next day she and Mike-the-rep had become an item.

'I wonder if Mike finds a lover on every trip?' I pondered with Leonie and Carol.

Not wanting to waste any time, the three of us made our bid for freedom and fun. We escaped from the part-lecherous leers and part-envious glances of our travel companions and caught a bus into Kos Town at about ten o'clock. Following the sounds of techno music, we found ourselves in a pedestrianised area lined with bars. Tables and cushioned chairs spilled out on to the paving stones, allowing the punters to enjoy their beers and cocktails alfresco. The area, we discovered, was appropriately known as *Barstreet*.

Upon reaching the first bar, we were stopped by a local guy. He invited us to sit down and have a cocktail. We made our excuses and walked on; wanting to absorb the atmosphere and see what was on offer before committing ourselves to a drink. The same happened in the next bar and the next, and we later learnt that these guys are the *kamakis*. Named after the harpoon used to catch a fish in one deft stroke, they are specifically hired to catch customers and are paid on a commission basis. What kamaki really means is Casanova. It's practically a profession in Greece. It's seasonal, and the commission pay is meagre, but it keeps the young men busy during the summer. Most of the victims are female Scandinavian tourists.

But I didn't know that at the time…

The Adonis who tried to pull us into bar number four was successful. Leonie, Carol and I took one look at him and decided this was where we wanted to play. This guy was a drop-dead gorgeous Greek god. He asked me what I'd like to drink and held eye contact as I ordered a Pina Colada.

'I think you should try a Sex on the Beach,' he suggested.

'Okay,' I said, coyly, 'That sounds interesting.'

I sipped the sweet blue cocktail through a curly straw, seductively plucked my Maraschino cherry off its fancy cocktail stick and giggled when the Adonis alluded to the possibility of 'Some *real* sex on the beach.'

He had an Australian accent because he'd lived in Melbourne until he was fifteen, and he told us his name was

Nick. I decided I wanted a photo of him to show my friends back home, and he was happy to pose with his arm around me.

This guy was a professional; a ladies' man, and unbeknown to me a charming gigolo who was looking at the bigger picture rather than immediate gratification. I was so flattered by his attention that I was blind to the fact that he probably made a play for half a dozen different female tourists every night. I didn't consider that his ultimate aim was to find an attractive, financially independent woman who could offer him a better life than that of a barman on a holiday island. I didn't know that he spent months of semi-unemployed boredom every winter in a Greek mainland town with strait-laced parents who were pressuring him into marriage with a traditional Greek girl.

Perhaps my naivety was a blessing. Otherwise, I might have missed out on all the fun and excitement of that first week with Nick-the-Greek.

After that initial meeting, Nick made me promise to come back to Barstreet the following night. I could hardly believe my luck. I had chosen to come on holiday alone so that I would be free to do my own thing. Unlike the needy Solos, I wasn't looking for love and marriage, but I certainly wasn't going to say no to a holiday romance.

On our first date, Nick picked me up on his scooter and accompanied by his little dog, he took me to the nearby thermal springs where we bathed in warm therapeutic waters that reeked of sulphur.

He then took me for dinner at a rustic taverna on the beach; we shared fresh fish and a Greek salad, which I watched him adeptly toss in olive oil. We sat at a blue wooden table on blue wooden chairs, listening to bouzouki music and feeding each other with black olives. He tried to persuade me to eat the head of the fish, telling me it was the best part.

Most of my days during the remainder of the week were full because I had arranged activities, sightseeing and daytrips, but I spent every evening in the bar where Nick worked. He was attentive and caring and I was well and truly smitten.

Saying goodbye at the end of the week was hard; I wondered if I would ever see him again. Nevertheless, we swapped addresses and phone numbers and promised to write.

It was the end of the season in Kos, the island was about to close down for the winter, but he assured me he would be back the following May and made me promise to return and visit him again. Over the next seven months he wrote to me every week and phoned me every weekend. E-mail was still a very new concept at that time, and in those days, we relied on the time-honoured postal system; there was something truly delightful about receiving his handwritten letters.

~*~

On the first of May the following year, I flew back to Kos. My Adonis met me at the airport and once again I became putty in his hands. To be fair, he looked after me well. He gave me free drinks at the bar, and we shared the cost of our meals out. It wasn't until nearly the end of my holiday that it dawned on me that this man was a gigolo. Numerous phone calls and letters delivered to him at work, snatches of conversation, jokes and light-hearted teasing from his workmates. In fact, one of his friends casually explained to me that for a Greek man there are two types of women:

'The ones that bring out great passion and with whom every man desires a tumultuous love affair…'

'And the others?'

'The ones that you marry.'

I soon got the message. I think Nick was keeping his options open with as many girls as he could dangle on one string, and I suddenly understood that this relationship was never going to develop into love. I had already, over-optimistically, booked another flight to Kos just three months later in August, but scared of looking too keen, I deliberately hadn't told Nick.

We kept in touch after I returned to England; I revised my travel plans, and one week before flying back to Kos in August, I informed Nick that I was going island hopping on my own through the Greek Cycladic islands for eighteen days, starting and finishing with a day in Kos Town.

It proved to be a transformative decision. Dolphins cavorted alongside the ferries that took me to Santorini, Mykonos, Naxos, Paros, Antiparos, and Ios. All the places that epitomise the picture-postcard image of the Greek Islands with dazzling white buildings offset by bright-blue church domes, perfect beaches, immaculate crazy-paved streets, hilltop windmills, and wrought iron balconies draped in morning glory and bougainvillea.

I plucked up the courage to enter the bars on my own. On Naxos, I met a real-life Shirley Valentine who assured me,

'The average Greek man doesn't want an equal partner. He wants a woman to support his image, make his coffee, cook his dinner, wash and iron his clothes, raise his children, and when necessary, massage his ego so that he still feels like a man.'

On Mykonos, I met a hunky American who seduced me not only with his good looks but also with his wisdom and his wit. My self-confidence soared.

On Santorini, I was pursued repeatedly by a Greek waiter called Cosmos who disowned me when his mother made an appearance; what a candyass.

Back in Kos for the final night of my holiday, as I confidently walked through Barstreet, being greeted by the locals I'd befriended on my previous visit, I was reminded of a scene in Shirley Valentine. Towards the end of the movie, we see Shirley confidently strolling through the market square, nodding and smiling at the locals. Although her brief affair with Costas, the charming gigolo, is over, they have remained friends and she has remained on the Greek island.

Shirley stares directly into the camera and reveals, 'I have fallen in love with the idea of *living*.'

It was the same for me.

Upon returning home to England after this soul-searching voyage of inspiration, I knew that my life would never be the same again. The seed had been sown, and a plan for a future life lived overseas began to take shape.

I kept in touch with Nick and over the next three years we met up again in both England and Greece. His dreams were far more limited than mine, but I made one of them come true by taking him to watch his favourite football team, Manchester United, play at Old Trafford.

The following year, after participating in a trade union training course in Athens, I took the train to Larissa, his hometown. He treated me to three nights in Larissa's best hotel, but he didn't join me there, he told me he now had a Greek girlfriend. He had bowed to the parental pressure – and no, he didn't introduce me to his mother, but that was okay, our attachment had run its course, he no longer fitted into my dream.

~*~

It was only a few months after this that I left my longstanding job, sold everything, and flew to a new life on another sunny little island many thousands of miles beyond the horizons of Greece.

Before I take you there, however, I'd like to go back in time and share a few more travel tales that took place during my six years of flying solo in between breaking up with Nigel and flying away.

9
THE BUTCHER OF ALCOBAÇA
1993

I have a very good friend called Barbara who used to teach at a language school in Portugal, and it was while she was living there – in a town called Alcobaça, 120 kilometres north of Lisbon – that we shared a very memorable holiday with our mutual friend, Lyndsay.

Lyndsay and I had both set out from home at six a.m. to catch the early morning coach to London's Gatwick Airport. It had been a long slow journey, followed by three hours in the departure lounge before boarding our short flight to Lisbon and arriving in the late afternoon. Barb had driven down to Lisbon to meet us and had booked us all into a little hotel in the Rossio district of the city. Our plan was to relax there for just one night, and then enjoy a leisurely drive up the coast to Alcobaça the following day.

Our timing was perfect. We found ourselves in Lisbon at the height of the 'Festas de Lisboa,' an annual festival of music and dance, which takes over the entire city every year throughout June. Our arrival had coincided with the highlight of the month-long celebrations – the 'Procissão de Santo António,' a street parade that dates back to the sixteenth century in honour of St Anthony, Lisbon's most beloved saint. The merry atmosphere of this event is akin to a party; a full-blown fiesta of colourful floats, dazzling fireworks, raucous street parties, music, dance, and the local Mateus Rosé wine.

We checked into the hotel, freshened up, and went out to join the fun on the lively streets of the old town. We were soon strolling along cobblestone alleyways through the mediaeval quarters of Alfama and Mouraria, which were once frequented by aristocratic Arabs and humble fishermen. The breeze was scented with the pleasing aroma of woodfires, so we stopped at a streetside café to eat grilled sardines served with corn bread and a sweet cherry liqueur called *ginja.*

After our long and tedious day of travel, Lyndsay and I had both been feeling quite tired, but we had been re-energised by our arrival in Portugal, our joyful reunion with Barbara and the highly charged atmosphere of the festival. The ginja went straight to our heads.

By the time we caught up with the parades, we had drunk six glasses of ginja and two bottles of Mateus Rosé between us. We stood in front of the traditional tile-clad buildings in one of the stone-cobbled streets of Baixa, gazing at the view. Above us was the magnificent Castle Sao Jorge, below us was the harbour, and to the west we could see the Tagus River and the Belém Tower, built during the beginning of the sixteenth century to protect the Port of Lisbon.

Abruptly, we got swept up by a boisterous crowd of revellers and were herded towards a broad tree-lined plaza. We were offered a fresh ’n fruity sangria served in plastic cups and we watched, enthralled, as the local people began dancing to some dynamic music performed by an old man on a squeezebox. Everyone seemed to be participating, including teenage boys and young children. There were more women than men, but gender didn’t seem to matter; old ladies had partnered with each other, and mothers were dancing with their daughters. The music was compelling, I was swaying in time to the rhythm, and I wanted to join in, but I felt way too self-conscious. Unexpectedly, Barb was whisked away by a sprightly old boy in a black hat, and Lyndsay was approached by an attractive Portuguese man who didn't look to be much more than twenty-one. By now my reticence had been overcome by drunken feelings of self-pity and envy. Why didn't anybody want to dance with *me*? The music stopped, and the dancers regrouped into a long line; a partner was no longer a requirement. I joined the end of the snake behind Barb and her ageing beau with his wrinkled smile, and the squeezebox puffed and exhaled the opening notes of the Conga.

Oooh, this was marvellous, round and round we went, singing and kicking up our legs. At one point I lost my grip on Barb's red T-shirt and the line broke. Barb's familiar outline was replaced by the enormous bulk of a rotund Portuguese widow. Clinging on to her black dress, I kept catching a glimpse of Lyndsay standing at the side in deep conversation with her admirer. And then it happened…

In my intoxicated enthusiasm, I stumbled slightly on the uneven ground, briefly lost the flow, and the fat lady's foot stamped down hard on my big toe – exposed and unprotected by my flimsy sandal. I felt a sharp stab of pain, but I was having so much fun that I chose to ignore it and kept on dancing. Finally, the music stopped, Barbara politely thanked her old man and made a dash for freedom and we both headed to the makeshift bar where Lyndsay was standing with the Portuguese hunk. After a brief introduction, our plastic cups were replenished with sangria.

Lyndsay then looked down at the ground and screamed, 'Oh my God!'

Following her gaze, I was horrified to see a river of blood, coursing between the cobblestones and dripping down the steps below the piazza, its source was my big toe. Somehow my toenail had been almost completely ripped off and was sticking up like the open page of a book at a ninety-degree angle to my foot.

It was well after midnight, we had just arrived in a foreign country, we were drunk as skunks, Lyndsay had pulled, and it looked like I was going to need surgery.

~*~

'You'll have to go to the hospital,' said Barbara.

It was a sensible suggestion, but it was already very late, Lyndsay was still getting chatted up by the young man, and I didn't want to break up the party. I figured that the injury wasn't too painful and maybe I could just cut the nail off later. My toenail had been dodgy for years, ever since the nail bed had been treated with trichloroacetic acid to prevent it from growing inwards. It was crusty and misshapen; it wasn't unusual for it to drop off occasionally.

I wrapped my toe in a paper serviette and decided to refrain from dancing, but I continued drinking to numb the pain. Barbara just couldn't *stop* dancing, and Lyndsay disappeared with her new friend, promising to meet us back at the hotel later. It was one of those unforgettable evenings, tattooed onto my mind forever. Weary from travelling all day, we had been revived and intoxicated by the colour and ambience of the festival, the music, the dancing, the singing, the enticing smell of fried garlic, the traditional pots of fresh sweet-scented basil for sale on every street corner, and the summery flavour of the chilled rosé wine.

Two hours later, Barb and I wobbled and limped back to our hotel, wondering how we could possibly have been so stupid as to allow Lyndsay to disappear into the night with a strange man in an unfamiliar city in a foreign country. Poor Barb, her two friends had been in Portugal for less than nine hours and already one of them had gone missing and the other was going to need surgery.

To our relief, the first problem was resolved soon after daybreak when Lyndsay returned unharmed, happy and flattered by her encounter with the Portuguese hunk. She told us that they had walked through the streets of the pulsating city and participated in some more of the festivities before he personally delivered her back to our hotel, accompanying her in a taxi.

I, meanwhile, had woken up in severe pain and upon examining my toe I discovered that it wouldn't be possible to simply cut the nail off. The bleeding had stopped but my nail was still attached by stringy filaments of secondary skin. My toe was swollen, grotesquely inflamed and far too tender to touch; it was impossible to flatten the nail against my flesh, and I had to borrow Barbara's Teva Velcro-strap sandals because I could no longer push my foot into my own pair.

We discussed our predicament over breakfast. It was a Sunday morning; I had to choose between finding the hospital in Lisbon or waiting until we got back to Barb's home in Alcobaça, where I could visit the casualty department of a hospital that was conveniently situated opposite her apartment. I didn't want to spoil our day by searching for treatment in Lisbon; the little cottage hospital in Alcobaça sounded like a much friendlier option, so I said I would hold on.

We loaded our bags into Barb's ancient red and white Citroen 2CV. The car suited her image with its canvas deckchair seats and an open roof. It certainly wasn't a sports car and was the subject of much ridicule from Lyndsay and me.

Nevertheless, it was invigorating to feel the wind in our hair and the sun on our faces. My toe was still throbbing like a sock full of grasshoppers, but I didn't want to make a fuss. After all, it was only 120 kilometres to Alcobaça, we could be there in about an hour and a half, and then I'd be able to get some medical attention.

Unfortunately, there was a small problem with the car. After she had arrived in Lisbon, Barb had noticed a pocket-sized pool of oil on the ground underneath the engine. Optimistically presuming that it had originated from someone else's vehicle, Barbara had ignored it, hoping that by the following morning there would be no further evidence of a leak. In the morning, however, the puddle was considerably bigger. We stopped at a petrol station and Barb bought a four-litre container of motor oil and tipped about half of it into the engine.

'It'll be alright,' she assured us, 'as long as it gets us back to Alcobaça. There's nowhere I can get it fixed on a

Sunday, but I can get it sorted out tomorrow at the service garage opposite my apartment.'

'But…,' I interjected, 'I thought the *hospital* was opposite your apartment?'

'It is,' Barb countered, 'and the garage is next door to the hospital.'

So, we set off, each keeping one eye focused on the temperature gauge, which left the other eye free to take in some of the pretty coastal scenery and typical aspects of Portuguese rural life. Barbara said she would drive slowly in an attempt to avoid overheating the engine and would stop every now and again to allow the car to rest, and that way we could relax and enjoy the journey. Earlier I had taken a couple of painkillers to combat the thumping ache in my toe but already the pain had returned, and I was wondering how the hell I was going to survive the trip.

~*~

Two hours later I was sitting on a glorious white-gold beach. The sun was beating down from a cloudless sky and the Atlantic Ocean was beckoning me to swim in its cool waters. Barbara and Lyndsay had stripped down to their bikinis and embraced the gentle waves with gay abandon, but I had to be content to merely watch from the shore. I was hot, frustrated and in extreme discomfort. I had a plastic bag over my foot secured with a length of orange raffia. The objective was to keep the sand away from my injured toe.

At any other time, I would have really enjoyed the drive and all the stops that we made along the way, especially this wonderful beach. I didn't want to be a burden to my friends, but

I was in so much pain; how I wished we had looked for a hospital in Lisbon.

At last, we all got back into the car, but not before Barb had topped up the oil for what must have been the tenth time. It was already late afternoon and my injury had been festering, untreated, for seventeen hours. The oil leak was getting worse, and the journey was turning into a nightmare. Barb didn't dare drive faster than about thirty kilometres an hour and all eyes were on the temperature gauge and the rising needle. We now had to stop every fifteen minutes, oil was draining out of the sump and Barb had to continually top it up. At one point, clouds of smoke appeared from under the bonnet.

'The car's on fire!' I screamed.

Luckily, it was just some surplus oil that had been spilt on the hot engine. I began to feel nauseous, clearly caused by a combination of anxiety, misery, pain, and oil fumes.

It was eleven o'clock and dark by the time we reached the outskirts of Alcobaça, where we stopped for a pizza at a fast-food restaurant. The car had survived the journey and Barbara said she would take me to the casualty department at the hospital right away. I knew, however, that having the toenail removed would probably be harrowing. I was exhausted, and I couldn't bear the thought of any more traumas until I had had a decent night's sleep. So, for the second time, I put off the hospital visit until the following day.

At nine o'clock the next morning, refreshed and relieved to be doing something positive about my predicament at last, I went to the hospital with Barbara. The place was full of people and there appeared to be no order, everyone was pushing to get to the registration desk at the front. I was used to a formal queuing system. *How was I ever going to get attended to?* Suddenly Barb spotted someone she knew, a hospital administrator, and I was rapidly whisked away into a back office to complete the paperwork. Payment, it seemed, took priority over treatment. I stared at the dirty white walls and inhaled the smell; it was a blend of garlic breath, stale sweat, cigarette smoke and disinfectant.

After a few minutes, I was instructed to go into the doctor's consultation room and lie down on the couch. To my surprise, the doctor wasn't there but I was not alone. A group of about ten people were sitting around talking and smoking, they didn't look like medical staff. I removed my borrowed sandals and pulled the temporary dressing – the paper serviette – off my swollen toe. It was a real mess. The door flew open and the doctor waltzed in. I gasped in dismay. Instead of a white coat, he was wearing a white plastic apron; he was carrying a tray of sharp implements and he looked more like a butcher than a doctor. Actually, he reminded me of the Barber of Seville, a huge man with a vast stomach and a fearsome handlebar moustache.

The Butcher of Alcobaça briefly examined my grotesque toenail, donned some surgical gloves and reached for one of his gruesome instruments. I recoiled in terror as I realised that he had no intention of giving me a local anaesthetic.

'Anesthetico por favor,' I begged repeatedly in my pidgin Portuguese.

My ten 'roommates' stopped gossiping and settled down to enjoy the show. Pokerfaced, the butcher ignored my pleas, turned his back on my face and swiftly performed his surgery on my toe. He must have been efficient, I nearly hit the nicotine-stained ceiling, but thankfully the searing pain only lasted for a few brief seconds.

My toe was then gently cleansed and bandaged by a compassionate nurse. Sadly, I could neither swim nor dance for the remainder of my holiday. However, I will never forget grooving in the cobbled streets of Lisbon, captivated by the sweet aroma of woodsmoke and fresh basil, and the cheerful melody of a squeeze box.

10
SHATTERED DREAMS IN LANZAROTE
1991

I had just met the man of my dreams… another one. He lived in my hometown. I'd seen him around for years and he'd always given me a friendly wave or a dazzling smile, but that was the extent of our communication; he was married and so was I.

It wasn't until I had unexpectedly assumed a new status of being single – and discovered that this guy was also newly single – that my interest in him was kindled and we spoke to each other for the first time. He told me that his wife had left him six months earlier and he was devastated. I idly wondered how any woman could leave someone as good-looking, talented, and successful as… let's call him 'Dick'. I think it might have been the first time he had ever been rejected. He had been with Kate, his wife, for ten years, he had helped her to get her first job and had then watched her blossom into a self-assured young career woman. I guess she didn't need him anymore.

My first date with Dick was a success – or so I thought. Maybe I was just in denial of the clues that were there from the very beginning. We had enjoyed a lovely evening together, but he bid me goodnight with a mere peck on the cheek and made no mention of wanting to meet again. However, after a fretful ten days of waiting and hoping, my phone rang, and we started seeing each other on a regular basis. I was impressed by his beautiful house; he had designed and built it, brick by brick, almost entirely on his own. He wined and dined me and took me out on weekend daytrips in his BMW. To be sure, he enjoyed my company, but in retrospect, I think he just saw me as a distraction from the memories of Kate. She had a new boyfriend, he was hurting, I made him laugh and lifted his spirits from time to time, yet I was a poor substitute for his perfect ex-wife.

It was Dick's idea to go away on holiday. He explained that he hadn't had a holiday for years and he thought it might do him good to get away and relax. Another distraction.

I remember thinking, *This is all about you, Dick, snap out of it and stop feeling so sorry for yourself.*

He was wallowing in self-pity, but I didn't voice my feelings, I was energised by the prospect of a holiday together, maybe he would overcome his depression and start to realise that I was his perfect woman after all.

He wanted to go on a package holiday. Oh, how I hated the thought of a package holiday. Where was his spirit of adventure? Furthermore, he didn't want to go to Italy, Portugal or mainland Spain because those were all places he'd visited with Kate. He didn't want to go to The Seychelles because that was where he and Kate had spent their honeymoon. That only left us with about one hundred and eighty-something other countries to choose from, but he said that Asia was too dirty, Australia was too far, and America was too dangerous – he remembered once reading a story in a newspaper about a British tourist who had been shot dead in Florida. I had to acknowledge that he was just a little bit too safe and boring for me. Scandinavia was too cold. Switzerland was too expensive, Africa was too hot, and he didn't think he'd like the food in Greece. My Mr. Perfect was turning into Mr. Pain-in-the-Arse. I suggested France but that was out of the question because he'd heard that Kate was planning to go there with her new fella. So, we eventually agreed upon a week in Lanzarote in the Spanish Canary Islands, and Dick gave me carte blanche to go ahead, choose a hotel and book the holiday.

The Canary Islands attract Scandinavian sun worshippers, German grannies, British lager louts and French family groups. Described by the Lonely Planet as *A seething mass of oiled flesh jiggling to the beat of discos, bars and gay nightclubs*, these seven Spanish islands – previously known as 'The Fortunate Islands' but not so fortunate for me as it would turn out – lie in the Atlantic Ocean only one hundred kilometres from the coast of Africa. I had been told that the islands were chockfull with tacky hotels and the sort of bars where you can pretend you never left home. I feared that we were about to experience mass tourism at its very worst.

Lanzarote is dry and arid; it hardly ever rains there, and its stark landscape is bizarre and fascinating. In 1730, the island experienced one of the world's greatest volcanic eruptions, which lasted for six years and spewed thousands of tons of molten rock into the air. The sand on the beaches, and the fertile volcanic soil in the flower-filled, white-walled gardens, is as black as coal.

My first choice of hotel was full. If it had been available, this holiday and Dick's future may have turned out very differently. Blissfully unaware of what fate held in store, I booked my second choice, an attractive *apartel* at Playa Blanca – the name means 'white beach' and boasts the only area of white sand on the island. The hotel comprised about two hundred small apartments with balconies and verandas overhanging a central courtyard with two large swimming pools. This wasn't exactly what I would call an adventurous trip; it was a middle-of-the-market package holiday to a place that has been embracing mass tourism for many years. The only adventurous part was in trying to win the heart of a man who was yearning to be reunited with his ex-wife. I had a week in which to try to make him see sense.

Arriving at our destination, happy yellow sunflowers nodded and smiled at us. We were shown to our immaculate accommodation where pink bougainvillea draped every entrance; Dick was impressed. Maybe he could now start forgetting about Kate and focusing on me. Maybe I could cure him of his OCD, his blinkered negativity, and his over-cautious attitude, by teaching him that travel broadens the mind.

For the first few days, I actually believed I was making good progress; Dick was relaxed, and happy to go with the flow. We rented a car, went everywhere and saw everything that this lovely little island has to offer. We were awestruck by the stark and desolate volcanic landscape of the Timanfaya National Park, reminiscent of a barren planet. Distorted, twirling stacks and tapered columns of solidified lava stuck out of the ground like black stalagmites, punctuated by volcanic cones. We relished a delicious lunch after watching our food being barbecued on a grill over the natural heat that was rising from the red belly of the volcano. We went out every night, drank jugs of sangria and ate tapas in romantic restaurants. Everything seemed to be going remarkably well.

On day four of the holiday, we took the ferry over to the nearby island of Fuerteventura. We relaxed on a white sandy beach, while I introduced Dick to the joys of snorkelling – although he didn't exactly take to it like a fish to water. Later, we drank sunset cocktails in a beach bar, and I squirmed when he discarded the contents of his almost-full glass of Negroni because a fly had briefly touched down on the rim. For me, this was confirmation indeed that he was obsessive, compulsive and anal-retentive, which I already knew were personality traits that wouldn't gel too well with mine. *Did this mean we were incompatible?* I was disappointed. However, little did I know that – for completely different reasons – day five would prove to be the beginning of the end.

Dick was a sociable soul, and often, during the week, while I'd been reading my book beside the pool, he had drifted off to chat to various other guests who were staying at the hotel. He told me he'd met two Welsh girls; he suspected that one of them was seriously ill, but he admired her positive outlook on life. Their names were Glenda and Lynn and he introduced them to me when we were on our way out to dinner; they seemed quite nice. The next evening, Dick asked me if I'd mind if he invited the two girls to join us for dinner. Unquestionably, I minded. I wanted Dick to myself. But I couldn't tell him that. I was still trying to play the cool, independent, laid-back girlfriend.

We all went out to dinner, and we learnt that Glenda was indeed, very sick. Lynn told us discretely that her friend was in partial remission from Stage IV cancer. She had been given just six months to live. She was only twenty-nine years old.

We had a pleasant enough evening with them, but Dick focused all of his attention onto Glenda, and Lynn appeared to be put out and I perceived a little bit jealous. I couldn't work out what was going on, I was wary of Lynn, but I was struck by Glenda's courage and zest for life. Dick insisted on paying the bill and the girls then insisted that they would treat us to dinner the following night. I didn't want to go. It was the last night of our holiday and I wanted to be alone with Dick but of course I agreed. How could I have refused without blowing my cover.

Everything that had been good about the holiday was over. Dick wanted to spend the final day hanging out with Glenda and Lynn beside the pool. I guessed that he had probably told them that our relationship wasn't serious or – even worse – that it had been a mistake. In the evening they took us out for dinner. I tried to laugh at all the jokes and posed for numerous photos, but I felt miserable inside. I knew by now that I had lost Dick; the mystery was to whom? Why was he focusing all of his attention on a woman who had been given only six months to live? *Surely, he couldn't be imagining a future with her.* We all swapped addresses and I pretended to be enthusiastic about keeping in touch.

~*~

I only saw Dick twice after we got back from our holiday. We went out for a drink, and he asked for copies of all of my holiday photos with some additional duplicates for Glenda and Lynn. I assumed that our relationship was over.

When I challenged him about it, he insisted it was just a friendship, there was 'No *relationship* to end.'

A week later, he called to tell me that Glenda had invited herself to come and stay with him the following weekend.

'I don't really understand why she's coming,' he confided.

'Maybe it's because you encouraged her,' I retorted.

He invited me to join them for dinner on the second evening of her visit, and through a mixed bag of emotions: indignation, displeasure, puzzlement and curiosity, I observed that things seemed to be awkwardly platonic between them.

Glenda invited Dick to visit her in Wales; I was excluded. Dick didn't hesitate. He took time off work and made the three-hour journey to Swansea to stay with Glenda and presumably catch up with Lynn as well.

When he got home a few days later, he called me to say that he and Lynn had 'hit it off' and had got 'something wonderful going on.'

I could only conclude that he had been deliberately and cruelly directing his attention upon Glenda in order to win the jealous Lynn's heart. How could he be so selfish and calculating? How come his broken heart had mended so quickly?

To my chagrin, six weeks later, Lynn put her house on the market, sold it, left Swansea, and moved in with Dick. They got married within a few months, had a baby, and moved to another town.

I was disenchanted and a tad humiliated but I was determined not to feel bitter. Although I disliked Dick's manipulative methods, I acknowledged that he'd met the woman he wanted to be with for the long term, and while it's true I didn't care too much for Lynn, she wasn't a homewrecker, she was just a woman who believed she had met her Mr. Right.

From the whole sorry experience, I learnt to lower my expectations and not to give my heart quite so quickly and easily. I was soon to realise that my priority and dream in life was not about finding a man but about finding a special place in the world. I heard that Glenda's brave spirit held the cancer in remission for considerably longer than the predicted six months, but I never saw any of them ever again.

~*~

11
ANCIENT WONDERS, MODERN WORRIES
1996

As the plane descended towards Cairo Airport, I sat with my face glued to the window, hoping to get a sneak preview of the pyramids. I was visiting the city on a four-day stopover en route to Tanzania, to be followed by a second stopover of twenty-four hours on my way home. This was barely enough time to explore Cairo let alone get a true feel for the country, but it would be a taste of somewhere I had wanted to visit ever since I was twelve years old when I'd achieved top marks for a school project on Ancient Egypt.

Much of my enthusiasm had been fuelled by my father's stories of his numerous visits to this country, both as an RAF pilot and as an airline pilot. He was also a writer, meticulously recording every detail of his travels on an old upright typewriter, and likewise, my twentieth century 'Flight into Egypt' had been exceptionally inspired by something he had once written. It was an account of an experience in May 1938, when the RAF sent out five 'London' flying boats to Australia as part of the 150-year, or sesqui-centenary, celebration of Australian Federation. The boats were twin-engined, with round open cockpits and an inner cabin. They each carried six or seven crew – captain, second pilot, third pilot, a fitter, a wireless operator and a rigger. On the last leg home, they had stopped off on the Egyptian coast 140 miles west of Alexandria at a place called Merea Matruh.

My father and another member of the crew went off on a daytrip, and the following is taken from his description of a village they passed through:

'...It was not long before we stopped, enthralled by its biblical aspect, at a Bedouin cattle market, where the shepherds carried crooks and sometimes a lamb across their shoulders. Towards sunset, we diffidently entered a mosque and, after exchanging courtesies with the dignified muezzin, asked to be allowed to accompany him to the minaret from which he would call the faithful to prayer. He graciously consented. In the red glow as the sun set over the western desert, whilst swallows fluttered about the tower, we listened to his moving cry, which was repeated from the four corners, being careful ourselves to remain out of sight from the ground, as he had bid us. Would it be blasphemously unchristian, I wondered, if I were myself to whisper a prayer to Allah for a strong easterly wind?'

Now, nearly sixty years later, I was learning that Egypt still maintains an atmosphere that is reminiscent of stepping back six or seven centuries. Bedouins still live in goatskin tents and farmers still plough the earth with the simple tools of their ancestors. I discovered that Cairo was where the mediaeval world and the contemporary western world meld together. Here, luxury five-star hotels, constructed of concrete, steel and glass, flank the banks of the mighty Nile, while towering office buildings compete to share the skyline with the domes and minarets of the mosques.

Entering the vast city, my ears were assaulted by a cacophony of shouts, car horns and ghetto-blasters, accompanied by the distinctive summoning cries of the muezzins. Later, as I walked the streets, I witnessed the chaos of the city traffic where the donkey carts were as terrifying as the BMWs.

Cairo is the biggest city in Africa. At the time of my visit, it was home to more than twelve million inhabitants. I noticed tiny alleyways lined with mudbrick houses, and I'd been told that due to the gross overpopulation of the city, even the ancient sprawling Necropolis, known as the 'City of the Dead', is a residential area. Nobody knows how many people dwell in the tombs, but the figure is estimated at over one million. This series of vast Islamic-era cemeteries provides living space for some of Cairo's poorest inhabitants and has become a city in its own right with shops, tea houses and even factories.

My accommodation was considerably more upmarket. As a lone female traveller, I had chosen to stay in one of the classy hotels on the banks of the river. It hadn't really been necessary to book in advance and I could easily have found somewhere a lot cheaper, but I didn't regret my decision; the view of the Nile from the window of my room was spectacular. Yet, there was one thing that was bothering me. I'd booked my hotel at the same time as I'd booked my flight, and because of this, I had been met at the airport by a representative of the travel company. Mr. Ali was a big man with a loud laugh, a balding head, and a hooked nose. He seemed kindly and knowledgeable, but he insisted on taking my passport in order to arrange another entry visa for me. This was because I was returning to Cairo for the second half of my stopover on my way home from Tanzania. If I had not been alone, I might have accepted that this was a formal procedure, and I might not have been quite so reticent. I argued with Mr. Ali that I wanted to keep my passport in my safe possession, but he maintained that another entry visa was a compulsory requirement. He gave me a receipt, together with his contact details, before dropping me off at my hotel. He promised that he would be back, with my passport, to take me to the airport the following Saturday morning at seven o'clock.

I was alone in a foreign country with no passport. *What had I done?*

~*~

The man in the long flowing robes and the strange headwrap was waving his arms at me, pacing to-and-fro in the hot sun and shouting.

'You told me twenty minutes; already I am waiting forty minutes.' He looked extremely angry, animated, and a little bit scary.

I decided that the angry man was probably just a good actor. He was a taxi driver who had insisted on waiting for me while I browsed the market in 'Islamic Cairo', the old mediaeval quarter of the city. I had known that my mission might take considerably longer than twenty minutes and when I arrived, I had tried to pay the driver and send him away but at that stage he had refused to take my money, assuring me that it was his duty to wait for me. So, I had wandered, enthralled, through the labyrinths of the covered market in search of a belly dancer's costume. I eventually found a shop where I was kitted out with a stunning heliotrope outfit complete with sequins and cascading beads, a string of gold coins to wrap around my hips and a yashmak to cover my face. My plan was to make a striking entrance at the next fancy-dress party I attended back home in England. Right now, however, I was feeling a bit foolish. I had been well and truly duped by the taxi driver. I calmly asked him how much extra money he would require for his time; we agreed on a somewhat inflated price and once again he was all smiles and charm.

Yes, I was loving being in Cairo, but I couldn't shake the fear of no longer being in possession of my passport. I was going hot and cold at the thought of it. Maybe things would be okay, maybe not. There wasn't much I could do about it at this stage, but in the meantime, I was permitting this magnificent city to envelop me as I walked through the streets lined with mosques and temples. Crossing the chaotic main roads was a death-defying undertaking. On one occasion, I allowed a kind man to help me. I was really grateful to him and in return I agreed to accept his invitation to visit his brother's shop; I bought a lapis lazuli cat. Yet again I was being fooled by traditional scams, falling into common tourist traps and feeling obliged to part with my money. I was later taken on a tour of an impressive perfume factory, and I spent far too much money on a bottle of jasmine oil; but it didn't matter. I inhaled the sweet fragrance of the jasmine, which mingled with the enticing aromas of street food, I detected coriander and cumin, which in turn merged with the smells of traffic fumes, animals and squalor.

Likewise, the two predominant colours of Cairo seemed stronger, deeper and more concentrated than anywhere else I had ever been. The view of the city exposed a striking contrast between the faded sepia brown of the sandstone buildings and the intense violet blue of the clear sky. During the late afternoon, as the sun began to drop, the sepia turned to gold; long shadows stretched over the stonework like a giant's limbs, and rich tones of chocolate brown spread across the picture, which was now crisper and clearer than it had been all day.

The next morning, as I stood in the flat desert, hypnotised by Khufu, Khafre, and Menkaure, the three pyramids at Giza on the west bank of the Nile, I felt like an infinitesimal speck in the history of humankind. There was I, alongside the Great Pyramid, Khufu, the oldest of the Seven Wonders of the Ancient World, which has been standing for more than four-and-a-half-thousand years. These pyramids have survived the rise and fall of great dynasties and conquerors. It was a humbling and overwhelming experience that made me realise that my missing passport was comparatively insignificant. My next trip was to the Egyptian Museum, and for a change, nobody seemed to be interested in taking any money off me. The treasures of Tutankhamen's tomb were heavily guarded; I acknowledged how privileged I was to see the four gilded shrines and the famous gold mask, together with chariots, gloves, and jewellery. Wandering through the remainder of the rambling building, I felt like an explorer. Many of the exhibits were unlabelled; others were unreadable and appeared to be almost as ancient as the antiquities themselves. In one dusty corner, I stumbled upon a whole heap of sarcophagi jumbled up with some rusty old electric fans.

On my last morning, I rose early and waited in anticipation for the arrival of Mr. Ali with my passport. To my relief, he was punctual, cheerfully presenting me with my re-entry visa. Strangely, I felt a little bit cheated, if I had known with certainty that he was going to turn up I would have had nothing to worry about.

Mr. Ali escorted me to the check-in desk at the airport for my flight to Dar es Salaam. I was feeling relaxed and carefree again. If I had been aware of what I would be bringing home with me from Tanzania, I would have had yet something *more* to worry about. On the other hand, I guess I might have been a bit more vigilant.

12
BOILED EGGS, BIG CATS & BLOODSUCKERS
1996

'So, I'll see you on Saturday week, is there anything else you'd like me to bring?'

'Yes, Cadbury's chocolate, Marmite, wine, and don't forget the vid…'

Our telephone conversation had come to another abrupt end; for the third time, the line had gone dead. I'd been talking to my dear friend, Jackie, who had recently moved to Dar es Salaam in Tanzania. Her husband, Andrew, was working for an engineering company, managing a pipe-laying project. They had jumped at the opportunity to live in Tanzania for ten months and I had jumped at the opportunity to visit them. It wasn't until they had arrived in Africa, however, that they discovered the lack of availability of so many essential commodities. For Andrew, as manager of a company that relied on technology, this was particularly frustrating. Telephone connections and communications were tenuous, corruption was rife, and his budget for the project was insufficient to pay the enormous import duty that was being levied on the essential items he was obliged to import.

Meanwhile, personal needs were equally important, and I had been given a long list of toiletries, books, and food products to bring with me. Also, in accordance with the audiovisual technology of the mid-nineties' era, I had purchased about a dozen blank VHS video tapes on which I had religiously recorded hours and hours of British television shows, dramas, documentaries, comedies, and movies for my friends to watch. They had correctly anticipated the lack of entertainment and nightlife in their new hometown and had brought their own VHS player with them from England.

It was a relief when the elderly aircraft landed at Dar es Salaam; I had changed flights in Muscat and boarded a small, dodgy looking plane. It had been a rough and bumpy ride and I'd been alarmed to see smoke emerging from under my seat. I'd pointed it out to a member of the cabin crew, but no one seemed concerned. I felt a bit nauseous and all I wanted to do was get out into the open air, but I could see that disembarkation was going to be rather chaotic. The plane was packed with local people, and everyone seemed to be carrying at least two, string-bound cardboard boxes and half a dozen plastic carrier bags each, all bursting at the seams. The international regulations regarding hand baggage had not been enforced on this flight.

I finally alighted on to the tarmac and felt like I had walked into a hammam. Having just come from Cairo where the weather had been pleasantly hot and sunny, the intense heat and humidity that greeted me in Dar es Salaam promised to be challenging. It didn't seem to be any cooler inside the airport building; I cleared immigration and then got apprehended by customs. I hadn't exceeded my duty-free limit and I wasn't bringing in any drugs or firearms, so what was the problem? The customs officer wanted to examine every item in my luggage but thankfully he didn't seem to be aware of the necessity of Cadbury's Dairy Milk Chocolate, Marmite, mascara, Germolene antiseptic cream, or Tampax, and he lost interest in my video tapes once he realised that the plastic cellophane had been removed and they were, therefore, no longer new. I later learnt that if he had been able to assess the value of what I was bringing into the country, he would have tried to charge me one hundred percent import duty.

Dar es Salaam is a hustling, bustling seaport that straddles some of the most important sea routes on this planet. Here, Arab dhows mingle with huge ocean-going vessels.

My friends were living the expat life in a colonial-style house provided by Andrew's company. I hadn't expected to see the security guards, the solid entrance gate and the impenetrable fence bordering the property. I was shocked when I noticed the metal bars on the windows and discovered the bolted iron gate at the top of the staircase, inside the house. They had been recommended to padlock it every night. Was Tanzania really that dangerous? Jackie explained that certain areas and activities were unsafe. For example, it was far too risky for a woman to go to the beach alone, so it had been necessary for them to join the expensive yacht club in order to have regular access to a private and secure beach. However, by joining this club, they had made many new friends and had smoothly integrated into the expatriate society. In fact, Jackie had truly embraced Tanzania and I was so proud of my friend. After only five months in the country, she could already communicate superbly in Swahili and had become involved with a local children's orphanage. She had also smuggled half a dozen electric deep fat fryers into the country and set up a fish 'n chip venture with a friend. On Wednesday nights they cooked beer-battered fish and chunky chips in the true English style for the expat community. The day after my arrival, Jackie took me down to the busy fish market at Kivukoni Front. Every morning at dawn, the dhows sail in to offload the night's catch and I stood back, fascinated, as Jackie bartered with the yelling fishwives, each of whom was brandishing a knife or a cleaver. The harbour was scruffy, and the smell of fish clung to the oppressively hot air.

On my second night, only half an hour after Jackie and I had slightly-drunkenly stumbled upstairs to bed, we were woken by the sound of gunshots and shouting. Terrified, I peered through the bars of my bedroom window and saw the security guards running around the garden in circles, flashing their torches and bellowing loudly. I had never seen them so animated; normally they were prostrate and fast asleep. To my further disquiet, Jackie then appeared in the garden, and told them all to shut up and calm down. As soon as she had heard the gunshots, she knew exactly what had happened. She had left some eggs on the boil in a saucepan, got drunk with me and forgotten all about them. The pan had boiled dry, and the four eggs had exploded.

We had a good laugh about it over another late-night beer. The hardboiled eggs had been intended for our picnic lunch the next day.

Tanzania is still Africa as it should be. A land of mountains, lakes and savannah plains, which are home to some of the world's largest game reserves, and early the following morning we were setting out on a safari. I had been told that nowhere else on this earth would I see wildebeest, gazelles, zebras and antelope in such enormous numbers. There are far more animals than people and, at the time of my visit, there were remarkably few tourists to enjoy these riches.

Jackie had already been on three safaris. She kept a notebook in which she was ticking off all the animals and birds that she had seen so far. She told me we could expect to see the big five: lions, gazelles, giraffes, zebras and cheetahs, but my greatest desire was to see a leopard. The previous day I had been talking to one of Andrew's friends, he had been going on regular safaris in Tanzania for fifteen years but had never seen a leopard. He explained that they were shy, solitary, nocturnal creatures and the chance of spotting one of these spotted cats was pretty remote. He mentioned that they slept in trees; I resolved to keep my eyes wide open in search of one.

Safari in Swahili means a journey, and our journey began early in the morning when Jackie and I left Dar es Salaam in a robust four-by-four with a driver-guide called Obi. Obsessed with my mission to spot a leopard, I asked Obi if he had ever seen one. He shook his head, sadly, adding that he had been on many safaris. As I polished the wide angle zoom lens of my camera, I concluded that I had better focus my attention, and my lens, on the other creatures instead. Obi warned us that it wouldn't be safe to open the windows or get out of the vehicle.

As we were only going on a short, one-day safari, we were heading for Mikumi National Park – a small oasis relatively close to Dar es Salaam, presenting an incredible game density. Before we even entered the park, we encountered monkeys and elephants. We observed a young herd of elephant bulls feeding off the trees. We were so close to them that I wondered if visiting a game reserve really counted as seeing animals in the wild. Jackie assured me that the beasts were most definitely undomesticated and explained that before the days of game reserves, wild animals used to roam into the towns and eat people.

So, I stayed in the vehicle, but I felt very honoured to be able to observe these majestic elephants so intimately. We were close enough to see their eyelashes and watch the nimble work of their trunks picking up tiny pieces of vegetation. They looked so benevolent that it was easy to forget that they can charge at speeds of well over forty kilometres an hour.

At first, we saw so many animals that the safari seemed all too tame and easy. We saw herds of giraffe, zebra, wildebeest, impala and comical warthogs but I soon found out that in between sightings we could go for long periods of not seeing anything. The birds were particularly striking, and I loved watching the greater and lesser flamingos paddling in the shallow waters of the lakes. We also saw Thompson gazelles, Grant gazelles, antelopes, jackals and a monitor lizard. Then we found a pond full of hippos, but despite hanging around for about twenty minutes we never actually saw the hippos, only the tips of their nostrils when they came up for air, and the bubbles they were blowing under the muddy water. It wasn't long before we encountered our first cats, a family of cheetahs.

In the meantime, I was still scanning the treetops, in the keen hope of sighting a leopard. Obi told me that only experts could discern leopards in trees.

'They are far too well camouflaged.'

It was in the late afternoon that my wish was astonishingly granted. The sun was beginning to cast dappled shadows across the savannah plain through the leafy trees, and fantastically I noticed a long, spotted tail hanging down from a lofty branch. It was so familiar, the very same colours and pattern that adorned my big floor cushion, a skirt, a dress, a pair of shoes and three pairs of knickers. My real-life leopard was beautiful; he had been dozing peacefully until we disturbed him. He looked a bit peeved at having been woken up and started to descend the tree headfirst – leopards being one of only a handful of cats that can do this. I had to be restrained from opening the window. I was desperately trying to focus my camera lens in an attempt to get the perfect photo, and only had time to snap one shot before he swiftly jumped to the ground and disappeared into the undergrowth. It seemed as if I had somehow manifested my greatest desire of the day; a wonderful experience for all of us.

Later, Obi shyly asked me if he could have a copy of the photo. I promised to send it to him when I returned home to England. It came out quite well and I had two prints enlarged, which I posted to Jackie with instructions to put one in a frame and give it to Obi. This was a man who had no access to a camera; he didn't even have photos of his wife and children. Jackie told me he was overwhelmed with his gift, and it was a real pleasure to learn that our safari had been as special for Obi as it had been for us.

~*~

Ahhh… Zanzibar. What is it about this place that makes it so exotic to people who haven't even been there and hardly know where it is? For years I had wanted to visit this bewitching little spice island that has lured travellers for centuries. Some of those travellers were in search of cloves; some were trading in ivory, while others were players in one of the darkest, most tragic and disturbing episodes in the history of mankind, when Zanzibar was regarded as the hub of the East African slave trade.

I didn't really know what I was in search of, or what to expect. At first, I was just attracted by the name; Zanzibar sounded seductive and mysterious, but now, I knew that my Tanzanian adventure would not be complete without a visit.

A spicy blend of African and Arab culture, with influences from China, India, Europe, Egypt and more, the island lies within the Zanzibar archipelago, which also includes Pemba, another bead in a necklace of islands that thread their way down the shore of East Africa. Historically a separate nation, nowadays Zanzibar is officially part of Tanzania, although it is still necessary to show your passport to get in, which is worth it for the stamp.

Jackie and I booked accommodation in Stone Town, the old city and cultural heart of Zanzibar, where little had changed in two hundred years. Then, bursting with enthusiasm, we set out early to catch the ferry from the port of Dar es Salaam. We secured a good vantage point on the boat and watched, engrossed, as the vessel was loaded up with fruit, vegetables, textiles, cardboard boxes full of electrical commodities, and a rainbow of plastic buckets, bowls and homewares. The activity was feverish and frenzied, tall graceful African ladies in brightly coloured attire were carrying mountains of merchandise on their heads; there was music, shouting, hooters were blaring, and aromatic smells filled the air. This was so exciting; before our journey had even begun, we were being treated to front row seats in a living, pulsating theatre of commotion.

The ferry took just over two hours to reach Zanzibar, and my spine tingled with anticipation as the little island came into sight. After the shantytown buildings that I had observed in Dar,

I was totally entranced by the once grand and extravagant architecture of Stone Town. It is a place of winding alleys, lively bazaars, palaces, cathedrals, mosques, and faded colonial mansions. We wandered the chaotic labyrinthine cluster of meandering streets, lined with crumbling whitewashed buildings and imposing three-storey Arab houses, with their crenellated parapets and magnificently carved, brass-studded, wooden doors. We browsed the markets and the little shops and bought traditional fabrics, a painting, sparkly sandals and a brass bell.

At lunchtime we found a pleasant café on the harbour. It had been constructed on a wooden jetty and once more we were entertained with the dynamic activity of the port. A fleet of small fishing vessels was returning from the open sea. The boats were similar to sampans with oars and no sails, and each was carrying a weighty catch of fish, together with four or five crew members. While two of the men on each decrepit craft were desperately trying to row and make some headway, the remaining crew members were bailing out the water that was rapidly filling the bottom of each and every boat. Their equipment was basic; just a few small plastic jugs and aluminium saucepans to save maybe a dozen, overloaded, leaking vessels from sinking. It was also a race against time in order to get these battered boats, crew and cargo safely into the harbour. We wondered who would have to work the fastest, the oarsmen or the bailers? This was clearly an everyday performance, accompanied by much shouting, panic and hilarity.

Freddy Mercury was born in Zanzibar. So, one evening, we paid him homage by having dinner at Camlur's Restaurant, which at the time claimed to be Freddy's former family home. We relished a spicy fish curry, listened to the haunting rhythm of Swahili drumbeats, and discussed our expectations of the spice tour that we had booked for the following morning.

Our hotel was as enchanting as the island. It wasn't expensive, but it would have once been a distinguished building. Now, like many of the other houses in Stone Town, it was badly in need of restoration. The coralline rock of Zanzibar was a good building material, but it also eroded easily.

I thought that the muslin-draped four-poster beds under the open-beamed ceilings were dreamy, and I didn't give much thought to the reason behind the nets. Malaria in East Africa is rampant but hey, I was taking the tablets, I'd be okay.

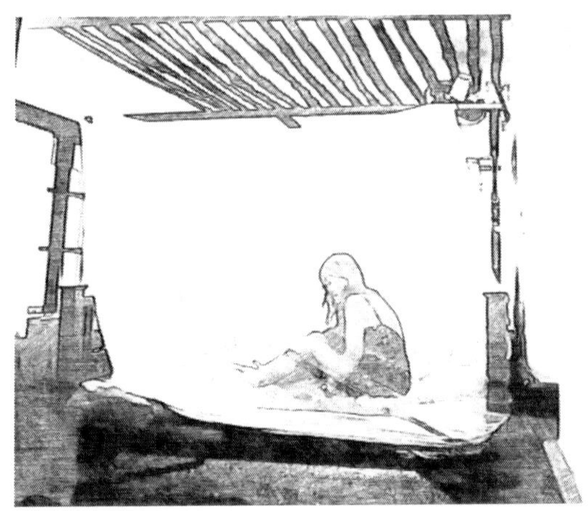

~*~

'Are you waiting for Mr. Mitu?' enquired the driver of the dusty old pick-up truck outside the Cine Afrique.

'Yes,' I replied, surprised and rather pleased.

I had been dreading that Mr. Mitu would turn up in a large, air-conditioned bus.

Jackie and I were about to embark on a spice tour and had no idea what to expect. Our enquiries had led us to Mr. Mitu, the most famous and knowledgeable spice tour guide on the island.

Mr. Mitu proved to be charismatic, charming and entertaining, with a genuine love of the environment and a pride in his island home. Our excursion was simple, enlightening and captivating; a close-to-nature experience that presented us with spices, plants, fruits and healing herbs that we had never even heard of. We learnt about their uses in cooking and cosmetics and their incredible value in curing numerous ailments. At Mtoni, in the overgrown gardens of the Maruhubi Ruins, we came across a neem tree. We learnt that chewing a couple of neem leaves every day reduces the possibility of contracting malaria. Mr. Mitu also gave us a guided tour of the ruined palace, built in 1882 to house the impressively large harem of Sultan Bargash.

At the end of the tour, we found ourselves in a small village, where the local women had prepared a magnificent vegetarian feast. Platefuls of rice were served with a delicious selection of curries cooked with many of the spices and plants that we had been introduced to on our nature trail. These ladies were not only artists in their makeshift kitchen, but also in their skilled application of henna and Indian ink. When we had finished eating, they painted our skin with temporary tattoos.

I was sorry to leave Zanzibar; this beautiful island proved to be one of the most appealing places I have ever visited. After a few more days in Tanzania, I returned home to England, stopping off once again in Cairo.

~*~

In Tanzania I had been plagued by mosquitoes. My hatred of these blood sucking, disease spreading parasites was justified by the reaction of my skin to their 'venom'... a multitude of angry, itching, red swellings that very often became infected, forming large blisters.

Just before my visit to Tanzania, there had been a lot of media exposure in the UK about the dangerous neuro-psychiatric side effects of the controversial prophylactic, Lariam, aka mefloquine hydrochloride, which at the time was the most prescribed antimalarial drug in the world and clearly the most effective. An increasing number of Lariam users had reported depression, nightmares, panic attacks, epileptic-type convulsions, headaches, visual and auditory hallucinations, paranoia and other psychotic symptoms after taking the drug, describing it as *a horror movie in a pill.* Other researchers claimed that the charges had been sensationalised, and that if patients were properly screened and the medication was prescribed with informed consent, then its benefits would far outweigh its risks.

Jackie had informed me that most of the expats in Dar es Salaam opted not to take Lariam because it was not viable for long-term stints, and after listening to the warnings of the media; I went against my doctor's recommendation and chose not to take it. Instead, I attempted to make do with some foul-smelling repellents and the prophylactic, Paludrine, and chloroquine.

Unfortunately, this was not adequate protection against the malaria carrying mosquitoes of Africa. There are more than 3500 different species of mosquito, of which two hundred species have developed documented resistance to at least one insecticide. These deadly creatures can smell us from as far away as fifty metres, their saliva contains an anti-coagulant to prevent the blood from clotting, and they will continue to suck our blood until they have had their fill. If I had taken Larium, I would have had a thirty-eight percent chance of experiencing some of the vile side effects but what the media had failed to mention was that by not taking it, I was risking a ten percent chance of contracting malaria.

Two weeks after I returned home to England, I got sick. I spent twelve days in bed with an unrelenting headache, liver pains and an intensely high fever characterised by violent shivering and demented sweating. It was diagnosed as malaria. The identical symptoms recurred two years later, and to a lesser degree every two years or so for the next decade. But hey, no pain no gain. I will always cherish my fabulous memories of Tanzania and Zanzibar.

13
SEEKING ALHAMBRA IN MALTA
1997

My maternal grandfather was a senior civil servant who held high ranking positions in a number of British naval dockyards overseas, including Gibraltar, Bermuda, and the tiny Mediterranean island of Malta where the family lived from 1930 until 1932, when my mother was in her mid-teens.

Twenty-four years later, my mother returned to Malta with my father and my brothers. My dad was based there for work, for a year. This was all before I was born, but I grew up hearing stories about sunshine, rocky beaches, limpid waters, and Maltese housekeepers. Even Dingli, the family cat, had been named after a district in Malta.

Forty years after my family left Malta, and over sixty years after my mother had lived there as a teenager, I decided that I wanted to visit the island country that had been their home. Both my parents had died, and I felt a burning need to learn a little bit more about the influences that had shaped their lives. It was like going on a treasure hunt but before setting off, I needed to find some clues. Without my parents to turn to, I had to get my information from my mother's brother and sister, and from my own brothers. I learnt that the house where my mum's family had lived in the early 1930s was called 'Alhambra'. I think it had come with my grandfather's job. I wondered if it would still be standing. An old school friend of my mother's,

Cella, still resident in Malta, had visited my aunt on a recent trip to England. I wrote to Cella and told her that I would be visiting Malta with my friend Lorrie, and she invited us to join her for afternoon tea when we arrived in the country. Lorrie was almost as enthusiastic as I was about researching my family history, and it was a pleasure to have her share my quest.

From the minute our plane touched down in Malta, I was surrounded by familiarity – and my parents. Nearly every entrance door in the capital, Valetta, boasted a shiny brass doorknocker; some were fashioned in the familiar shape of a dolphin, just like the doorknocker that my father had brought back from Malta in the 1950s. It had graced the front door of every house we had lived in since, and I remember my dear old dad lovingly polishing it on Sunday mornings. I recognised the handmade Maltese lace; it was the same as the lace cloths that had adorned the tables in the houses where I had grown up.

Lorrie and I stayed in a tacky hotel, but it didn't matter. The kitsch aspects of Malta are all connected with tourism and didn't exist in the days when my family lived there. Even now, the island's staunchly Roman Catholic culture has helped the Maltese maintain a tight-knit community and control on runaway development. The capital, Valetta, is a beautifully preserved sixteenth-century walled city, and the Grand Harbour is breath-taking. After a hotchpotch of cultural influences, which included being a British colony for 150 years, Malta gained state independency in 1964. Yet the British influence remains throughout, and my mum's old school pals, Cella and her friend Mary, turned out to be eccentric, comical caricatures of elderly colonial Brits who had never left. They were both seventy-nine years old and had attended a convent school with my mother and her sister. We were made very welcome at Cella's yellow-walled house in Sliema and drank Darjeeling out of bone china teacups as we listened to the two old ladies telling stories about life in Malta in the 1930s. Cella informed us that Alhambra, my grandfather's tied house, had been empty for some time and was looking rather neglected these days – apparently a property developer had bought it but couldn't get the necessary planning permission to enlarge it. She directed us to the house; it was only a few minutes' walk away from her own home. The street was very ordinary, and the houses alongside were fairly simple and a little bit shabby.

Nothing had prepared us for Alhambra; certainly not Cella or indeed my uncle back in England. Yet the name should have given us some clue of what to expect. There was no garden at the front, no long driveway; the property was set only a few feet back from the road, with just a gate and a low wall topped by a wrought iron fence between the narrow pavement, a set of crumbling steps, and the front door.

When Lorrie and I reached the house, we gasped in astonishment; loudly and unashamedly exclaiming words that would have horrified Cella and Mary. It was a petite street-side palace, faded and decaying, but not beyond redemption.

Once it would have been grand and splendid; now it was rundown, romantic, exotic and delightful. The Moorish architecture, complete with highly intricate stone carvings, horseshoe arches, graceful columns and perfect symmetry was in a very small way reminiscent of the famous Alhambra Palace in Granada, Spain. I tried to imagine my mother and her sister as teenagers, running down the hill and entering the house through that same front door. We peered through the grimy windows at a domed ceiling, and a dusty floor of geometric mosaic tiles; it was enchanting. It was strange to think that my mother probably just took it for granted along with her privileged childhood and household servants.

Later Lorrie and I visited the house where my parents and my brothers had lived in 1956, it was far more ordinary. We sought out Dingli Street and the imposing Dingli Cliffs on the southwestern coast of Malta, and I was reminded of our family cat of the same name who had lived to the old age of seventeen. We visited magnificent Catholic churches and tried to tone down our language when we once again gasped in amazement at the opulence and splendour of the frescoed interiors.

On the next-door island of Gozo, we both got a little bit sozzled in the heat of a Mediterranean afternoon when we entered a wine cellar and sampled some of the local Gozitan wine. It was wickedly sweet and potent. While we were there, Lorrie found herself spellbound by a heavy stone statue of a fertility goddess, whose pagan representation was in stark contrast to the Catholic paraphernalia and bling that dominated the souvenir shops.

'She's speaking to me,' claimed Lorrie, 'I just *have* to have her.'

She purchased the fertility statue, carted her home in her hand luggage, became instantly and unexpectedly pregnant, and has ever since been loaning her goddess out to any friends in need of a little bit of help in conceiving a child.

In contrast, my choice of souvenir was a brass dolphin doorknocker. I placed it on my front door and rather pretentiously renamed my house 'Alhambra'. It was a private acknowledgement of the time that my family had spent in Malta. My treasure hunt had yielded a hoard of riches.

14
A FORTUNE TELLER TOLD ME
1997-1998

'You are about to change your life completely,' declared the fortune teller, a kindly grey-haired gentleman who appeared to be receiving messages from the 'other side'.

'You will be moving east.'

I didn't believe in all that clairvoyant mumbo jumbo. I had only agreed to see the man because he had scheduled a day of fortune-telling at my friend's house, and he needed to have at least six clients in order to make his journey worthwhile. He claimed to be a medium who communicated with the spirits. What intrigued me was the way in which he was listening and then thanking his invisible guide for each new piece of information, and his uncanny accuracy had already grabbed my attention.

'Your reason for being in Plymouth will shortly no longer be there.'

'Yes, that's right,' I replied earnestly, 'the office where I work is closing down, and I'm going east to Exeter.'

Two weeks earlier, I had learnt that the corporate bank where I worked was undergoing a restructuring process and streamlining its administration. I had been privy to this restricted information in my role as National Vice President of the company's trade union. I was living in a small town and on the days when I wasn't attending union meetings, I was commuting fifteen miles to work at an admin centre in Plymouth. All fifty members of staff had yet to be informed of the forthcoming closure, which would take place the following year. We would be presented with the option of remaining in Plymouth and working in one of the bank's sales offices, or alternatively relocating to the Exeter admin centre – forty miles away – with the benefits of a generous relocation package. The third option was to commute to Exeter daily with travel expenses paid, and the final option, if we wished, was to apply for voluntary severance – and get a big redundancy pay off and leave the company altogether. However, this was not a guaranteed option, just a preference that we could apply for; there was a limited budget for severance and therefore a limit to the number of staff that the company was prepared to let go of and pay off.

I hated the idea of working in sales and I didn't want to move from my beloved home, so I had already decided to opt for the daily commute to Exeter – a journey that would take less than an hour each way and could probably be shared with two of my commuting workmates.

The fortune teller interrupted my thoughts. 'No,' he said, 'you will be going a lot further than Exeter.' He then proceeded to tell me that I would be moving east to somewhere much warmer, 'Where the sun shines, beside the sea.'

He explained that I was already sorting things out in my life and having a major clearing-out process, building myself up for a lot of blossoming change.

'You and your values are readjusting, and you are getting ready for something major because you are about to change your life completely.' He added, 'You will be forced to stand on your own two feet, you will let go of all your security; there will be a removal van coming and you will sell everything and leave.'

I shook my head and smiled at the man's ignorance. 'My plan is to commute to work each day at the new office in Exeter.' The thought of selling my house and all my possessions was inconceivable.

Mr. Fortune Teller smiled too – knowingly. 'This will be your window of opportunity through which to fly,' he advised me, 'you must be adventurous and not take the easy option.'

Yet he reassured me that the move would bring me a lot of happiness and a lot of love.

'You will meet someone in your new life who will make you very happy, he will bring love into your life, and you will walk on the beach together, kicking pebbles in the sand.'

The psychic predicted that the preparation, transition, and settling-in period would be three or four years, and then, at that point, my creative talents would be unleashed like a raging torrent, and I would make millions. He said, 'The whole picture into the future is sunshine apart from the initial period of change. Your life hasn't really begun yet and you are still waiting for the start.'

I pondered over his words; I was thirty-eight-years-old. *How could my life have not yet started? How could I possibly earn millions?* The advice kept coming.

'You must grab this opportunity with both hands, you will feel like you have been thrown into the sea, but you will walk out of the difficult patch onto dry land. You must be like a dog with a bone, and you will not let go of where you want to be.' He then added that there would be a lot of hanging around waiting for it to happen.

Poppycock, I scorned silently, dismissing everything he had said. I was going to work in Exeter. East, yes, but there was absolutely no way that I would ever consider selling my precious house.

I had recorded the man's prediction on a cassette tape, but I'd just tossed it aside. It was to be nearly four years before I listened to that tape and the clairvoyant's words again.

Any sceptics reading this might suggest that, despite my absolute certainty that this was not going to be my path, the fortune teller could have planted a seed within my subconscious. I don't think he did, I knew exactly what I wanted at that time. I wanted the security of my job, and my comfortable home and my life in England. However, four months later I changed my mind. I didn't want to sell my home, but I had a large mortgage on my house and a personal loan, and I figured that if I applied for the redundancy package and was lucky enough to get it – there were no guarantees – I could pay a lump sum off my mortgage and clear my debts. Furthermore, after nineteen years of working for the bank, I was fairly confident that I would easily get another job with another company. It was July 1997 when I volunteered for the severance, and my years of service meant that the package would be the equivalent of more than two years' tax-free salary. However, I was told that no decisions would be made until the following March. In the months that followed my application, I started giving some more thought to the opportunity that it afforded and decided that I'd like to take a year off to travel the world. I had no intention of selling my house and obviously it would also mean that I would spend the money on travelling instead of reducing my mortgage debt.

Travel and life experience is more important, I convinced myself.

A sleeping desire was beginning to stir in my heart. My mother had died two years earlier, and my father had passed away twelve years before that. I had a brother in Australia, a brother in America and a brother in England, I had no children, and I had no partner. Travelling was my passion. I was free. My only commitment was my mortgage.

By November 1997, I had decided that I would like to do more than just travel around for a year, I now wanted to pursue my teenage dream of living and working overseas.

Maybe I could rent the house out?

That, however, would put me in a vulnerable position, I would still be obliged to pay the mortgage each month and the money that I would receive in rent might not cover this, together with the cost of maintaining the house, buildings and contents insurance, and paying fees to a letting agent.

What if something were to go wrong? What if I got the tenants from hell? What if they wrecked the place? The house was more than seventy years old. *What if I had to suddenly find the money for new windows and a new roof?*

Meanwhile, some of my furniture and personal effects would have to go into storage, which meant yet more ongoing expenses. I concluded that if I really wanted to live in another country, then I would have to sever my ties and sell my house.

Yet I couldn't possibly sell my home, it was too special; I had put so much of myself into it...

It took me two weeks to make the agonising decision to sell; it was one of the hardest decisions I have ever had to make in my life. Yet I still had to wait a further four months before I would know if my application for voluntary redundancy had been successful.

By this time, I had forgotten all about the fortune teller, yet his prediction was already proving to be eerily correct –

'Lots of hanging around waiting for it to happen.'

In February, I put my house on the market, by now I had decided that even if things didn't go according to plan, I would still leave my job and sell up. Yet, in reality, I desperately needed the severance money because property prices had plummeted, which meant there was almost zero equity in my house. All I would gain from the sale would be freedom from my obligation to pay the mortgage. Additionally, it was a very difficult time to sell houses. The market had slumped, finding a buyer could take a long time, and despite the fact that it was a charming house with a gorgeous rural view, it was a bungalow. Nothing wrong with bungalows except that the people who tend to favour single-storey houses in the UK are generally older people who perhaps can't cope with climbing stairs; this bungalow was built on the side of a hill and there were twenty-two concrete steps leading up to the front door. It wasn't an old person's house, and nor was it a potential family home, the steps would have been unsuitable for prams and pushchairs, and dangerous for young children, while families with older children might have been deterred by the fact that it only had two bedrooms.

Nevertheless, there was still plenty of time; my plan was to try to sell the house by September, the month of my fortieth birthday. I didn't want to leave England before then because I wanted to have a big farewell birthday party before I set off.

In March, the bank finally let all of the staff who had applied for severance packages know if their applications had been approved. I was so nervous on the day; my appointment with my boss was scheduled at four-thirty in the afternoon. I felt sick, my stomach was in knots, and I couldn't stop running to the toilet. This was someone else's decision, and it would change my life.

The fortune teller had told me that this would be my 'Window of opportunity through which to fly.' This was my destiny.

I was trembling when I entered the boss's office, and I was shaking when I came out. He asked me why I was looking so worried, and after he had given me the answer I was aching to hear, he'd commented, 'Did you really think your application might be declined?'

The relief was immense, and when my body calmed down, my anxiety was replaced with pure elation. I would receive my big payoff soon after the office closed on the first of June. Now all I had to do was sell the house.

During the weeks that followed, everybody who was leaving the company was offered the opportunity to go on an exit course. This was professional advice and counselling on what sort of employment or career we might now be suited for, including help on how to write a CV, how to apply for a job, how to approach a job interview, how to retrain for a new career or start one's own business. There was even advice on working overseas. It was one hundred times better than the terrible advice that Mrs. Pengelly, my careers teacher, had given me at school. The first thing I was asked to do was to complete a multiple-choice questionnaire to assess my strengths and my skills.

The result was clear-cut. I was creative and I was a communicator, the exact requirements for being a writer – the path that I would have followed had Mrs. Pengelly not scoffed at my 'fantasies' of wanting to become a novelist and live on a tropical island.

So far so good, although before I could even think about being a writer, I had to sell my house and then decide on where in the world, or more appropriately whereabouts in the tropics, I wanted to live. The happiest moment of my life-up-until-that-point occurred when I packed up my desk and left my job at the bank, forever.

For the next few months, I relished the freedom of being unemployed for the first time since I had left school. I went to my nephew's wedding in the US, I visited a buddy in Cyprus, and I travelled all over England, as well as visiting Wales, Scotland and Northern Ireland to say goodbye to my many friends before heading off for my new life.

I had some interest in my house, but the estate agent was very pessimistic about its marketability. There was a problem with it. The large retaining walls below the house, which were holding back the hillside, were cracked in several places and I was informed that they had not been built properly. I was confident they were not going to fall down; they had already been standing for fifteen years, but I also knew that no building surveyor would risk his reputation by confirming that they were sound. I also knew from working for a bank that any offer of a mortgage of over sixty percent would be subject to a condition that the walls were rebuilt, and a large portion of the loan would be withheld until the work had been completed. This would be enough to deter most buyers and make it almost impossible to get a mortgage on the property without having to put down a large deposit.

Granted, I wasn't in any great hurry, I was quite happy not to sell my house until I was ready to leave the country after my fortieth birthday party in September. In fact, I decided the perfect date for the completion of the sale would be one week after my party. I didn't plan to have the party at home, but I knew it would be good if I could enjoy the house right up until the last possible minute. Of course, these were just my personal feelings; I had no intention of influencing or delaying the date of sale. I knew I would let the house go at any time if only I could find a buyer.

Incredibly, my estate agent found a cash buyer, someone who had enough money to pay for the house outright. She didn't need a mortgage and she wasn't fazed about the cracked walls. Moreover, without any input from me, we completed on the sale six days after my fortieth birthday party. It was meant to be.

My *I'm Forty and I'm Fucking Off* party was a blast; it was held in a private function room at my local pub and 120 people attended. Naturally, I invited my estate agent, a lovely woman called Kate, who, it's worth mentioning, was the ex-wife of the anal-retentive Dick. My good friend, Allison, made me a beautiful birthday cake fashioned in the shape of a rucksack and a pair of hiking boots, yet I still had no idea where on Earth I was going to go.

~*~

During my months of happy unemployment, I had busied myself with research on living and working abroad. I applied for VSO – voluntary service overseas, but my application was turned down on the basis that I didn't have a profession. I wasn't a doctor or a nurse or a teacher or a dentist or an engineer. I also made enquiries about living and working in Australia because my brother, Jeremy, was there. However, I knew in my heart that I wanted to live in Asia.

Two weeks prior to my party, my friend Carolyne had called me to report that she'd seen a job advertised in The Daily Mail looking for timeshare sales reps in Bali. I assured her that I had no desire to sell timeshare.

To which she replied, 'Well, it would get you started; you'd make contacts and maybe you'd find something better when you got there.'

I had been to Bali once before, for a two-day stopover en route to Australia in 1982, but I hadn't considered the possibility of living there, and I really didn't want to apply for a timeshare job. If I had seen the ad myself, I wouldn't have looked at it twice, but because Carolyne had taken the trouble to think about me and call me, I felt that the very least I could do was to make some further enquiries.

I contacted the company and was told to send them my CV, which I did. I didn't even receive an acknowledgement and I didn't care; I really had no interest in pursuing the job. However, ten days after my party, just after I'd moved out of my house, I received a phone call from the timeshare company inviting me to a seminar in London, which was four hours' drive away. I probably wouldn't have bothered except by strange co-incidence, I had already arranged to travel to London on the day before the seminar and stay with my newly married nephew and his wife for a couple of nights. My plan had been to check out some specialist long haul travel agents and the possibility of purchasing a budget round-the-world air ticket. Remember, at this time the Internet was still very much in its infancy, and it was long before the days of on-line bookings. I asked the lady from the timeshare company where the seminar was taking place and she told me it would be at the Hammersmith Novotel; a mere five minutes' walk from my nephew's house. The Universe was making it uncannily easy for me.

Of course, I got the job; timeshare companies will take on anyone who is willing. There were no terms of employment, and all earnings would be on a commission-only basis. The company provided no contract, no salary, and no work permit, but I didn't care, I embraced the adventure because I had nothing to lose.

Three weeks later, with my house sold, my furniture in storage and my life in a suitcase, I was on my way, bound for the sunny nirvana of Bali.

15
THE WINGED MESSENGER
1982 - 1999

I first became aware of the winged messenger when I visited Bali for the first time in 1982. He is a prominent figure in the ancient Hindu culture, and his name is Garuda, which, in the Indonesian language, means eagle. Believed to represent the sun's rays, he is the devourer of serpents and the king of birds, books describe him as 'mythological' – legendary yes, fabulous yes, but this guy is no myth in *my* book. Half human and half bird, he is the vehicle of the supreme god Wishnu, and an ever-watchful go-between with the power to swiftly travel between the worlds.

Garuda, what a great name for an airline. I always used to think it was a special compliment to the tiny Hindu island of Bali that in 1950, about a year after naming its flag-carrier airline, 'Garuda Indonesian Airways', the Republic of Indonesia chose a complex symbolic representation of Garuda as its national emblem. Actually, the symbolism goes back way before the invention of jet engines, back to the thirteenth century when Islam first arrived in Indonesia and adopted some of the traditional ornaments for its own use.

It was probably because I flew to Bali with Garuda Indonesia that my interest was aroused all those years ago. I remember seeing wooden statues and stone carvings of the mystical, anthropomorphic Garuda perched upon a pedestal, and when I returned to England, I wished that I had purchased a memento of him to take home with me.

It was some six years later when I was browsing through the Oxfam Christmas gift catalogue, full of handicrafts from Bali, India, Thailand and South America, that I saw him again. I could have sworn he flew out of the page at me. Mail order Christmas gifts for my friends forgotten, I just knew that I had to have the hand-carved, wooden Garuda mask. The price was only five pounds, yet it was so important to me, I would have paid a lot more. Two weeks later he arrived. No, he didn't fly, he just landed on my doorstep, packed soundly in shredded paper and polystyrene chips in a large cardboard box delivered by Parcel Express.

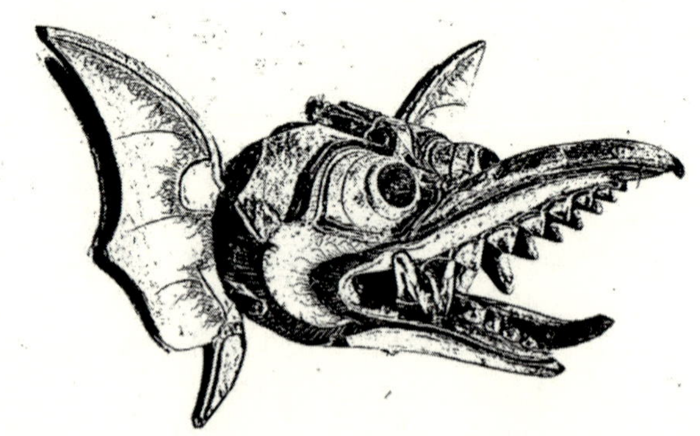

I hung him up in my hallway where there was an imposing archway, positioning him in the centre on the apex. With his long beak, prominent pink tongue and sharp teeth, big ears and bulging eyes, all my visitors noticed him as soon as they stepped inside my house.

'Arghh! What's that?' people used to ask.

'That's Garuda,' I would reply, 'he's from Bali, he's a protector and he brings good luck.'

After a particularly difficult period in my life, one of my friends commented, 'Well, he didn't bring you much luck did he.'

It was food for thought, but now I reckon he helped me through the hard times and gave me the strength to prepare for what was coming next. I believe the winged messenger-between-the-worlds – in my case, the contrasting worlds of England and Bali – had a plan for me. He didn't want me to languish in a small town in England. Instead, he wanted to take me back to his earthly home in Bali, so that I would have the opportunity to embrace some of the many alternatives that this life has to offer.

It took the winged messenger ten years to deliver his message; to coax and cajole me, convince and prepare me, but after that it was easy. Allow me to explain…

The set of circumstances leading up to my new life was unprecedented. I had always wanted to live and work overseas, but the time had never been right, and then suddenly the time was just so very, very right; everything was pointing to, and leading me in, a very precise direction. I knew I wanted to travel, but I had no plans to sell my house and then abruptly it seemed to be the most obvious way forward. I had to sever my ties, no point in doing it half-heartedly, I had to be fully committed but I still had no idea where I wanted to go. Yet, following a series of bizarre coincidences, everything just very simply slotted into place. I received an unanticipated offer of a golden handshake from my longstanding job. I sold my house, despite pessimistic predictions from the estate agent about its lack of marketability. I received a couple of unexpected telephone calls. I got swept up in a great wave of unyielding energy, jumped at an unsubstantiated offer of work, and found myself bound for a faraway tropical island.

In the end he didn't come with me, he sent me on ahead of him, alone. I left my magical guardian in a storage warehouse, but I never forgot him. I was poignantly reminded of him nearly every day in Bali; Garuda was all around me in the form of statues, stone-carvings, woodcarvings, paintings, insignias and souvenirs. A year later I returned to England in order to sell my furniture. Although my flimsy job hadn't proved to be fruitful, I had no doubts that I wanted to stay and live in Bali. I carefully retrieved Garuda from his cardboard box in the warehouse and together we flew back to our island abode. Inferior jobs gave way to something good, and my new life in my new world came together.

My protector has long held pride of place in my Balinese house; my visitors notice him as soon as they walk in, but nobody squeals, 'Arghh! What's that?'

His face is far too familiar in Bali and, for me, an enduring reminder of how the island came to be my home.

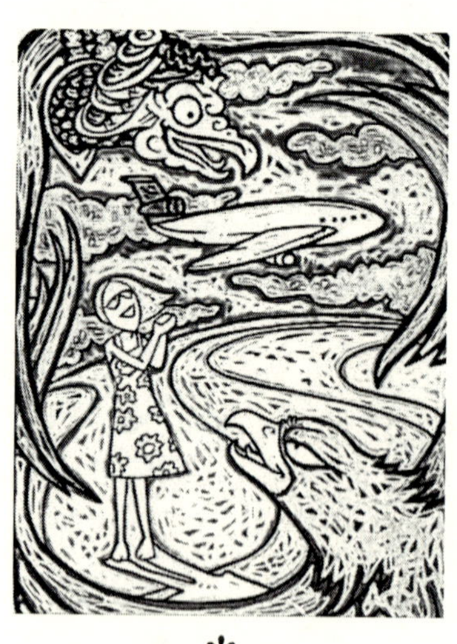

~*~

16
FLOWERS FOR GANESHA
1998

The captain had announced our descent into Bali, I could feel the pressure building up in my ears as I peered out of the window at a thickly forested area and my first perception was that the island was not as overrun with tourists as the guidebook had suggested.

Abruptly, the land gave way to the ocean, the plane banked steeply and for a few minutes all I could see was the sky. We turned sharply back inland, and I realised that my twenty-hour journey was almost over as we flew at just a few hundred metres over white-capped waves towards a golden crescent-shaped beach, which I later learnt was Jimbaran Bay. Glancing down I could see a myriad of tiny fishing boats shaped like canoes with outriggers on either side. The beach appeared to be almost deserted. A quiver of excitement ran down my spine and my eyes pricked with emotion as we approached the runway. *Could this sunny little tropical island really be my future home?*

The heat hit me like a furnace as I walked down the aircraft steps onto the tarmac. Wide-eyed, I had arrived and was inhaling the first breath of my new life. I patiently queued with the other passengers in the arrivals hall and cleared immigration. Removing my heavy suitcases from the carousel reminded me of the fact that my luggage was well overweight; I certainly needed a lot more than if I had just been coming for a two-week holiday and it was lucky that I hadn't been charged excess baggage at Heathrow. I was waved through customs and proceeded out through the open doors into a sea of faces, scanning the crowd for Jay, the man who had interviewed me in London for my new job. He had told me on the phone that he would be at the airport to meet me in person; tall and handsome I knew he would be easy to spot. Someone stood directly in front of me and asked if I was Miss Rachel? It was only then that I noticed he was carrying a signpost with my name written across it in large letters. Unfortunately, he was neither tall nor handsome, and he certainly wasn't Jay.

'How did you know it was me?' I enquired as he introduced himself as Agus.

'Oh, it very obvious,' he replied, 'you no tourist, you alone, lots of luggage.'

Agus procured a taxi and we set off together for my hotel. He sat next to me and barraged me with dozens of questions, 'You have husband? You have children? You want me take you on tour of Bali?'

I didn't want to talk, I wanted to gaze out of the window and regard my new home. We were soon heading along a wide street with narrow pavements, where large hotels were displaying a flutter of long tapered flags, shimmering in the breeze, their shape and bright colours reminding me of jesters' hats. We should have had right of way, but at every junction cars pulled out in front of us, horns blaring.

Dozens of noisy motorbikes overtook us on all sides and the taxi driver was silent as Agus continued to pump me for information. 'This your first time in Bali? How long you plan to stay? What your programme for tomorrow?'

I tried to be polite. 'I visited Bali once before, but it was only for a two-day stopover and it was many, many years ago. I plan to stay for a long time – if I like it here, and tomorrow I think I will need to sleep and relax.'

I was feeling a bit cooler now, the air conditioning in the taxi was a relief and I apologised to Agus but I wanted to look at what was going on outside.

'You have a McDonalds here.' I exclaimed.

'Oh yes,' replied Agus proudly, 'McDonalds always very busy.'

We were now passing some smart designer shops; I hadn't expected this, I had no recollection of any modern, glass-fronted buildings in the Bali of sixteen years earlier. Past the Hard Rock Hotel and we were beside the beach. *Surely this had just been a sand road the last time I was here?*

To my relief, the sea hadn't changed, massive breakers were rolling in towards the shore; the sand was the colour of rich honey, and a lapis sky was reflected in the water. I was mesmerised by two surfers riding the waves.

'How old are you?' was the next question.

'Don't you know it's rude to ask a woman her age.'

The taxi had ground to a halt and the traffic was at a standstill. Four, lean, sexy, young men, all with long black hair, were crossing the road in front of us and a small thin man was manoeuvring some sort of a food trolley to my left. Meanwhile, a couple of red-skinned sunburnt tourists seemed to be having an argument with a local guy carrying a small suitcase.

'What's he selling?' I asked Agus.

'Watches. You want? He sell Rolex and Tag Heuer, anything you like. I get you good price.'

'No thanks Agus, I already have a watch.'

We inched forward slowly and were overtaken by what I believed was a bicycle, its rider completely obscured by a rainbow of beach balls and inflatables. I looked back at the beach. Sun, sea, sand, and surf. The excitement was building up inside of me again. Palm trees lined the street and we moved towards a group of women gathered in the shade of a white-blossomed tree. They were all dressed alike in sarongs, sashes, and lace blouses. I wondered why, but I really didn't want to ask Agus any more questions, plenty of time for discovering answers at a later date.

'I don't think you're going to enjoy selling timeshare very much,' the irritating voice interrupted my thoughts.

Well, I didn't think I was going to enjoy selling timeshare either, but it was the last thing I wanted to hear within an hour of my arrival.

My hotel was a peaceful oasis, shielded from the chaos outside. Ornate fringed parasols flanked the intricately carved wooden doors. Outside my room was a statue of Ganesha, the Hindu god of making things happen and the remover of obstacles. There was a red hibiscus flower on my pillow and two cockroaches in my bathroom.

During the next forty-eight hours, I was attacked by an army of mosquitoes, I awoke during the night to find my bed shaking violently in an earth tremor, and a moneychanger with the hands of an illusionist short-changed me by the equivalent of twenty pounds. I breakfasted on banana and honey pancakes and drank avocado juice laced with chocolate. Wandering around the haphazard street stalls and shops, I was amazed that there was so much to buy: shorts, T-shirts, woodcarvings, kites shaped like galleons, wind chimes and photo frames. I tried to relax on Kuta Beach.

'You want massage?'

'Plait your hair?'

'Paint your nails?'

Women carrying baskets of fruit on their heads, their faces wrapped up in sarongs to protect them from the fierce sun.

'You want pineapple?'

'You want coconut?'

'You want cold drink?'

On my third day, I escaped from Kuta in a scruffy old car with a driver, and discovered volcanoes in the mist, pink water buffaloes, hot springs, lush tropical jungle and emerald-green rice terraces that were rivetingly beautiful – I was enrapt. Moreover, I was aware of a powerful spiritual energy; a force so strong in Bali, yet lost in the Western world, deeply buried under a strata of consumerism and commercialism.

Smiling happy faces greeted me on the streets, everyone at the hotel seemed to know my name and offerings of flower petals were placed outside my door each morning by a young girl wearing a *kebaya,* a *kamben* and a sash

Meanwhile, every day, I placed flowers behind Ganesha's ears, and by day five, I knew with absolute certainty that I was in Bali to stay.

17
TIMESHARE SCAMS
1998

Having decided I was in Bali to stay, I now needed to focus on earning some money. It appeared that the timeshare company had kindly given me a few days to settle in and get over the jetlag, whereas in reality, I had just missed the start of one training course and was having to wait six days until the beginning of the next one. Nevertheless, I was keen to start the training and meet the other new recruits. From having observed the guests at my hotel and overheard a few loud conversations, I was aware that I had already seen some of the workforce, but they were part of the previous influx of newcomers who had landed in Bali a couple of weeks before me and already finished their initiation and started work. They all seemed to be very self-confident for young people who had just arrived in a strange Asian country to begin a challenging new job. I say *challenging* because if we didn't sell, we wouldn't earn, yet allegedly there was some excellent money to be made by those who were good at it.

The first day of my training course dawned and I got a taxi to the training centre in Kuta. I'd been told it was opposite the Ramada Bintang Hotel, which was easy to find, but I had been so worried about getting lost and arriving late that I got there about thirty minutes' early. As I whiled away the time and tried to calm my nerves by sipping a banana juice in the hotel lounge, I brooded on how vital it was to make a success of this job. I had burned my bridges back in England; I already knew that I wanted to stay and live in Bali. My redundancy package was not going to stretch as far as I'd hoped, so I had to find a way to survive.

The training centre was just a room in an old and poorly maintained building, but at least it was airconditioned and cool. My hotel room only had a fan. My four classmates were all middle-aged Englishmen, all older than me. They were staying in a hotel in Kuta and were a complete contrast to the cool, cocky, twenty-something-year-old Australian dudes I'd scrutinised at my hotel in Seminyak. These old guys looked like burnt-out used-car salesmen, which is actually almost-exactly what three of them were. I could see that, like me, they were suffering from the heat, their shirts were dripping in sweat, and on first sight none of them looked to be a very appealing representation of the company that we were about to start work for. *Would anyone really consider buying a timeshare apartment from one of these slobs?* .

Steve was stocky and heavily built with thinning hair and a London accent and had indeed been a car salesman although he could have equally been a bouncer in a nightclub. He told us he was in Bali to make a quick buck and had no plans to stay long-term; he seemed to be right out of his comfort zone.

Ted was also a former car salesman; he was tall, lanky and bald, with a North Country accent and a cheerful, gentle demeanour. I warmed to him immediately. He told me that his wife was coming to join him in a couple of weeks.

'Our plan is to stay in Bali for a bit if the job proves to be a money-spinner, or alternatively we can just enjoy a long holiday together.'

I envied Ted's happy-go-lucky attitude and wished that I didn't feel quite so dependent on the need to make a success of timeshare.

Then there was Andy, he was the youngest of the four, and very full of himself. He told us he'd been a very successful double-glazing salesman in London. He was quite confident that he could 'make a financial killing in timeshare,' while also enjoying the Bali sunshine and what he perceived would be a party lifestyle. I could see that he would be well capable of selling; he had that outgoing, charming, attractive personality, a cheeky smile, and the cockney gift of the gab; it was hard to imagine him taking life too seriously.

Tony was the opposite; he looked anxious and insecure. He told us that he had failed the final exam of his training course a few days earlier, so he was back for a second attempt.

A shiver ran down the back of my spine, this was the first I had heard of an exam. *What would happen if I failed?* I might not even get a chance to start selling and making money, I had to be successful; I had to stay in Bali. I instantly resolved to spend every evening that week studying whatever it was we were about to learn. Tony told us how difficult he'd found the course, he confessed he'd never worked in sales before and didn't think he possessed the right qualities for it. I liked his openness and honesty but Jay, our young, handsome tutor – the guy who had interviewed me for the job in London – warned Tony, 'Shut up before you neg them all out.'

From this, I grasped that in order to be good sales reps, we needed to feel fired-up, inspired and positive. There was no room in this business for negative energy or pessimism.

Tony humbly apologised, and said, 'Oh dear, I've messed up again.'

Lacking in looks, poise and self-assurance, he didn't appear to have much going for him, but he seemed like a nice bloke, and I felt a bit sorry for him.

Andy whispered to me, 'He's never gonna make it in sales.' It was my first hint of the ruthlessness of the timeshare industry.

I turned my attention to Jay. Australian, six-foot-tall, twenty-eight years old and gorgeous, he was immaculately attired. He told us that he'd been in a lucrative role as a manager for the company and now he'd been given a salaried position recruiting and training the newcomers. I cringed at the mention of a corporate structure within the company, I'd just escaped from nineteen years of climbing the lower rungs of the corporate ladder and now I was right back down at the bottom again; a mere pleb. However, it was encouraging to learn that there were some salaried positions within the organisation; it wasn't all commission-based.

Jay told us he had recently hosted two well-attended seminars in London, which was where I'd met him, and four in Australia, out of which he had handpicked about fifty new recruits to work on the company's sales' decks in Bali, India and Thailand. He admitted that he could never really tell at interview stage whether or not someone was going to fit into the tropical lifestyle, but he knew a potentially good sales rep when he saw one.

I later learnt that there had been no handpicking procedure. The company's policy was that anyone who had enough get-up-and-go to chuck in whatever they were doing back home and fly to a far-away place, was a good enough candidate to start with. Therefore, everyone who requested an interview got offered the job. Jay was a good role model. He appeared to be a man who loved his job and he seemed to be very driven and successful. He proudly told us that he drove a BMW and lived in a beautiful, four-bedroom house in Sanur, complete with a swimming pool, air-conditioning and a team of three staff.

I had no idea of the whereabouts of Sanur but concluded it must be a very upmarket neighbourhood. The following week I found out that most of the timeshare crew chose to live in a hotel in Kuta or in shared rental houses in Seminyak so that they could enjoy the nightlife, whereas Sanur was quiet and family oriented. I also gathered that Jay shared his house with five other people, and apparently every expatriate in Bali employed a maid and a gardener, and potentially a security guard, while many others also employed a handyman, driver, nanny and cook. I was told that there was an expectation to give back to Bali by providing work for the local people, it didn't cost much, and it was lovely not to have to do one's own cleaning, washing, and ironing. Besides, many rental houses came with staff anyway. The story about the BMW was bullshit. Our tutor was a high-powered salesman who had studied the psychology of the industry in which he excelled. He was merely selling us the *idea* that we could make enough money from selling timeshare to live very comfortably indeed.

Yes, Jay was good at his job, I came out of my first day of training believing that the 'shared ownership' company for which I had been 'handpicked' was internationally acknowledged and respected as the most productive in its field.

As Andy, Ted, Tony and I sheltered from a torrential thunderstorm – the first storm of the rainy season – while waiting for a taxi to take us to a local restaurant, which Ted had discovered the night before, I erroneously felt rather proud to be part of this promising new timeshare world.

The rest of the week was spent learning the timeshare pitch, the sales techniques, and the universal timeshare jargon. For example, the OPCs (Off Premises Contacts) were the hustlers on the street who would stop tourists – the potential buyers, who were known as UPs (Unqualified Prospects) – ask them a few leading questions and present them with the remarkable possibility of winning a holiday. The tourists would be offered a free scratch card, which would instantly declare them as winners of the grand prize – five hundred dollars in cash, a camcorder, or a holiday, the OPC would gleefully jump up and down as if this was a very rare occurrence and then kidnap the UPs by whisking them away in a taxi to collect the prize, with the assurance of a free taxi ride back to their hotel afterwards.

The operators working the streets were all Indonesians, and I was soon to discover that this was because we foreigners were working illegally and therefore couldn't risk being seen out at work in public. Upon passing our exam, we were all to become *liners,* working on the *cold line*, cold selling an unseen villa, apartment or hotel suite to the kidnapped prospects. A daily, randomly selected list of our names would denote the order in which we would be picked to pitch the visitors, this was to ensure that each liner was given an equal chance and that the people most likely to buy were not necessarily paired up with the most competent or deserving reps.

Everything operated on statistics in timeshare. As long as the company had enough hustlers on the street, they would statistically be able to entice enough tourists indoors to sit through a presentation. If the kidnapped tourists didn't stay for at least an hour, they would not qualify for their prize. We were told that each pitch must last at least two hours, ideally three hours because the longer the liners could keep the visitors sitting at the table listening to the spiel, the greater the chance they would buy. Statistically, an average ten percent of the tourists that the OPCs brought through the door would buy a timeshare property.

Essentially, the potential buyers had to meet a specific criterion in the first place. In order to qualify for a presentation and the prize, which was never the cash, the UPs had to be a couple, on holiday in Bali, and married or living together for at least three years. One member of the couple had to be at least twenty-eight years old, and ideally, they should be people who took regular overseas holidays, with an income at that time of at least fifty thousand US dollars per year, with children and a mortgage. Statistically, these were responsible, stable people who were most likely to buy timeshare. Gay couples were also a good bet because of the probable double-income-no-kids factor. The free holiday was a complimentary stay – excluding airfares, food and beverages – at one of the company's mediocre timeshare resorts, where they would have to endure yet another three-hour-long timeshare presentation. For every qualifying pair of tourists that they got through the door, the OPCs would receive fifty dollars. Likewise, there was a team of telemarketers who would call guests in their hotel rooms to convey the happy news that they had won a free holiday in a prize draw. The timeshare company would bribe an insider in each of Bali's major hotels to supply the names and room numbers of all the newly arrived guests. After countless complaints, the hotels would, of course, get wise to this and refuse to put calls through to the guests, but very often the insider would also be able to supply a direct dial number to the hotel's guestrooms in order to avoid going through the switchboard. Another scam was to bribe an immigration officer at the airport to supply the company with a list of new arrivals and the names of the hotels where they were staying in Bali; this information was obtained from the immigration landing cards. At the time of my arrival in Bali, there were more Australian tourists than any other nationality, so we rarely had to deal with the complication of non-English speakers.

During our training course we were taught a lot of sales' techniques; the psychology proved to be interesting. First of all, there was the *Sizzler*.

'Excite your potential buyers with a Sizzler,' instructed Jay, 'paint a picture of a beautiful tropical holiday, with swaying coconut palms and crystal-clear waters lapping a white sand beach. Throw in an immaculate family-sized apartment or villa within a well-managed resort with all the bells and whistles, show them a photo, and tell them that all of this could be theirs.'

Then comes the *Takeaway*...

'The minute these people start to show an interest,' said Jay, 'you must take the dream away from them by telling them that the property you have just shown them is unfortunately no longer available, this will make them want it even more; it's only human nature to want something we can't have.'

'What happens next?' I asked.

'You pull a rabbit out of the hat and bring their dream back to reality with an even better option.'

This all made perfect sense to me; Jay had made it sound so easy. He reassured us by telling us that our line managers would be on hand to jump in and help us if we felt like we were in danger of losing what should be a deal. As soon as the couple agreed to buy, they would be taken to the *Button Up* department where another rep would explain the legalities of the purchase; and contracts would then be signed.

'And Bob's your uncle,' concluded Jay, 'you can expect to earn an average of six hundred US dollars in commission from each deal, most reps will make two deals per week to begin with, so you can expect to make five thousand dollars per month. In a few weeks' time you'll be achieving a deal every day, which amounts to fifteen thousand dollars per month based on our six-day week. If you want to make a career of this – which you will – you can progress to management level and earn commission off each sale made by each member of your team, and you will also have the option of working in other countries.'

It was beginning to sound very exciting, although I had to admit I was rather concerned about working illegally.

'Don't worry about that,' said Jay, 'the company bribes the immigration department to leave us alone.'

'We're here on two-month tourist visas, what happens when the two months is up?' I queried.

'You have to leave the country,' replied Jay, 'but it's all very easy, you simply fly to Singapore and when you re-enter the country, you will automatically be given a new tourist visa.'

'Why Singapore?'

'Singapore is the closest and cheapest place to get to. You can fly there and back in one day if you wish. In fact, you don't even need to leave the airport, you can just do a quick turnaround and fly back on the same plane.'

'So, is that *really* okay? Will Immigration *really* allow us to do that?'

'Ah look, it's kind of breaking the rules, but all you have to do is slip a Rp 20,000 note in your passport, and the immigration officer will let you in without giving you a hard time.'

I was annoyed that Jay hadn't been upfront about the visa situation at the time of my interview with him in London, and I found the idea of bribing an official to re-enter the country was both frightening and thrilling. I was also a bit disappointed to hear about the six-day working week. Our only day off was Friday, which meant we had to work on Saturdays and Sundays. Our working day was officially nine to five with two pitches per day, and there was no going home early if there were no customers. Moreover, we were expected to stay late if our tourists arrived late in the afternoon; this meant that we could be there until eight p.m. Having spent many years as a national executive of a trade union, looking after the very best interests of a workforce of thirty-six thousand, I knew I was now going to have real trouble adjusting to the controlling tactics of a company that provided no contracts and offered no employee rights whatsoever.

I wanted to explore Bali, and the rest of Indonesia and Asia; I wanted to visit Jeremy in Australia, *would there be any time for this?*

'What's our annual holiday entitlement?' I asked.

'If you're good at the job, you'll be able to take plenty of holidays,' reassured Jay, 'but you'll be so hooked on making money that you won't want to take time out.'

What was not explained to us, however, was that we would not receive our ten percent commission of the purchase price of the timeshare apartment until the clients had paid, and because many people requested a twelve-month payment plan, this meant that we would have to wait for the commission, which we would receive in stage payments. This was fine if we really were going to make numerous sales per month as it would provide a steady monthly income, but what if we left the job? Would we still receive the money that was owed to us after we left? Was it really okay to work illegally in Indonesia? Would we really be allowed back into the country on the strength of a two-dollar bribe? In my head, I was already likening Bali to

Narnia: *What if I couldn't get back through the wardrobe?* Would we really be earning fifteen thousand dollars per month, or was Jay working some sort of perverse psychology on us, his trainees?

There was no choice but to bite the bullet for now, knowing that maybe one day soon I would probably spit the dummy.

After each day of training, I would have an early dinner with Tod, Andy and Tony – Steve didn't seem interested in socialising with us – and I'd then return to my hotel room to swot, but I didn't tell the others. Nobody seemed to be taking it quite as seriously as me, apart from Tony who was a bundle of nerves. I wanted to be the star pupil and let everyone else assume it had been effortless.

On the morning of our exam, Andy turned up late with a terrible hangover, and Steve walked in relating a story about how someone had tried to mug him in a dark backstreet the night before. The luckless assailant hadn't anticipated that his prey would fight back; Steve had retrieved his wallet and given the thief a good beating. I was shocked. Initially because I hadn't realised that street muggings occurred in Bali, and secondly because I feared Steve could have seriously hurt the man. Andy, meanwhile, told us that he'd been out most of the night at a beachside nightclub called Double Six. Apparently, this was the most famous nightclub in Bali and the place where all the other timeshare reps liked to hang out, especially on Thursday nights before the company's day off on Friday. Andy had overheard some of our future workmates discussing it at his hotel, so he'd decided to quietly check it out on his own. I couldn't believe that he could be so irresponsible to stay out all night before an exam; he had such a cavalier attitude.

Well, we sat our exam and as far as I was concerned it was easy. Jay even gave us a few clues. I whizzed through it, Ted whizzed through it, while Steve, Tony and Andy sweated their way through it. Yet, we all passed, and to my glee I came top of the class.

After lunch, Jay took us to the salesroom. Known as the *deck*, this scruffy upstairs space was where the liners, as we would now be known, were expected to cold-sell the timeshare apartments to Bali's visitors. As we entered our new workplace, I could barely hide my dismay. The room was hot and crowded, sweaty and smelly. It was crammed with about thirty small wooden tables and hard wooden chairs, most of which were occupied by a rep and the recipients of the sales pitch that I had strived so hard to learn. Most of the tourists looked hot and uncomfortable, having been provided with only a glass of water to drink. Yet, the reps, many of whom I recognised from my hotel, appeared animated and confident. Some of them had captivated their potential clients and were holding their attention and making them laugh, but the majority of the other tourists looked bored or exasperated. I couldn't understand how a business could operate like this. Fresh from working in a bank in England, I had been accustomed to a spacious modern office with all the bells and whistles, a comfortable working environment designed to please the staff and impress the customers, to reassure them that this was a reliable, esteemed company where they could safely invest their money.

About eight of the reps were waiting for new victims to be brought through the door. Therefore, Ted, Andy, Tony, Steve and I were each hurriedly introduced and partnered with someone, allowing us to sit and observe a presentation. I was paired with a young Australian woman called Julie, she told me she'd been working for the company for about a year and that on average she accomplished about two deals per week. She looked quite straight compared to some of the other old timers who looked more like partygoers than diligent company representatives. Nevertheless, sitting through Julie's presentation was an encouraging experience for me, reaffirming my confidence in my knowledge of the techniques and the spiel. I could tell straightaway that Julie's victims were bored and disinterested. In fact, they couldn't wait to get out of that shabby room and back to their hotel. This was a bit disheartening, but Julie was unfazed.

'Only ten percent of them will buy,' she reminded me, lifting my spirits, and reiterating that there was a possibility of making some seriously good money.

Observing my classmates, I noticed that Andy was buoyant and empowered at being on the brink of selling and making money. Ted's reaction was similar to Andy's, and Tony seemed relieved to be finally starting work, but Steve appeared downcast. Julie's couple eventually made their bid for freedom at four o'clock and I was allowed to leave at the same time.

'Be back here tomorrow morning at nine,' ordered Jay, 'there will be a team meeting for everyone before we start work and then you're on your own.'

The following morning, I punctually reported for duty on deck. My fellow workers were a mixed bunch. Unlike my classmates, most of them were younger than me; everyone was well dressed, in a summery, smart-casual sort of way as required by the company. Some of them were very self-confident and others positively arrogant, several seemed rather bewildered and there were a few who looked vulnerable and lost. Apart from two eloquent Indonesians, nearly all of them were either Australian or English, and at least half of them had started work only a couple of weeks earlier. Steve was notable for his absence.

Our first task was to stand up and introduce ourselves. When my turn came, I informed everyone that I'd taken voluntary redundancy from my job in a bank and sold my house to follow my dream of living and working overseas. It was only later I learnt that I was not the model of a potentially successful timeshare rep. The company wanted people who were highly motivated to make money; ideally people who were either living beyond their means or had a major financial goal. Anyone who desperately needed to make money was a good bet, but my talk of a redundancy pay-out and the sale of my house implied that I had a comfortable stash of cash in the bank and probably lacked the required motivation. Chrissie, who I was soon to befriend, was a much better blueprint of someone who might do well. She was a former singer, who had been suffering with serious throat problems and vocal cord damage; she badly needed an expensive operation if she was to ever sing again, and she believed that she could get rich quick through selling timeshare. She was needy, motivated, determined, and like me, she was desperate to make it work; the only difference was that I had inadvertently led everyone to believe I was cashed up, when in fact I had very little money to invest in my new life. I had made zero profit on the sale of my house, and my redundancy money had gone towards paying off my loan, a trip around my home country, two foreign holidays and an expensive fortieth birthday party. Indeed, I'd been merrily living the high life during the five months since I'd been voluntarily unemployed.

Thus, anxious to start making money again, and trying to convince myself that I fully believed in the product I was selling, I began work on the deck. We only once saw Steve again, he came into the office on our first day of work to tell

Bob, one of the company directors, that he was leaving; apparently his mother had suddenly been taken ill and he had to return to London. Nobody found his story very convincing, but he was able to claim back one third of his airfare on the basis that, like us, he had completed the training course. We were each told that another chunk could be claimed back on the accomplishment of our first deal.

Incredibly, on that very first day, I concluded my second 'tour' – the timeshare word for presentation – with a deal. I couldn't believe it as I watched the young Australian couple being escorted into the button-up department to complete the transaction with the signing of forms and the payment of a deposit. All of my hard revision must have paid off, this was so easy. Mentally hugging myself, I remembered the words of a dear and wise, much older friend who had once told me I could achieve anything I wanted in life, as long as I believed that I was capable. Most of my fellow workers heartily congratulated me although Murray, one of the managers, and some of the more experienced reps looked less enthusiastic.

'Doing a deal on your first day,' declared Murray, 'gives you a false sense of security. You got lucky but now you're feeling cocky, and it will make you think you don't have to try so hard.'

I was crushed. A minute earlier I had been floating on air, pumped up with a mixture of joy, self-satisfaction, self-esteem, disbelief at what had happened and yet a newfound belief in my own ability to succeed. Now, Murray had popped my balloon.

There was more soul-destroying news to come. Murray proceeded to tell me that the couple would probably renege on the agreement as they had only paid a fifty-dollar deposit – a lot less than the four-hundred-dollar deposit required to seal the deal. This was yet another blow, but it was then that I remembered I would now be entitled to claim back two-thirds of my airfare, so I still went back to my hotel with a smile on my face.

~*~

Over the next few days, I started making friends with some of the other reps, especially the other newcomers. I was drawn to gentle Chrissie who so badly wanted to resume her singing career, and I liked scatty Mandy, Ted of course, and Lloyd, who was a bit of a nerd but always happy to chat. Meanwhile, I also attempted to befriend some of the old-timers so that I could find out more about what went on behind the scenes in timeshare. I was equally eager to learn everything possible about Bali but none of my workmates seemed to be interested in the island or its culture. There was one person, however, who I'd not yet met.

'Brad will be here on Saturday,' announced Bob, at our first staff meeting, as he divided the reps into two teams, advising us that one team would be reporting to Brad and the other, my team, to Murray. 'Brad and Murray are your line managers. Whenever any of you need help in completing a deal, Murray and Brad will be on hand to assist or take over; the last thing we want is for any of you to lose a potential deal because you are unable to answer a question that your prospective buyers might ask.'

Despite Murray's negativity about my first deal, he seemed to be a nice enough guy, so I was happy to be in his team, but I wondered what Brad would be like.

'Brad's worked for the company for a long time,' explained Murray.

'Brad's brilliant,' confirmed Shelley, one of the brash, experienced reps, 'he really knows his stuff, he's always willing to spend time helping others with ongoing training, and he's made so much money from timeshare. He's a real success story and a credit to the company.'

I was looking forward to meeting Brad.

The previous day, some of the timeshare girls had been telling me how hard it was to find a man in Bali.

'Most of the men here are only interested in the local women.'

Yet it hadn't escaped my notice that our workmate, Andrea, had already hooked up with the gorgeous Jay, who had been her tutor on the training course only two weeks earlier.

I hadn't come to Bali to find a man; it was more about finding myself and making a new life for myself. My first priority was to earn some money and find a place to live after my one month of free board at the hotel. I wondered if the good-looking timeshare guys, Aaron and Toby and Will, were into the local ladies. They were all confident men from Australia, and it was pretty obvious that they regularly indulged in party drugs. This was what fed their ability to sell; cocaine was what they spent their money on.

A few days later I was introduced to Brad. I could see immediately that he was Mr. Popular. He was lively and funny and loved to be the centre of attention, yet somehow, I had expected him to be tall and sexy like Jay. Instead, he was short and not very attractive at all, with a receding hairline, close-set eyes, and a bulbous nose. I felt disappointed.

~*~

18
DEATH ROW
1998

I was being bitten by mosquitoes and had huge, red, infected welts all over my legs. The rainy season had arrived with a vengeance, I was suffering from the oppressive humidity, and my hotel room was dirty; there were cobwebs around the bedside lamps and the washbasin hadn't been cleaned once since I had arrived. Six days a week I was going into work and trying to sell timeshare and every day I was coming home having earned nothing. My workmates were either successful, cocksure bon-vivants or desperados like me who were useless at selling timeshare and becoming increasingly unhappy and preparing themselves for the inevitable.

'If I haven't done a deal by the end of next week, I'm going home,' announced James, one of the other newcomers.

'But surely you need to give it a bit more time?' I commented.

'Nah,' said James, despondently, 'my month is up next Friday and after that I'll have to start paying for my hotel room.'

'Murray had a word with me today,' said Tony. 'I've got two weeks left and if I don't do a deal in that time, I'll be kicked out.'

'What? 'I cried, incredulously. This was the first I'd heard of the possibility of anyone getting the sack. 'Why would they bring us all the way here and then sack us?'

'They're only interested in reps who can sell,' explained James. 'We are mere statistics in the mix, just like the holidaymakers out there on the street. Out of all the reps who come and work for the company, only a certain percentage make the grade. They give us all a chance but if we can't do it then we'll be discarded. Chewed up and spat out.'

I felt that recurring shiver running down the back of my spine; it hadn't occurred to me that all the non-sellers were on Death Row. Sure, I'd made a deal on my first day, which had afforded me the one-third refund of my airfare, but according to Murray the timeshare transaction was highly unlikely to be completed as the about-face buyers had made no attempt to pay the remainder of their deposit. I wasn't sure whether or not to believe Murray, maybe this was another cruel timeshare scam that had been dreamt up in order to avoid paying the reps.

Mulling over my pessimistic situation, I wondered if I could find any other sort of work in Bali. The problem was that foreigners were not allowed to do jobs that the locals could do, and even when there was an opening available, most companies, depending on their size, were only allowed to employ three or four foreigners, and must have at least ten Indonesian employees for each expatriate hired. I'd been told it wasn't always easy to find an employer who was prepared to pay for a work permit, and the only real way forward would be to set up my own business, which would require a substantial investment. Then, just as I'd decided that my future in Bali was looking bleak, I had a sudden flash of inspiration. The timeshare company employed a certain number of salaried staff in the form of administrators together with the accounting team. Okay, so maybe they weren't legally employed but nor were the reps; if only I could get transferred into the admin side of the operation, I'd be alright. I was skilled at both admin and accounting, I'd get a salary every month, and that would be enough to start with. I'd be secure; I'd be able to stay in Bali.

Feeling a little bit buoyed up by my plan, I joined Tony and Ted's discussion about the possibility of a sightseeing trip on our day off. I'd already been on the island for three weeks and as yet had only been out on one daytrip; there was so much more to see. I was surprised that none of the other timeshare reps were interested in visiting the temples, lakes, rice terraces and volcanoes, all they seemed to want to do was party. Meanwhile, my other objective was to get out of my hotel, I didn't like it very much; I wasn't enjoying living out of a suitcase and I was already craving somewhere that I could call home.

It was Thursday evening, and as Friday was our day off, nearly everyone it seemed, was into going out. The evening was to begin with a few drinks in Kuta, followed by Double Six nightclub later on. However, I had no plans to go clubbing because Tony, Ted and I would be setting off early the next morning on our sightseeing trip.

I chose my outfit carefully, wanting to prove to the rather intimidating timeshare party girls that I was every bit as capable of having a good time as they were. We met at Paddy's Pub, and then moved on to The Bounty, which turned out to be a nightclub in the guise of an old pirate ship. It was there that I allowed myself to be dragged onto the dance floor by Aaron – another timeshare man, who I'd nicknamed Mr. Gorgeous. He was very attentive and when he encouraged me to come along to Double Six with the rest of the crew, I threw caution to the wind.

Arriving at Bali's most famous nightclub, I was awestruck by the size of the place. It was a vast, open-sided, grass roofed pavilion beside the beach, complete with open-air terraces, a huge swimming pool and a forty-eight-metre-high bungy jump. I had never seen a nightclub like it. I stuck close to Aaron but to my surprise, Brad asked me to dance. Happy enough to oblige, I was even more surprised when he asked me if I'd like to go out for dinner with him.

'Okay,' I spluttered, wondering why I was saying yes and therefore jeopardising any possibility of a date with Aaron. I wasn't attracted to Brad, and I had been told that a relationship between a manager and a rep was against the company's rules. My calculating mind, however, was remembering my goal of getting transferred into the admin department. It would be nice to be wined and dined, I thought, and all I have to do is develop a friendship with Brad and he might be able to help me.

'When?' I asked, expecting him to suggest the following night, or Saturday.

'Wednesday,' he replied.

Wednesday was six days away, I couldn't work out why he wanted to wait so long, but I stayed cool and nodded my head.

'Sure, that'll be nice, thank you. I'm going home now because I've got an early start in the morning, but I'll see you in work on Saturday.'

In truth, I was confused and unsure if I'd made the right decision. *Did I really want to go out with Brad?* The nightclub was atmospheric; its dark interior rhythmically penetrated by flashes and corkscrews of light, the house music emotive and loud. Wandering outside, I sat on a low wall overlooking the beach and watched the hypnotic green lasers cavorting with bullets of rain. I needed time to think. I then turned my gaze to the four parallel lines of white surf racing towards the shore. Each time the closest line disintegrated upon meeting the sand, another one, bigger and bolder, danced in from the shadowy horizon.

A local guy came and sat down beside me.

'What your name? Where you come from? You have husband?'

Ignoring his questions, I told him I'd come outside for some peace and quiet.

'Ahhh, peace and quiet,' he repeated with phoney charisma, and remained next to me without saying another word.

Another local guy then came over and sat on my other side. As he opened his mouth to speak, the first boy muttered something about 'peace and quiet.'

'Ahhh, peace and quiet,' repeated boy number two, and remained quietly seated beside me.

~*~

Tears pricked my eyes as I stared in disbelief at the threatening three-letter word, which Murray had scribbled down on a piece of paper and thrust at me from his side of the table:

'Bye.'

I was back at work after a fabulous day out exploring the Lake District of Bali. I had walked onto the deck feeling positive and happy, Brad had given me a secret smile and asked me about the sightseeing tour, and Murray had just burst my bubble. He had taken me to one side, told me that my presentations were not lasting long enough, and targeted me to achieve at least six, three-hour presentations out of my next ten.

'What happens if I don't?' I'd challenged.

It was at this point that Murray had replied by writing down his single-syllable reply. I could only conclude that he was an unprofessional arrogant bully.

It was looking increasingly unlikely that I was going to be able to survive in timeshare, but I was falling in love with Bali and had to find a way to stay. I still had reservations about whether or not I should enter into a relationship with Brad – if indeed that was on offer, he had made no further mention of our potential date – and yet Brad was possibly my only hope.

Later in the day after completing two presentations, both of which lasted two-and-a-half hours, albeit neither resulting in a deal, I felt I'd done alright but Murray once again vented his displeasure and threatened to sack me. Brad was present at the confrontation although his only contribution was to nudge me a couple of times under the table with his foot. He could see I was upset and was obviously trying to reassure me. I appreciated his gesture but still wondered if I would be wise to enter into a forbidden relationship with a man who worked in timeshare. Meanwhile, Ted and a couple of the others had been waiting outside for me, and in the taxi on the way back to the hotel, they tried to console me.

'Murray's not really angry with you,' comforted Ted, 'he's just working his perverse psychology on you.'

'He's a control freak,' added Chrissie, 'it's all a ploy to frighten you into becoming a successful sales rep.'

Personally, I didn't comprehend Murray's cruel technique and surprised myself by bursting into floods of tears.

The stress was taking its toll...

~*~

Two days later, I found myself a house. My potential career in timeshare was in tatters but I was more determined than ever to find a way to stay in Bali. After all, I had no choice. How could I possibly go back to England with my tail between my legs, with no job and no home. At least the timeshare company had honoured its agreement to refund two-thirds of my airfare for the completion of the training course and my contentious first deal. Upon receipt of this money in cash, millions of rupiah, the equivalent of about four hundred pounds, and feeling like a millionaire, I suddenly remembered the fortune teller's words,

'You will make millions'…

Cracking a wry smile at the irony, I decided I was ready to go house hunting.

Ted took me to look at a hotel called Dwi's.

'But I don't want to live in a hotel,' I protested.

'Wait 'til you see it,' responded Ted.

Dwi's Hotel turned out to be a little oasis in the heart of Kuta with thirty rooms situated on two levels around a swimming pool within a delightful tropical garden. It was just five minutes' walk in one direction from the bars, restaurants and shops of the main street, and five minutes', in the other direction, from the beach. The owner, Felix, was an affable German-Swiss man married to a Balinese woman called Dwi. I decided to take a room and went back again the next day to leave a deposit.

'Have a look at the house,' suggested Felix as he greeted me.

He'd explained the previous day that there were two fully furnished houses on the premises; he and his family lived in one of them and an Australian couple rented the other, but they were going back home for five months and wanted to sublet. They were flying out the next morning. I then met the couple, John and Val, and all their cats, and Val showed me around the house, which I immediately fell in love with. Undoubtedly romantic, it had a walled garden, open-air living and dining spaces, a cosy lounge room with a spare bed in the corner, a kitchen, a quirky open-air bathroom, an upstairs bedroom with a massive bed and a balcony, a telephone, a cable TV and a music system.

'All of the hotel facilities are included,' explained Val, 'the swimming pool, room service, electricity, gas, and daily housekeeping. You can use my bicycle, and you can get all your washing done at the laundry around the corner for next-to-nothing.'

When she told me the rental price of the house, which amounted to the equivalent of a mere 178 pounds per month, I nearly fell through the white-tiled floor.

'Our only request is that you look after our cats – a mother-cat and her four, eight-week-old kittens,' she added.

'Absolutely,' I responded eagerly, 'I'm crazy about cats.'

We agreed that I would move in the next day. I had been in Bali for four weeks, and for the first time I was feeling really happy. I was at last moving out of my grubby hotel into my own little boho pad, close to the timeshare office, and close to where my workmates and newfound friends were living in Kuta. What's more, and as far as I knew, I had a forthcoming date with Brad, who just might be able to help me work out a way forward.

I'd given a lot of thought to the possibility of a relationship with Brad. Initially, I hadn't been interested in him, I wouldn't have given him a second glance if I'd seen him on the street, but in the four days since he'd asked me out, I'd become increasingly attracted to him. Maybe it was because I was needy and vulnerable, or maybe I just really liked him. I was magnetised by his success and self-confidence and impressed at how much everyone else seemed to like and respect him. However, I was frustrated by his lack of attention and the fact that he had made no further mention of our date. I wondered if he was applying some of the timeshare psychology to the situation, the very stuff that he, Murray, and Jay had been teaching the new reps…

'Endear yourself to your clients, stroke them, fascinate them, make them laugh and befriend them. Excite them with a sizzler, and finally, as soon as they start to show an interest, employ the takeaway technique as this will make them want it even more; it's human nature to desire the things we can't have.'

It was so true. Now that I was no longer sure that Brad wanted me, I was excited at the prospect of having a clandestine relationship with him, one that none of the staff or management could know about. My hope that he might be able to help me get a salaried desk job within the company was now of secondary importance.

After another frustrating day of no sales at work, and Brad leaving the office early having hardly spoken to me, I moved into my new house. Clementina and Lloyd had offered to help me, but Clem was ill, and Lloyd had disappeared. At least the kittens were happy to see me. Over lunch that day with Chrissie, I had learnt that Clementina had been sacked for being off sick, and that James had just got his first deal, otherwise he too would have been sacked. If I hadn't been feeling so enthusiastic about my new house, I would have been feeling very scared indeed. I slipped into the comfort of my mosquito-netted bed and dreamed of love, success, and wealth on my tropical island.

On Wednesday, the day of our potential date, I made an extra effort with my appearance and hoped that Brad would notice my newly painted nails and my cool white dress.

By mid-afternoon, I couldn't stand the uncertainly any longer, and when Brad smiled at me, my resolve to remain aloof evaporated.

'Are you still taking me out tonight?' I mouthed.

He nodded and came over to my table, 'Yes, if you like.' he replied. 'Write down your address and I'll pick you up at eight-thirty.'

I put Brad's apparent lack of enthusiasm down to timeshare psychology, and for the rest of the afternoon I was so excited that I didn't dare look at any of my colleagues for fear of giving the game away. My stomach was heaving, my head was buzzing, and my heart was fluttering.

After leaving work, I raced home, showered and got dressed in a spaghetti-strap top and a short skirt. I was so hyped that I could barely apply my make-up. At eight-fifteen, when I was finally ready, I put on a 'Faithless' CD and waited for him. At nine-fifteen, I moved onto my balcony from where I would be able to see him approaching. At nine-forty-five, I shifted onto my roof. Finally, at eleven-thirty, long after I had given up all hope and acknowledged that I had been stood up, the house phone started ringing. I'd not yet got a local number for my mobile, and while Brad and I hadn't exchanged phone numbers, I knew he could have easily found out the number of the hotel. I flew downstairs to answer it, full of anticipation and forgiveness. To my immense disappointment, humiliation and embarrassment, the caller was not Brad but Dwi, Felix's wife.

'Please will you turn your music down; you're disturbing the hotel guests.'

With a wail of dismay, I dissolved into a sobbing heap of tears.

Walking into work the next morning, my stomach churned with a mixture of fear and hope. Fear of further rejection combined with the hope that Brad had a good, defensible reason for having let me down.

As I entered the room, he held up his hands, shook his head and apologised.

'I'm so sorry, I couldn't find your house and I didn't have your phone number.'

I was amazed that he should even mention this in front of the other reps, surely our potential relationship was meant to be a secret.

'That's the first time I've ever been stood up in my life.' I retorted. 'I'm not impressed,' and with a flourish of private triumph, I swept out of the room and up the stairs to deposit my handbag in my locker.

Five minutes later, I returned to his desk and apologised for giving him a hard time as he recounted his evening, using words such as 'terrible' and 'frustrating,' which led me to believe that the experience had been as bad for him as it had been for me. When he suggested that we should try again that evening, I smiled and gave him my phone number and a map.

Meanwhile, I didn't seem to be any closer to making any timeshare deals but Murray was full of encouragement, telling me he was well pleased with the length of my presentations. I couldn't help wondering if this was something to do with Brad; after all, the cat was now out of the bag and most of the staff probably knew we were going out on a date that evening. Just to make absolutely sure, as I left the office, I told Murray to tell Brad to call me, which he did, twice, first to tell me what time he would pick me up and then to tell me he was on his way.

When Brad arrived, smiling, I offered him a Bintang and proudly took him on a tour of my house. I showed him my bedroom with its huge super-king-size bed and as I closed the door behind us and we headed back down the stairs, I felt empowered, remembering how in timeshare terms this would be called a sizzler; a little taste of what could be on offer, designed to tease, entice and excite.

Sitting in Brad's car, I was struck by the realisation that I hadn't been out on a real date in years. I'd forgotten what it was like to have someone come pick me up at home and take me to a nice restaurant for dinner.

He took me to a place in Seminyak called Goa 2001, which proved to be a massive semi-open pavilion with two bars, a sushi counter, and a coffee bar, under a soaring thatched roof. Even at that early hour the place was rocking, trance music playing through the speakers, and dozens of people sitting, eating and drinking at an assortment of colonial-style marble-topped tables. My attention was caught by a pair of colourful characters with deeply lined faces and hippy clothes having an animated conversation at the bar, and I suddenly felt a quivering thrill to be living on this diverse and fascinating island with its Hindu culture and tourism, friendly local people, sunshine, foreigners, and from what I could gather, an amazing nightlife.

The waitress arrived to take our orders from Goa's eclectic menu; an Indian shrimp curry for me and a pizza for Brad, while I listened enthralled as he told me stories of his motorcycle racing days and his travels around the world.

I spotted some of the timeshare squad, Aaron, Murray, and Toby, standing at the bar, and when our food arrived, each of them approached our table independently to say hello and smirk.

'Is this cool?' I asked.

'I don't give a shit about company protocol,' replied Brad, 'I'll be upfront about you, and they'll have to accept it.'

Glowing with pleasure and revelling in his company as we headed off to the A-Bar with a plan to go on to Gado Gado Nightclub and then the fabulous Double Six, I couldn't help but wonder what the future might hold in store.

~*~

Sadly, as it turned out, the future held nothing in store for Brad and me. He was a man who enjoyed the thrill of the chase, he was a good guy, and he was fun company, but after two months together, it became painfully obvious that he was not prepared to make any sort of commitment to anyone. I also realised that he wasn't in a position to throw me my perceived lifeline of a salaried job with the timeshare company.

Murray, Aaron, Shelley and the other long-term timeshare people all told me the same thing, 'Brad's a timeshare man, don't expect too much from him.'

I resigned from timeshare, I jumped before I was pushed, and I left, according to the big boss, 'With a clean slate.' He said I was welcome to come back and work for the company at any time.

Fast forward five months, and I was still living in Bali, but I had earned no money, I'd lost the friends I'd made – Chrissie, Lloyd, Ted and Brad – because they'd all left the island. I was missing my family; I was missing my friends in England.

I was also almost out of money, desperately hoping that the ATM would keep paying out, and I was fretting because not only did I need to find a job, but I would soon need to find somewhere else to live.

Regularly walking the expansive sands of Kuta Beach all the way up to Seminyak and beyond, I'd watch the surfers riding the waves, people walking their dogs, running, exercising, practicing yoga, meditating, playing, and probably praying.

I prayed too.

I prayed to Ganesha, the remover of obstacles and god of making things happen.

'Dear Ganesha, please make it happen that I can find a way to stay in Bali.'

19
SO, YOU THINK YOU'D LIKE TO LIVE IN BALI?
1998 - 2000

Breaking away from the stressful city life and escaping to a sunny tropical island sounds like an idyllic fantasy. Most people

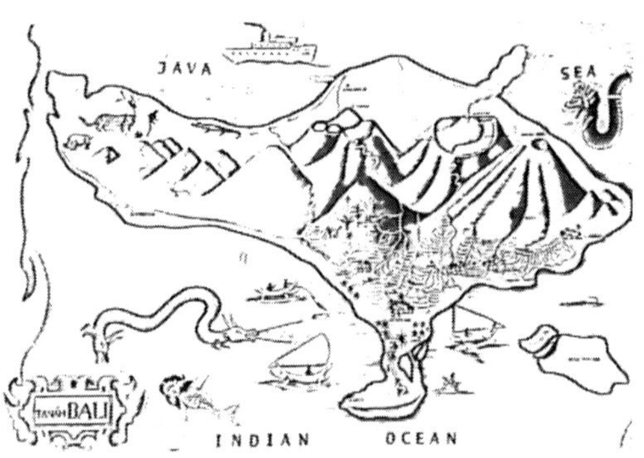

acknowledge that it's just a fantasy and would never pursue the idea. Many of Bali's visitors say they love the place but couldn't live there. Others, however, claim to have developed a strong affinity with the island, or even that they found the experience to be so profound that Bali has captured their soul forever.

> 'As soon as I arrived, I just knew that I wanted to stay.'
> 'I felt very strongly that I was meant to be here.'
> 'Immediately I got off the plane, I felt as though I had come home.'

'I have found my Heaven on Earth.'

During my first few months in Bali, I spent many hours talking to a fair number of the old-timer expats who'd been living on the island for twenty years or more. I heard some incredible, heart-warming, magical stories, I was told about the great business possibilities as well as the numerous business initiatives that had failed. I heard some scary stories and some horror stories. I gleaned that a lot of people couldn't handle the inexplicable coincidences and mysterious energy of the island. The truth is that Bali is not entirely the paradise that people imagine, it's stressful – but in a different way from the West – you can't expect things to run smoothly. It is expensive – for sure you can buy street food for a couple of dollars, but imported commodities, medical treatment, medical insurance, education for foreign kids, and visas are all expensive requirements. Paradise is hot, wet, dangerous, exciting, challenging, scary, and wonderful. You can fulfil your dreams in Bali, or you can drown in a treacherous sea.

I'd made the momentous decision to move to Bali on my own, and initially I only had myself to consider, but during those difficult early months, I had a lot of challenges to face alone. There was so much to deal with, such as making friends, finding somewhere to live, securing a means of making some money, learning my way around, grasping the language and gaining an understanding of how things worked.

My first landlord, Felix, had told me, 'In Bali, money talks louder than anything else,' and undeniably it does, but I didn't *have* any money.

My first six months was a culture shock. I didn't think of it like that, I thought I was coping well, but I wondered why my emotions were so intensified. *Why did I feel so happy, joyful, tearful, angry, frustrated and scared?*

I was struggling to survive on a tight budget, I had eventually found a job and a new abode, but I soon realised I was living in fear of the immigration department, in the house from hell, with an unreasonable landlord and a demonic employer. I learnt that if I tried to fight the system, I would just stress myself out, there was no point in getting angry with every taxi driver who said he hadn't got any change, or the supermarket check-out girl who gave out small change in the form of boiled sweets instead of coins. The frustrations of living in Bali and attempting to conduct business are enough to try the patience of a saint. Why was everything so complicated? Why wasn't it possible to pay the bills by direct debit? Why did so much incoming post go astray? Why didn't things work properly? Why was everybody always late? Why were there so many power-cuts? Why was the internet so slow? Why was the traffic so terrifying?

I knew that if I wanted to stay in Bali, I needed to make friends with the local people, learn the language, acknowledge the dangers, take care on the roads, accept the things that I couldn't change, embrace the challenges, explore the island and the culture, and be open to the intense spiritual energy. Bali is full of magic and wonder.

I was assured by my new friend, Pam, 'If you truly want to be here you will find a way to make it work. There are a lot of lessons to be learnt along the way, but if you have a passion for Bali, the joy and rewards of living here are immeasurable.' She added, 'The first two years are the hardest.'

~*~

During my first two years in Bali, I lived in six different houses, three of which were houses from hell. I had my handbag snatched on the street, and my home was robbed three times. I found another commission-only job selling medical insurance to expats but I had to borrow money to pay for my work visa because my boss was unwilling to cough up the required fee. Ironically, I couldn't afford to protect myself with the medical insurance cover that I was selling to others.

So why didn't I just give up, count my losses and return to England? The reality is I never gave up on my dream. I loved this friendly island and its devout smiling people, I loved the nature – the birds, the wildlife, the beaches and the ocean, the mountains, the waterfalls and the lakes, the rice terraces, the rainforests and the river gorges. I loved the climate, the culture, the colourful Hindu ceremonies, the ever-present creative force and the gorgeous artwork.

I wanted to stay in Bali more than ever, and I believed that if I faced the challenges I could make it work. I got a puppy, a Kintamani mountain dog called Lily. She proved to be a great guard dog and I never got robbed again. I couldn't afford a car, and a motorcycle didn't appeal so I bought myself a bicycle and got super fit cycling a round trip of eighteen kilometres to work and back each day. I was constantly struck by the friendliness and benevolence of the Balinese, if I ever got a flat tyre or a broken chain, some kind soul would always stop to help me. Both the warm-hearted man in the warung-shop close to my house and the sympathetic owner of the internet café across the road were trusting enough to occasionally give me short-term credit on food and services. As long as I stuck to the well-lit main roads, I always felt safe when walking alone on the streets at night, and twenty-five years on, I still do.

Bali is an easy place to make friends. Most of the fickle timeshare crew had moved on but it wasn't long before I was making what I believed could be lifelong friendships. Seminyak sunsets are legendary, and in the late afternoons, my friends and I would partake in the daily ritual of heading to the beach to enjoy what would hopefully be another spectacular *matahari terbenam*. My social life was pumping yet by the same token I had no problem going out alone in the evenings, it was easy to mingle with the tourists, and with a relatively small expat population in my neighbourhood, I was guaranteed to bump into the people I knew.

Every weekend, I'd go to Double Six; in the immortal words of Maxi Jazz, this was "My church", this was where I'd "heal my hurts".

If I was on my own, I'd skip the evening cocktail bar scene and head to the club around midnight, and I soon had a whole team of people watching out for me every step of the way. Even at such a late hour, a Balinese couple with a *kaki-lima* food cart, would be cooking and serving *nasi goreng* on the street just a few metres from my house. The first time they saw me, they smiled and asked where I was going, and the husband offered me a lift to Double Six on the back of his bike for Rp20,000 – the price of a nasi goreng. He was soon to become my weekly *ojek* motorbike taxi. There was another nice man, Indra, who worked on the door of the club, and as I was a regular, he would let me in for free and would always make sure I got home safe. Once inside Double Six, I would head straight to the expat corner, where I would be surrounded by my buddies.

I found myself a Balinese boyfriend called Ari. Although both of us were aware that our relationship wasn't going to last long-term, we had a fun, love-filled, three years together and I will always be grateful to him for helping me to understand so many aspects of the Balinese culture.

During my second year, I scored a job working as a PA to the Italian owner of a garment factory, which fulfilled orders for fashion houses such as Dolce & Gabbana, Armani, Calvin Klein, and Trussardi. I know I should have been grateful to have a salaried job, and it was interesting at first but it wasn't what I wanted to do. I acknowledged that although my dream was almost in sight, I still had a long way to go; there were still many obstacles to overcome and indeed, many lessons to be learnt.

Despite my almost-lifelong desire to be a writer and live on a tropical island, I didn't think about writing for my living until I climbed Mt Agung in 2000. Reaching the top of Bali's highest volcano was one of the most incredible and inspirational experiences of my life. Afterwards I wrote an account of my adventure and e-mailed it to my friends and family in the UK. My friend Suzi sent the story to the local newspaper in my old hometown in England and it was published.

That was the beginning.

If my work is good enough to be published in the UK, it's good enough to be published anywhere.

I decided I would try to make a living from writing.

I soon got gigs writing travel features and artist profiles, as well as sampling tourist activities, nightlife, restaurants, spas and hotels and reviewing them for a number of local and overseas English-language tourist and travel magazines. At last, it seemed, my life was starting to get easier.

20
SEEMS LIKE 'A NICE ENOUGH BLOKE'
1999, 2000

It was while I was working for the garment factory that I moved into house number four.

In Kuta, I had been treated like a tourist. After all, I had been living in the grounds of a hotel, and the people I'd met were all transient, visitors mainly. So, I'd decided to migrate to Seminyak, the trendier, more sophisticated option to Kuta, frequented by the beautiful Italian and Brazilian visitors.

The first two houses I found in Seminyak proved to be houses from hell; in each case I was scammed by a deceitful landlord. One was a Balinese man who didn't understand my expectation of, and my need for, running water; I moved out after two nights and lost a month's rent. The other was a financially challenged French conman who likewise rented me a place where nothing worked – the toilet flush, the electricity, the hot water, the cold water. He asked me to pay sixty dollars for my share of the village council fee, which I later learnt should have only been about two dollars, and I also found out that I was paying *his* power bill – he lived in the adjoining property. I put it down to my own naivety and moved out after two months.

My next house, however, was enchanting. One of an enclave of four Balinese bungalows, with a shared swimming pool that none of the other tenants were interested in using, the house was large, rustic and romantic, built in the *lumbung* or rice-barn style, with a bonnet-shaped *alang-alang* grass roof carried by bamboo rafters and hardwood pillars. Open to the garden, which was filled with hibiscus, heliconia, palms and banana trees, the living area was an expansive veranda; there was a pond in the kitchen, and a bathtub under the stars. The bathroom and three small bedrooms were the only rooms with doors, the walls were un-plastered, white-painted brick and the interior partition walls were made of woven bamboo, a process and product known as *bedeg*. It was a bungalow with an upstairs bedroom in the roof space, complete with a shaded balcony accessed via a spiral staircase; I claimed it for my own. In the early mornings, I would gaze out of my bedroom window across the rice fields and watch the sun rising from behind the revered volcano, Gunung Agung.

There was no air-conditioning, and the basic kitchen offered nothing more than a two-burner hob fuelled by bottled gas and positioned upon a concrete workbench. There was no electric kettle or microwave, the electricity supply was inadequate, which meant that high wattage appliances would overload the electric current and trip the circuit breaker. Fortunately, the pool pump was on a different power supply. There was no oven and no hot water heater in the kitchen. But the point was that this was normal in mid-range rental properties in Bali in the late nineties, lamps were too dim to read by, and every time there was a thunderstorm – a frequent occurrence during the rainy season – there would be a power cut. Although most of Bali's villages were connected to the electricity grid by 1995, it was several more years before many of the smaller, more remote *banjar* (village hamlets) gained electricity. Nevertheless, this was a time of reform in Indonesia, and the forerunner of the mass development of Bali's land for tourism.

Throughout the next decade, changes would be happening very fast.

Despite its lack of modern comforts and facilities, I loved my new house which, back then, I described as my 'modest boho dreamhouse.' I also loved the wild civet cats that used my roof and garden as a thoroughfare for stealing fruit off the mango trees lining my entranceway. My first six months of living there were joyful, but until I was able to supplement my income by writing articles for magazines, my salary from the garment factory was barely enough to cover the monthly rent. I needed to find a lodger.

I put the word out, and my friend, Pam, got back to me, 'I've just met this guy called Mark; he's looking for somewhere to live.'

'What's he like? How old is he? Where's he from?'

'He's in his mid-thirties, and he has a Kiwi accent but I think he said he was English. I don't know much about him but he seems like a nice enough bloke.'

The problem with making new friends in Bali is that nobody comes with any references. These days, the rapidly-increasing expat population sits at several hundred thousand, commonly-unregistered, often-temporary, foreign residents – crypto-capitalists, entrepreneurs, digital nomads and influencers – many of whom are fleeing the violence, or the draft, of the war in Ukraine.

However, when I first arrived in Bali, the number was considerably smaller. Excluding tourists, but including short-term visitors, the figure was estimated at only about ten thousand, which was a little bit less than the population of my old hometown.

In my hometown, most people had attended the same school, we knew each other's brothers and sisters, parents, partners, lovers and children, we knew where they worked, whether or not they'd gone to university, how much they'd paid for their house and where they bought their underwear.

In Bali, it seemed that the only foreigners who arrived with credentials were the ones who worked for internationally branded hotels, or long-established and well-respected NGOs. Most of the other legitimate foreigners were business owners, and many of them were highly successful, creative souls who had lived in Bali since the seventies or eighties. These were the savvy expats who had filled a niche and found a way – through investment, talent, skill, luck, business-acumen, hard work and determination – to fund a dream lifestyle, which gave back to the island, the environment and the local people. Of course, plenty of people had failed with their endeavours and moved on. In fact, about eighty percent of wannabe expats leave within the first two years, but what remains is a pool of extraordinary talent and philanthropy. Although an entrepreneurial business can grow quickly, its credibility is always very much dependent upon the ethics of the company and the way in which the owners treat their Indonesian staff.

When it came to new arrivals, we knew nothing about a person's integrity; nothing about their family, mental health, qualifications, or employment history. People came to Bali to reinvent themselves; some ran away from broken or abusive relationships, debt, or crime. Some changed their names; they came to escape, and to hide. There were villains and outlaws, swindlers and charlatans, conspiracy theorists, and a whole load of bullshitters. Some claimed to be aristocrats or scientists, others described themselves as entrepreneurs, many said they were architects, interior designers or fashion designers. Some became timeshare reps. A fair few of the reprobates overstayed their visas and laid low, while the wealthier, dubious strangers were quick to legitimise their illegal gains by investing in a seemingly doomed business, a restaurant perhaps, where no one seemed to be too interested in turning a profit. Indeed, money laundering was rife.

In those days, there was no verification process – at least, not outside of our home countries. The worldwide web didn't become mainstream until the late nighties but even then, less than seven percent of the world was online. Access was via dial-up, connection speeds were painfully slow in Bali and the service was patchy at best. Wikipedia didn't exist, Google had not yet become a verb, business owners didn't yet showcase their portfolios or market their services on company websites, the 'Information Superhighway' was still exasperatingly short of material. There were no online forums, and social media had only just been invented, no one used it yet, so it wasn't yet possible to delve into the background of a stranger's life.

In truth, Bali doesn't give a shit about what we might or might not have done – good or bad – in a former life. She only cares about how we behave and what we do, or achieve, in Bali. Her main concern is our respect for the local people and the culture, and what we give back to the island. An old belief among the expat residents is that Bali will test you, and she will challenge you, and if she doesn't like you, she will 'Suck you in, chew you up and spit you out, dead or alive.'

And so, this 'nice enough bloke' called Mark, who no one really knew, moved into my house.

He paid me a month's rent in advance and told me was working for an Australian travel & tour operator, writing the company's package tour brochures. He said he would occasionally have to fly to Perth for a meeting, or to Vietnam or Thailand to experience some of the hotels and tours. It sounded like a dream job, I was curious, I asked him for more information, but he brushed my questions aside.

'I've only just started working for them, so I don't know the details yet.'

I assumed he was protecting himself from the possibility that I might jump in and try to score a job with the same company.

I didn't see Mark very often, and therefore spent very little time with him. He was a party animal. He'd regularly go out clubbing, usually to Double Six. He'd get high, stay out all night and sleep all day.

He was a liability. It wasn't that I disliked him, I couldn't deny he was 'nice enough'. I just didn't trust him, and I wasn't keen on the *kupu-kupu malam* 'butterflies of the night' – the hookers that he brought home. I decided to ask him to move out at the end of his first month; although I wondered how much notice I should give him. I never saw him doing any work and after three weeks I asked him if he still had a job.

'Yeah, I have a meeting with the big boss next week. I'm flying to Perth on Sunday night.'

And then, as an afterthought, 'Is there anything you'd like from Australia?'

'Could you get me a pocket English dictionary and some mature cheddar cheese?'

'Sure thing,' he replied.

The following Sunday afternoon, he brought a friend to the house; a polite, good-looking Brazilian man who introduced himself as Andre. The pair of them disappeared into Mark's bedroom for more than an hour. I was convinced they were snorting coke, and indeed when they re-emerged, I noticed that Mark seemed jittery and wired. He had changed into a collared shirt, black jeans, a smart jacket and leather shoes. He was carrying a small suitcase and announced that he was heading to the airport. There was a classic Yale lock on the door of his ground-floor bedroom and as he slammed it shut, he realised he'd left his key inside... and he'd forgotten something else too. Andre looked as worried as Mark. I didn't have a spare key, I couldn't do anything to help them, and time was against them, Mark had a flight to catch. Eventually, after about ten minutes, Andre managed to force open the window from the outside and was able to get into the bedroom to retrieve the key and Mark's phone. He smiled and muttered 'Goodbye,' as Mark raced off to grab a taxi.

'I'll probably be gone for about ten days, see you when I get back.'

To my surprise, Mark returned only two days later, upbeat and smiling. He handed me a Collins pocket dictionary and a generous five-hundred-gram slab of mature cheddar cheese in a brown paper bag. I asked him how much I owed him, and he said, 'It's on me.'

I enquired about how he'd got on with his work meeting, and he replied, 'Great, I'll be going to Thailand soon.'

Later, after Mark had gone out, I opened the pack of cheese. There was a receipt in the bag indicating that it had been purchased at a deli in Brisbane. *I thought Mark had flown to and from Perth?*

The next day, I got home from work to find Mark's bedroom door wide open. Looking inside, I could see that all his belongings were gone. I tried calling him but his phone was 'out of range.' There was a note in the kitchen.

I've decided to move out, sorry, I found somewhere else that will suit me better. I'll come round at the weekend and give you some money in lieu of notice. Mark.

'Yay.' I punched the air in relief; glad to be free of him.

True to his word, he rocked up the following Saturday with six weeks' rent and told me he had moved to a house near Jimbaran. He said he'd lost his phone but would message me with his new number. I was grateful for the money but I was under no illusion that he'd stay in touch.

A few weeks later, Pam – who had introduced me to Mark in the first place – informed me that Mark had been busted at Brisbane Airport with three kilos of cocaine, worth more than a million dollars, strapped to his body.

'It happened yesterday, he was brought down by the sniffer dogs and he's looking at an eight-year jail sentence.'

Pam had heard it from someone who'd heard it from someone else. 'I'm so sorry Rachel, I put you at risk by introducing you to Mark, but I had no idea what he was up to and nor did anyone else. We all thought he was a travel agent.'

I learnt later that Mark had been working for Bali's Brazilian drug barons, and they had been paying him ten thousand dollars per run. Thank goodness he hadn't been living in my house at the time of his arrest.

~*~

Three years on, I was sitting in a bar in Seminyak, and to my astonishment, in walked Mark. He didn't look well; he was thin and gaunt with a grey tone to his skin. He was on his own and seemed keen to talk. He said he'd got out of jail on parole after serving one third of his sentence. He told me he had two passports, one British and one Kiwi, but the authorities had been unaware of his dual nationality. They had taken possession of his British passport but he had been able to jump parole and skip the country using his New Zealand passport. I wondered how that was even possible. *Maybe his Kiwi passport was a fake*. I asked him why he had chosen to come back to Bali, and he explained that he needed to make a quick buck distributing some ‘goods’ for a friend but had no plans to stay long. I never saw him again.

21
HOUSEMATE FROM HELL #2
2000

My second 'housemate from hell' moved in soon after Mark had left. This time, I had placed an ad in The Bali Advertiser newspaper, 'Looking for a lodger.' Once again, I was taking a risk and would be sharing my house with a stranger.

Her name was Régine. She was a beautiful-looking girl, French, only twenty-two, and she seemed 'nice enough.' I was impressed that she'd come to Bali on her own, had found herself a job and spoke Bahasa Indonesia superbly after only eight months of living in the country. I was struck by her apparent understanding of the culture. How could she be so self-assured and independent …and yet so young? However, she turned out to be yet another chilling liability.

I had expected Régine to become a friend but she was very private. She was uptight. She was demanding, and she was mean; way too mean to even lend me a teabag. I was soon to learn that she was only working part-time, illegally, of course, and her mother was supporting her financially. She was petty and irrational, expecting me to instantly resolve all issues with the house; trivial things such as the purchase and replacement of a broken lightbulb in her room. This wasn't always easy for me, I was working a forty-eight-hour week, she was only working eight hours a week, but she always expected me to deal with the landlord. I had to buy her a transformer because she whinged so much about the electricity overload at night. When the garden flooded in the rain and the water level rose up over our ceramic tiled floor, she complained bitterly because I hadn't warned her that it was a possibility.

I said, "Sorry, it's never happened before."

When she discovered a small leak in the roof, she demanded a refund of her rent and threatened to move out, I vehemently wished she would. She was neurotic. I dread to think what would have happened if she had caught sight of the cobra I chased out of the pond in our kitchen.

Régine had a Balinese boyfriend called Dhuta. He used to turn up late and often stayed the night. I thought he was a 'nice enough bloke' but I would often hear them arguing. Through the bare boards of my bedroom floor and Régine's ceiling, I would listen to her screaming at him in Indonesian, making unreasonable demands. Twice, she threw a full cup of coffee at him; and on both occasions, I heard it smash against the wall, leaving brown stains running down my fresh duck-egg-blue paintwork, which I later had to re-paint.

Surprisingly, she apologised to me after the first incident, and in a rare moment of vulnerability, she admitted that Dhuta was married; he had a Balinese wife and three kids.

I was out one evening when I got a text message from Régine: *Urgent, come home now, house has been robbed, I'm very scared, I think he's hiding in the garden.*

She was waiting for me outside the entrance gate.

'What happened?' I asked.

'I went out to buy some cigarettes and I saw this man on a motorbike watching me from outside the gate and he was carrying a large black bag with handles. When I came back the gate was unlocked. Some money is missing from my room as well as my camera and my CD Walkman.

'Did you leave your bedroom door unlocked?'

'No, I always lock it.'

I went upstairs to check my room. My door was still locked but the intruder had stolen some music CDs along with my VCD player from my TV-watching area on the balcony.

Régine insisted I check the garden, *why me F.F.S?* But our robber was long gone. Unexpectedly, she started crying, the vulnerable Régine was back and this was confession time.

'I had two more keys cut, one to the front gate and one to my bedroom door, and I gave them to Dhuta so he could let himself in when he arrives late at night.'

She paused while I took a moment to digest this disconcerting revelation. The next admission was even more disturbing.

'His wife found the keys in his pocket and has been threatening to pay someone to burn the house down.'

'Well, it's lucky that you came home before he had a chance to start the fire,' I retorted. 'Régine, I can't live like this, you're a liability, you have abused my trust and I'd like you to move out.' I was surprised by my assertiveness but I'd had enough of housemates from hell.

Régine was gone within a week, and I heard that she left the island soon afterwards. This was the last time I would ever share a house with a stranger.

22
A RAGS-TO-RICHES STORY
2001

It was three days before Christmas, a Saturday night in Bali, and I was on my way out for an evening of fun. I was close to home, waiting for a friend, when I spotted a tiny, dirty kitten, foraging in the rubbish beside the busy main road. Street cats and dogs are a common sight in Bali, and I couldn't afford to be too soft, but this poor little thing didn't stand much chance of survival; she was either going to get run over by a car, mauled by a dog, or starve to death. She looked no more than about five weeks old, but she had long gangly legs and I realised later that she was probably closer to eight weeks. There was no sign of a mother cat, and she was so skinny it was clear that she hadn't been nourished by her mother for some time. I picked her up and took her home, knowing that this was an irreversible move. I had no idea whether or not she was sick, she certainly didn't look very healthy; she was literally skin and bone and most of the fur on her back had been worn away from where she had been scratching numerous fleabites. Her belly was completely hairless and through her pink translucent skin I could make out the dark shapes of her internal organs. She reminded me of a baby bird, she certainly wasn't pretty. My big cats hissed, growled, snarled and spat at her, resenting the intrusion. The kitten arched her bony spine and spat back. At least she had spirit. I gave her fresh water and some expensive cat food:

Whiskas seafood platter with prawns and calamari in aspic jelly. I was worried that it might be too rich for a starving animal, but she had an appetite like a horse, and everything seemed to be functioning normally.

The next day I bathed her. I cleaned her ears and her eyes and her little face and removed forty-one fleas and three ticks. Her condition improved daily. Her emaciated belly swelled and became distended, a normal occurrence in mammals that have progressed from starvation to a healthy regular diet. To begin with, she wasn't interested in playing and didn't bother to wash herself. I guess she had been too concerned with the struggles of survival, but within two or three weeks she started growing a new coat, not a fluffy kitten coat but a velvety smooth, ginger and white, adult coat; as thick as a teddy bear and soft as a rabbit.

And WOW! She was so affectionate. She started following me everywhere, purring like a well-oiled engine and wrapping herself around my legs. After just six weeks of shelter, food and love, my dirty malnourished little street kitten was transformed into a beautiful, healthy, friendly, playful puss. Even my big cats accepted her. She was so pretty that Ari, my Balinese boyfriend, was worried she might get stolen, which was rather ironic because he really hadn't been too keen on her when she was flea-ridden, scrawny and hairless.

My lovely 'Littlepuss' went on to live a long and healthy, happy life, and never stopped showing her gratitude for being rescued.

23
DRAGONS, DOLPHINS & HOURGLASS SAND
2001, 2009

The late afternoon sun was casting strange shadows across the parched, angular hills. There appeared to be no sign of life on the narrow beach that skirted the half-circle bay, the crater of an ancient volcano, where we had anchored. We were about to set foot on a mysterious island, which due to its fearsome residents, had been a former place of banishment for transgressors of the law.

As we disembarked from our dinghy, I was struck by an eerie sense of desolation. However, I noticed with amusement that we were not alone, hundreds of tiny hermit crabs in a multitude of stolen homes of varying size, colour and design, were dancing between my feet close to the water's edge. The tension in the atmosphere remained as a lone figure came to greet us.

And then we saw them…

Curious footprints in the compacted sand, showing clearly defined claw marks accompanied by the tell-tale tracks of a rear appendage, without doubt a dangerous carnivorous monster. The man informed us that, yes indeed, there had been a dragon on this very beach only half an hour earlier. I followed its tracks down to the sea noting that it had turned around and gone back through the thorn trees into the scrub. Our only visible place of refuge was a nearby weatherworn hut, with a black thatched roof crafted from sago palm fibre. Dare we intrude further into this remote and hostile territory?

Despite my trepidation, this was not the reception that I had anticipated on Komodo Island. I had expected the national park to be more commercial with sophisticated facilities, but this was 2001 and tourism on Komodo was still in its infancy. I took delight in the island's lack of refinement; its peculiar ambience gave me the feeling of being on a par with the early explorers.

Mindful of the tracks in the sand, we cautiously moved inland and discovered an office where we purchased our entry tickets, valid for three days, at a nominal price.

It was too late in the day to trek into the interior of the island, so we were told to return early the following morning. That night, with the permission of the park rangers, we lit a fire, fuelled by driftwood and coconut shells, on a designated spot just behind the beach. We barbecued our freshly caught fish and baked our potatoes in the hot ash. Strange noises emanated from the scrub, animals crashed through the undergrowth and the evening was enlivened by tasteless jokes about the man-eaters with whom we were sharing our environment.

I was on a voyage of adventure, cruising from Bali to Sulawesi on a beautiful *phinisi* sailing boat with a group of people I barely knew. After Gili Trawangan we had left telephone lines and civilisation behind for the tranquillity of the arid eastern Indonesian islands; dolphins had danced in our bow waves. Stopping at the island of Moyo, off Sumbawa, we had consumed fresh coconuts, as guests of the villagers, in a sea-green house on stilts. We had photographed some laughing children who were bathing in a cool river accompanied by their water buffaloes, and we had leapt from a high rock into a deep, waterfall-fed swimming hole. On another island, we had cast wishes into a magical volcanic lake.

The next morning, the scene on Komodo Island had become more industrious; a boat arrived at the beach and deposited a small group of western tourists. A few hawkers had set up some makeshift stalls selling pearls and woodcarvings, and I noticed that the glass souvenir cabinet in the reception building displayed some postcards and key rings in addition to the solitary stock of painkilling tablets and bandages that had slightly unnerved me the night before.

I decided to have a look around the information centre; it was a little museum, quaint, charming and neglected. There were a number of dog-eared functional displays describing the evolution and lifecycle of the dragons, but very little else apart from a rusty filing cabinet and some large oil paintings reminiscent of illustrations out of a 1950s' *Boy's Own* comic.

One depicted a small ferryboat about to be crushed in the embrace of a giant Komodo dragon, against the backdrop of a blackened sky and a raging sea. The statement on the wooden sign underneath the picture declared: 'Management Objectives.'

The statistics on the wall confirmed that in 1995, there had been 25,000 visitors to the 1,733 square-kilometre national park, which incorporates twenty-nine islands, but unfortunately the figures had not been updated for six years, all giving credence to the enduring prehistoric atmosphere.

Our guide, armed only with a pronged wooden stick, led us inland; a hot and dry monsoon forest surrounded by open savannah grasslands. Timor deer and wild boar nervously darted through the prickly palms; prey to the dragons that have no enemies apart from their own kind. The reason why these primeval monsters have survived is attributed to the fact that the treacherous whirlpools and rip currents in the seas around Komodo have ensured their isolated survival in a habitat free from invading predators.

Heading up the dry riverbed towards Banu Nggulang, we were accompanied by the sounds of birdsong and chirruping cicadas. There was a curious sweet smell, which I couldn't identify. I observed strange yellow snails clinging to the thorn bushes, rare orchids, distinctive lontar palms and kapok trees. A flying lizard landed on my shoulder, disturbed by a screeching gang of sulphur-crested cockatoos. I spotted a jungle chicken and a pair of megapodes, butterflies, and a swarm of bees hanging in a deadly mass from the bough of a tree. With a thousand species of fish in the waters off the shores, over 150 species of birds, water buffaloes, as well as macaques and wild horses on the island of Rinca, there is so much more to this wildlife reserve than just dragons.

Nevertheless, the Komodo dragons were our objective and we eventually found one under a thorn tree. A scaly, armour-clad monitor with spiked claws, snake-like head, and fierce jaws from which flicked a yellow forked tongue amid vile strings of drool. Two and a half metres in length, his menacing beady eyes regarded my orange T-shirt as he stretched his neck towards me, replenishing the folds in his thick loose skin. We saw another one a few minutes later; the most dangerous predatory lizards in existence; we had no desire to get too close, but it was awesome to see them in their natural environment.

In the afternoon, we sailed over to Pantai Merah, the pink beach to the east of the bay. My first impression was that it didn't look particularly pink, but on closer inspection I could see the soft hourglass sand was mixed with minute particles of deep-crimson foraminifera, with the colour more concentrated at the water's edge. It reminded me of sifted white flour mixed with chilli powder, as if in preparation for a spicy batter. The sea was cool and crystal clear, and the water garden beneath the surface was so perfect it looked as if it had been lovingly manicured by human hands; carefully planned and planted in the style of an English winter rockery.

~*~

Since that first trip, I've returned to Komodo National Park more than a dozen times. You'd think that once you've seen one dragon you've seen them all, but each of my Komodo adventures has been a unique and wonderful experience.

My second visit was in 2009; two friends and I chartered a small fishing boat and slept on plastic mattresses on the upper deck. There was a crew of three, a captain, a mate, and a cook who served up the most delicious meals. After exploring

Komodo and Rinca islands, we swam with giant manta rays at Karang Makassar. Manta rays are exceptionally graceful swimmers, they must keep moving in order to keep water flowing over their gills, and they appear to fly through the water as they beat their enormous wings. Drifting on the current with my mask and snorkel, just two metres above one of these beautiful creatures was an unforgettable experience; one that keeps drawing me back, again and again.

Later, we moored off Kalong Island, where we witnessed an arcane sunset mission as hundreds of thousands of flying foxes emerged in a steady throng from the forest. I likened them to a fleet of enemy aircraft intent on avoiding radar detection.

Our boat dropped us off at Seraya Kecil, a tiny crescent-shaped island with a coral reef just off its white sand beach. At the time, this little patch of paradise was home to nine weatherworn huts with grass roofs and woven bamboo walls. Each housed a fan-cooled bedroom and an ensuite bathroom equipped with a cold saltwater shower, a bucket and an unplumbed toilet. Whenever one of us felt the urge, we had to carry our bucket down to the water's edge, fill it up with seawater and use it to flush the toilet. The process was the cause of much merriment and ridicule, endearing us to the handful of other guests, with whom we'd mingle while drinking Bintang beers at sunset. Meals were served in the simple restaurant, which offered a menu of *nasi goreng – fried rice*, fried noodles, omelettes, chips and seafood. The mobile phone signal was almost non-existent, but the owner told us to take our phones up the hill behind the restaurant. Here, an old TV aerial was attached to a post and a washing line, onto which was pegged a colourful collection of hand crocheted and knitted purses, each about the size of a cell phone.

She instructed us, 'Write your SMS message, press send, and hang your phone on the line. Approximately every fifteen minutes the satellite will swing around, and your message will be transmitted.'

To my amazement, it worked, and sometimes there was even a reply waiting for me when I returned to pick it up. I had a new squeeze at the time, Michael, and I wished I could send him photos of this gorgeous place, but this was still the very beginning of the digital telecommunication phenomenon we know today. He saw my photos later, of course, which were enough to entice him to accompany me on another fishing boat cruise around the waters of Komodo National Park and a three-night stay on Seraya. A fun little third-time-to-Komodo trip, fuelled by laughter and Bintang. But more about Michael later…

24
THE CABARET SHOW
2003

It was a Monday evening in Bali, not late but the sun had already set, and I was on my way out to join a group of friends for dinner. Erik and his driver Kadek had picked me up, and Erik had then left us for a few minutes in the car, while he delivered a bouquet of flowers to another friend who was recovering from dengue fever. We were parked outside the old Gado Gado Nightclub; a place that had long been one of my favourite haunts until it had closed for renovation works. We all assumed that it would reopen again as a nightclub, and we were hoping that it wouldn't lose its original character and charm.

The renovations had begun at least a year earlier but the building work had now stopped; probably because of the horrific Bali bombings, which had occurred at two busy nightclubs in Kuta on Saturday 12th October 2002. Two hundred and two people died that night and more than three hundred were injured. The island was grieving, the economy had crashed and tourism had come to a grinding halt.

Gado Gado had ceased operating a long time before the terrorist attack; it had been a legendary nightclub; open to the beach with an alang-alang grass roof and living trees growing within and around the multi-coloured dance floor. It had originally opened in the early 1980s as *Le Marmite Chez Gado Gado*, a restaurant and once-a-month venue for full moon parties. This, in turn, had evolved to become Bali's hottest party spot, complete with a noisy generator and an even noisier tape deck.

I knew Erik would be gone for a few minutes, so I got out of the car and wandered into the former nightclub. I was wondering what changes had been made to the building and I was keen to see the progress of the renovations. Weaving my way around the *aling-aling* – a short screen wall designed to deflect malign influences because, in Bali, it is an acknowledged fact that evil spirits have great difficulty in turning corners – I found myself facing a raised plinth. It reminded me of a church altar, and I assumed it would be the site of the new DJ booth. The roof had gone, and the structure was open to the sky, but it was now hemmed in by three walls and completely dark inside, no lights, and no moon.

I had foolishly entered a dangerous construction site; the floor was a layer of compacted hardfill covered with sand and steel reinforcing mesh. I felt a sense of unease. Bali's heart beats in mysterious ways. Could it be that I was sharing the space with the ghosts of those who had partied there in the past? Or was I feeling the presence of evil spirits? I remembered the aling-aling, which meant the evil spirits couldn't enter the building via the front door, but that didn't stop the sea demons coming in from the beach.

Suddenly I heard a noise, the clank of something metallic and the crackle of dry leaves underfoot. Startled and a little bit scared, I ran towards the sound of the ocean waves, the living trees were still there next to what had been the old dance floor, but the area had been sealed off, there was no way out onto the beach. My only option was to go back through the building. I turned around and froze as I saw a flickering light and a nightmarish shadow rising above the 'altar.'

The shadow approached me.

I think I let out a scream.

The shadow morphed into the silhouette of a man in uniform, wearing a cap. To my relief, I realised it was a *satpam* – a security guard.

'Hello,' I said weakly.

The man shone his torch in my eyes and then deflected the beam so I could see his face. He looked very young. He wordlessly approached me and very incongruously attempted to kiss me. I screamed again and ran, but the building had changed shape since the time of its nightclub persona, and I ran blindly into a wall and then tripped over a piece of steel mesh before finding myself back at the main entrance.

Erik and Kadek were waiting for me in the car.

'Are you okay?'

'Not really. There was a satpam inside and he tried to kiss me.'

To my surprise, Erik was laughing. 'Can you imagine what it's like for the poor man? He's on duty there, night after night, all on his own, bored and lonely, never seeing anyone and fantasising that one night a beautiful naked woman might walk in and make his dreams come true.'

'That's a sweet compliment but I wasn't naked.'

~*~

Six days later, I was assigned to write a story for *The Beat* – Bali's nightlife and entertainment magazine – about the Cabaret Show at *Musro*, a dance club and live show venue in Kuta. For some reason I was expecting white satin costumes and ostrich feather plumes, troupes of girls performing the can-can and boys in sailor suits dancing to songs that were popular more than eighty years ago. However, this was no burlesque family show, this was modern cabaret, and there is nothing else in the pantheon of performing arts that punches with quite the same force. I love that cabaret can explore almost any subject, and flit effortlessly between different styles, emotions and themes. It can be camp, crass, humorous, tragic or refined; this show was all of those things.

The progressive house music was loud, vibrant and provocative. The show was energetic and compelling, full of sexual innuendo and fantasy. Aliens danced for their enigmatic sadistic mistress as she towered above them, with a satisfied smile, in her thigh-high boots. Belly dancers in yashmaks mixed suggestion with tradition. The lasers became falling stars as an interpretation of Madonna's *Frozen* was performed with a Japanese backdrop and lithe Samurai fighters. Far removed from burlesque, was the street scene with street kids dancing in urban groove hip hop gear.

Yet it was the final act, the climax of the show, that really blew me away, shocking me to the core, not because it was raunchy but because it was eerily familiar.

Performed to *Voulez vous coucher avec moi, ce soir?,* the scene opens with a uniformed security guard alone on the stage. He is already yawning, and preparing for yet another boring, lonely night on duty. While sitting there upon a hard uncomfortable chair, he drifts off to sleep and dreams about being joined by four beautiful women. To his astonishment, his fantasy becomes reality. The women appear wearing glamorous evening gowns and then proceed to strip down to their sexy underwear. The security guard is amazed, delighted and scared – especially when the women start to remove his uniform…

~*~

It was another year before Gado Gado reopened, reincarnated not as a nightclub, but as a fine-dining restaurant, with tables spilling out onto a beachfront terrace complete with the original living trees. The ambience has mellowed and matured since the crazy party nights, but the spirit and magic remains.

25
A DAY AT THE RACES
2005

It is known as Jembrana, or *Jimbarwana,* meaning the great forest; it is Bali's least populated regency and is characterised by impenetrable highlands. Not so many visitors make it this far, but those who are bold enough to venture away from the humid and crowded southern plains, the traffic, and the late nights and excesses of the hedonistic tourist areas, will discover another world. For here, in this Wild West, the local people race buffaloes.

The famous bull races, or *Makepung*, are staged every year during the dry season near the town of Negara to please the god of the harvest. The sport is said to have originated as a simple ploughing contest, introduced by migrants from the island of Madura.

One Sunday morning in August, my fellow-adventurer, Kristen, and I set out from Seminyak at six a.m. The slow drive to Bali's Jembrana regency took nearly three hours, we were sharing the winding main road with convoys of heavy trucks, which were heading for Java via the port of Gilimanuk. Our early start had been of necessity; we knew that by late morning the races would be over because the midday heat would make the buffaloes sluggish. We also knew that our excursion could end up as a wild bull chase; despite telephoning several travel agents and four tourism offices we had been unable to establish the exact date and location of this regular event. At this juncture, we realised that the races are not staged for tourists. I'd read that the heats, leading up to a grand final, take place at various race circuits, every second Sunday, after the rice harvest, between July and November. We had no idea whether or not we had picked the right Sunday, but at least we had a fifty percent chance of achieving our objective. Our route took us past rice terraces reminiscent of amphitheatres, and the splendid surf beaches of Soka, Balian and Medewi.

Upon reaching the outskirts of Negara, we stopped at a *warung* – a local shop – to ask for directions to the race ground. At the sight of two foreigners, a little crowd quickly gathered beside our car, eager to help. The people we spoke to knew nothing about the Makepung, and we began to wonder if we were pursuing an obsolete event. Two men directed us to Perancak, ten kilometres to the south. We duly headed south but within minutes we were passed by an open-back truck carrying two fabulously ornamented buffalo heading in the opposite direction towards the town centre. At least we'd picked the right Sunday. By the time we'd turned the car around, we'd lost sight of the truck.

Twenty minutes later, we were still looking for information. Finally, we found someone who could help us; for a small fee and five cigarettes he offered to lead us to the race ground.

'Can't you just point us in the right direction?' I protested.

'No, it's a very long way,' he replied as he pocketed his advance payment and set off on his motorbike with us following in the car. Our destination proved to be a mere three hundred metres around the next corner.

Loudspeakers and *dangdut* music heralded the race ground, but all we could see as we approached were colourful umbrellas and thousands of people lining the banks of a track. We jostled our way past dozens of makeshift food stalls selling Fanta and *nasi jingo*, past a man with a bicycle festooned with bird cages, and past what appeared to be the betting station, before taking our position above a ditch bordering the rough, narrow, racetrack. Within seconds, a loud jingling of bells drew my attention to something approaching from my righthand side, and camera in hand I leapt down from the bank to source a prime position for what could have been a great cover shot.

Suddenly, I was being dragged out of the path of two magnificently decorated pink water buffaloes as they thundered towards me in a cloud of dust. The other spectators all seemed to find the incident highly amusing but were quick to steer me towards a slightly safer outlook. I certainly got a better view of the next wave of contestants. This time it was a pair of brown buffalo; they were harnessed together and pulling a gaily painted chariot marked by a green flag. The precariously balanced jockey was standing in the cart, he was clad in a green shirt and was brandishing a stick; just a few metres behind him and marked by a red flag, the opposing team was in hot pursuit.

Set against a backdrop of mountains, the contest features Bali's sleekest, most handsome water buffaloes. Teams are divided into two clubs, from the eastern and western sides of the Ijo Gading River – hence the green and red flags – and as many as two hundred buffalo may take part. Each race is comprised of two pairs of bulls running against each other at speeds of up to sixty kilometres per hour along the erratic two-kilometre track.

In the days leading up to the races, the bulls are fed as many as fifty eggs per day; they are given herbal potions, massaged and sung to sleep. Before the start of the contest, chilli paste is applied to each animal's anus to give it that extra push. The winning bulls then go to stud, based on the theory that fast bulls can also plough fast. Festooned with strings of bells, silks and decorative harness, every winning team gains a point for its club, with the most stylish contenders picking up bonus points for the splendour of their presentation.

We watched the races for over two hours, illegal betting was rife, and the level of excitement and hilarity increased to an even higher pitch every time an unfortunate jockey was catapulted out of his two-wheeled cart. If only we could have understood the rules.

As the races drew to a close, we walked over to a special area where the buffaloes were resting and feeding after their exertion. We stroked their gentle faces and watched them being unharnessed from their carts and coaxed into large open trucks for the journey home. One man loaded his wife and kids into one of the little chariots and led his triumphant team home by foot. Weary, we also headed for home, it had been a truly spectacular and thrilling event. All that was missing was a beer tent and a row of Portaloos!

26
THE BALINESE DAY OF SILENCE
1999, 2003

The Balinese New Year occurs in March, on the day that follows the dark moon in accordance with the Balinese *Çaka* or *Saka* lunar calendar. The day is known as *Nyepi*, and the way in which it is celebrated is totally unique and something that you will never experience anywhere else in the world.

Nyepi is when all of the island retreats into silence for twenty-four hours. On this darkest of nights, the Balinese Hindus will not cook, work or travel. There will be no flights in or out of Bali on this day, shops will remain closed, all streets will be deserted, and no lights will be switched on, even after the sun has set. Nyepi is perhaps the most important of the island's religious days and the prohibitions are taken very seriously. Hotels are exempt from Nyepi's rigorous practices but the streets outside are closed to both pedestrians and vehicles – except for emergency vehicles – while village wardens, or *pecalang*, are posted to keep people off the streets and the beaches. For the Balinese, the purpose of the day is to teach control of excess, the idea being to spend the day in quiet contemplation and meditation. Any demons and evil spirits will be deluded into thinking that Bali is deserted, prompting them to leave the island. The days before Nyepi, however, are filled with activity. The Balinese Hindus dress in gorgeous traditional costume and take religious objects and effigies of the gods in long, colourful, lavish processions from their village temples to sacred springs, rivers, or the sea, for purification.

On the night before Nyepi, which is known as *Pengerupukan*, the Balinese try to simultaneously appease and scare away the evil spirits, and some of the temples will hold large exorcism ceremonies at main village crossroads, the meeting place of demons. Then, after dark, exciting street carnival processions take place as the evil spirits are driven away with gongs, drums, cymbals, firecrackers, and huge and menacing, highly creative papier-mâché monsters called *ogoh-ogoh,* with fangs, bulging eyes and scary hair.

My first experience of Nyepi was in 1999; new to Bali, I had no comprehension of what it was all about. In those days the airport was still open during Nyepi, and it just so happened that my friend Lyndsay was visiting me for a holiday and would be flying in on that very day. I was alarmed to learn that she wouldn't be allowed out of the terminal building unless she had prebooked accommodation at a five-star hotel in possession of a special dispensation to pick up its guests. Budget accommodation was out of the question.

I phoned Lyndsay, 'Can you change the date of your flight?'

'No,' she replied, 'Why?'

I attempted to explain that the island would be closing down for twenty-four hours, work and travel would cease, all shops and businesses would be closed, and no one would be allowed out on the streets.

'Uhhhh?' Eight thousand miles away in England, she didn't get it.

I told her not to worry, I'd work something out. I booked myself into an upmarket resort at Nusa Dua for two nights and booked Lyndsay in for the second night. I was thrilled to be invited to accompany the hotel driver on his journey to the airport to meet her. He was stopped on the way and had to produce his special document of exemption. I asked him if we could drive through Kuta but unfortunately, he was only allowed to travel between the airport and the hotel, and he was obliged to report to the *banjar* – the village security officials – again on his return journey.

When we got to the airport, we met some bemused and frustrated tourists, 'We're being held here against our will.'

Lyndsay told me that the captain had made an announcement on the plane, somewhere south of Singapore, 'We have just learnt that there is some sort of a curfew in Bali. We don't think this is any form of political action, it doesn't appear to have anything to do with civil unrest or the forthcoming presidential election.'

Apart from the pecalang, and a gang of naughty kids who were daring each other to sit in the fast lane of the bypass, we saw no-one and no other vehicles on the streets. Lyndsay was witnessing something exceptional; it was quite an extraordinary welcome to Bali. The following year the airport closed for Nyepi, and this initiative has continued every year. An airline pilot told me that it was almost unheard of for an international airport to close, but it's a much better idea.

~*~

One year, I spent Nyepi with Ari and my Balinese family at Kedonganan. I was looking forward to an enchanted candlelit experience, shared with folks who really understood what it was all about. Food was prepared in advance, and every window in the house was blacked out with thick cardboard, thus enabling the family to break the rules with the use of electric lights. The fridge was full, and we spent the evening of Nyepi in so-called 'quiet contemplation' watching movies and drinking Bintang beer. So much beer, in fact, that I had to get up twice on this darkest of nights to use the toilet, located behind a sheet of corrugated iron at the bottom of the garden. It was here, only a week earlier, that the head of the household had been bitten by a snake. It's not only the ogoh-ogoh that strike fear into our hearts at Nyepi!

~*~

Every year, this unique and wonderful day is pure joy for me. I wake up in the morning and know that something is different. Relishing the silence, all I can hear is the birds singing, even the street dogs don't bark because there is no one to bark at. I open my gate and tell my dogs they can go out and play in the road all day long, but very soon they sneak back into the garden because there are no pedestrians, motorbikes or cars to chase. One year I noticed my Javanese Muslim neighbours walking through the rice field with their prayer mats, defying anyone to forbid them to practice their faith. After nightfall, I sit in my bale pavilion, listen to frog song, and look at the magnificent stars, unadulterated by streetlamps. The rice field next door teems with fireflies; I guess they're always there but normally rendered invisible by electric lights. Later, looking west, from my bedroom window, I see the only line of lights – Javanese fishermen on the horizon, sailing beyond the boundaries of Nyepi.

27
MANGOES, DURIANS & THE GREEN-EYED MONSTER
2003

It was midnight; I heard him get up and I waited for the sound of the toilet flush, instead there was a click from the telephone and a whispered conversation. Three times recently I had answered the phone and someone had hung up on me. Twice he had been late home. He slipped back into bed beside me, I pretended to be asleep.

The next afternoon, when I was cycling past Jimbaran's traditional market, I saw him talking to the girl at the fruit stall. Later, when I returned home, I expected to find our fruit bowl full of the mangoes he knows I love so much, but there were none there, I was disappointed… and suspicious! Surely there couldn't be anything going on with the fruit seller. She wasn't his type, neither cute nor sophisticated, but she had magnificent breasts. I tortured myself, picturing them naked together, breasts like perfectly-formed mangoes. I wondered if she was like a ripe rambutan, a juicy watermelon, or an emotional passion fruit?

I already hated her with a vengeance, now I had to try to intimidate her. I cruised the designer boutiques of Seminyak and bought a slinky silk top and some tight black jeans. I thought I looked cool, but I knew my cleavage wasn't as good as *hers!*

On Saturday night she was sitting on the wall opposite the A-Bar and we exchanged glances, in my paranoiac state I was convinced that she was waiting for him. I noticed her looking at my man, but there was no visible eye contact. I was desperate to check my makeup, my hair. But I couldn't allow them the opportunity to talk to each other.

Sunday was normally *our* day. We'd always enjoy a late breakfast together and walk the dog on the beach. Instead he announced that he was going out on his motorbike, alone. I didn't protest, but I was churning inside, my guts were twisting. I was tormented with doubt but I couldn't confront him. He would just say I was being unreasonable, jealous. Worse still, he might admit that there was someone else. *Maybe that would be his cue to leave me?*

I searched his pockets. I went through his wallet and three pairs of jeans before I found what I was looking for. With grim satisfaction I examined a crumpled piece of paper containing a scrawled phone number. I called it.

A female voice answered. I hung up.

I also found a condom, but it was unopened and therefore unused; was that a *good* sign? Deranged and wretched I paced the tiled floor, dug my fingernails into the palms of my hands. *What should I do?*

I destroyed the phone number but the condom would be my means of monitoring the situation, so I replaced it.

Later he returned smiling, gave me a kiss and suggested going out for some sushi. He commented on how sexy I looked in my new jeans.

The mysterious phone calls stopped.

The condom remained unopened.

Maybe the smell of durian had turned him off!

28
RELEASING THE FISH
2004

A Balinese friend was hosting a fortune telling evening at his restaurant. For the equivalent of about ten dollars, I could have a thirty-minute session with a magic man, plus a complimentary drink.

Despite having been the recipient of an extraordinary psychic prediction seven years earlier in England, when I was told I was about to 'change my life completely and would be selling everything to move east to a place where the sun shines beside the sea,' I really wasn't the slightest bit interested in having my fortune told again. It just wasn't my thing. *What if I was given bad news?* Nevertheless, I'd been feeling a bit down in the dumps of late and I needed an evening out, so I reluctantly agreed.

The man was waiting for me when I arrived. Dressed entirely in black, with long black hair, eye makeup and long black-painted fingernails, the famous fortune teller from Jakarta had the appearance of a slick showman. He looked more like a conjuror than a clairvoyant. All that was missing was a tuxedo, a top hat and a swishing black satin cape. For some reason I had been expecting an elderly Balinese *balian*, a traditional healer who would use his ancient wisdom, magic, and wrinkled smiling eyes to mend my broken heart, but this guy was much younger than I'd anticipated, probably in his early thirties. We sat down together and he told me his name was Zebedee, and that he was a spiritual consultant. All he asked was my name and my birth month. I crossed his palms with silver – or rather an advance payment of Rp 100,000 – took a gulp of my complimentary mango juice, and awaited his revelation of my destiny.

He looked at my hands and began his spiel.

'You're a long way from home.'

Yes, that's true, I suppose, I'm eight thousand miles away from my birthplace but Bali is my home now.

'You're struggling financially but money is coming soon.'

Jolly good, I need some of that.

'You're looking for love but...,' he hesitated, 'you're not going to find it... until...,' he put his hand on his forehead, feigning confusion.

I hadn't wanted to hear this, so I decided the guy was an imposter.

'Until....' He stopped as if recollecting his thoughts before the next sentence poured out. 'There's somebody out there who is not letting you go.'

I leaned forward, startled. I hadn't thought of it like that, but maybe he was onto something.

'Are you sure *he's* the one that's not letting me go?' I queried, 'or could it be the other way around? Because... because we had no closure, and I haven't been able to move on. He's Balinese,' I explained. 'We were together for three years. Before we met, he was living in Japan. Six months ago, he moved back to Japan for work. His contract was for only three months, so I was expecting him to come home but he's still there. He calls me often, but I really don't think he'll be coming back any time soon. You're right, he's not letting me go, and I'm struggling.'

Zebedee looked at me and smiled, 'It's him, but you can help him to set you free,' and he proceeded to tell me what to do.

'Go to the supermarket and buy a fish.'

What an odd command.

'What sort of fish?' I asked.

'A live goldfish,' he replied, and explained that if I went to the big Indonesian supermarket just around the corner, I would see a tank of freshwater carp, ready for the cooking pot. 'It'll cost you about Rp 20,000, and you must take it away alive.'

I had this horrible fear that he was going to tell me to sacrifice it in a bizarre ritual, but his instructions turned out to be way kinder than that and way more inspiring.

'Buy the fish, take it to a river, and release it.'

Instead of predicting my future, Zebedee had surprisingly hit upon a significant stumbling block, a barrier in my life, and he had offered me a powerful ritualistic solution.

I pondered over whether or not the fish would be able to survive in the wild but figured I'd be rescuing it from the pot. So, a few days later. I did as Zebedee had instructed. The bloke behind the fish counter sunk a little green net into the tank and caught two big carp for me.

'No, no, I only want one.'

He placed the largest of the two on the scales and I watched in dismay as it flopped and writhed on the cold hard surface.

'Oh, no, please don't hurt it, don't let it die, please hurry…'

He filled a plastic carrier bag with water, dropped the fish inside, placed the bag inside another plastic carrier, tied a knot in the handles, slapped the price – Rp 19,780 – on the outside and told me to pay for it at the check-out counter.

There was a river relatively close to the supermarket but also quite close to the sea. *Would the fish swim upstream?* I wondered. *And if it got swept downstream, could it survive in brackish tidal water?* I've since been told that yes, carp will happily live in brackish water but will return to fresh water to spawn. The river was a bit too dirty for my liking, so I decided to release it in another river, which runs through Umalas; a twenty-minute drive away but close to my house. My next challenge was when I got into my manual-transmission car, and realised there was no headrest or hook of any description on which to hang the bag. Holding it in one hand while also gripping the wheel and attempting to change gear proved to be impossible. So, I just had to rest the bag on my lap, while the fish thrashed around inside with water sloshing out in all directions. It was a slow, wet journey.

Arriving at the village of Umalas, I parked and got out of the car. My shorts and my legs were soaked. I walked to the riverbank but there was a group of people close by, staring at me. They didn't know what I had in the bag, but it must have certainly looked like I'd wet myself. Not wanting to attract any more attention, I got back into the car and drove to a smaller river, upstream from the main river, which provided a much more private spot for my liberation ritual. I scrambled down the steep bank, paddled into the knee-deep water, released my fish and silently asked for strength, closure and the ability to move on. My scaly friend hung around midstream for a few minutes, treading water so to speak, while allowing me to conduct my own brief and private letting-go ceremony, before gliding into the lush green riverbank weeds.

I hope you survived little fella. At least I saved you from the frying pan.

As for me, I moved forward with my life and I've never looked back. Thank you, Zebedee.

29
AT THE ALTAR OF SKULLS
2006

The small boat rocked precariously as I alighted onto a rickety wooden landing stage and walked the few metres to the entrance of the tiny cemetery. Shrouded by the broad canopy and aerial roots of a towering tree, the stone steps and narrow split gate were almost hidden from sight. A pair of green-painted statues, the cemetery guardians, surveyed me silently as I entered their domain. The air was clammy, dense and viscous, the atmosphere heavy and eerie, and as I stepped forward, it became harder to breathe; I felt like I was pushing my way through thick treacle. Ducking around the undergrowth, I recoiled in shock at the macabre sight of about fifty moss-encrusted skulls, artfully arranged upon a ghoulish altar.

I was on the eastern shore of Lake Batur, where the village of Trunyan lies, cut off, beneath the rim of an ancient caldera. The residents of Trunyan are the Bali Aga people, descendants of the aboriginal Balinese, who inhabited the island long before the Majapahit invasion in the fourteenth century. The Bali Aga sought refuge from imperialistic strangers by choosing to live in isolated seclusion.

Not many people visit Trunyan; most are discouraged by stories of touts demanding extortionate boat fares that increase halfway across the lake. Tour guides from Kuta claim that taking tourists to Trunyan is more trouble than it's worth, generally proving to be full of unnecessary hassle and unreasonable expense for the visitor.

Most of the villagers are lake fishermen and sustenance farmers, growing cabbages, onions and corn in plots near the lakeshore, although a proportion of the younger men have had to leave the village in order to find work. By chance, I had met such a man only a week earlier. Yan Pulen told me he was the only Trunyanian living in Kuta, where he was working as a tour guide, returning to his village twice a month to spend time with his wife and kids. I felt very honoured when he invited me to visit Trunyan as his guest.

When we arrived at the lakeside, Yan's friend was waiting for us with a boat. It was a calm, sunny day and the surface of the water was like glass, reflecting the steep slopes of Mt Abang rising sheer behind the rusty corrugated iron roofs of the village. The spectacular view of this green mountain backdrop and deep blue lake with the active Mt Batur to the west was a treat; few get to see the volcano from this angle.

In the village, I was received with a mixture of grace and curiosity. Not everybody returned my smile, but as Yan's guest I was treated with respect; nobody – apart from a group of kids – followed us on our tour of the village, and nobody asked me for money. However, I was required to pay a hefty fee to the head of the village for sanctioning my visit. After introducing me to his family, Yan led me past a massive eleven-hundred-year-old milkwood tree in the centre of the village, and showed me the imposing *balai agung*, where the council of elders make their decisions.

To this day, the people of Trunyan retain a social order aligned with prehistoric traditions; cremation is not practiced here. The village actually has three cemeteries: *Sema Bantas* – the burial place of those who have committed suicide or died in an accident; *Sema Nguda* – the burial place of children or other young people who have not yet married; and the *Sema Wayah* – the kubutan where the dead are not buried at all. This shadowy cemetery is situated about five hundred metres outside of the village, and accessible only by boat. Here, the bodies of the dead are wrapped in cloth and simply left in bamboo cages on the ground until they have decomposed. Strangely, there is no stench due to the presence of the encompassing *Taru Menyan* tree. The tree is believed to produce a fragrant smell, while its roots, buried deep beneath the rotting bodies, mysteriously eliminate any trace of odour. Yan explained that the cemetery only ever accommodates a maximum of eleven decomposing bodies at one time. When a fresh body is brought in, the bones of the longest-dead body are kicked aside, and the skull placed upon the altar.

I was relieved not to find any fresh bodies on the occasion of my visit. I didn't stay long, a strong wind had suddenly blown in from across the lake, so I hastily returned to the boat and endured a choppy voyage back to more familiar shores.

30
A MILLION DOLLAR VIEW
2005

Puffing up the steep slope to the village-hamlet of Cegi, I needed to stop every few minutes to catch my breath, the sun was intense, and the sweat was dripping off my face. We had parked our cars at the end of a track lower down the mountain. Already sixteen kilometres from the nearest asphalt road, our four-wheel drive vehicles could go no further, the incline was too sheer and the loose gravel too hazardous. A small troop of kids had been waiting for us. Entwined within the shady branches of a tree, they had greeted us with giggles of excitement. They had then eagerly helped us to unload our provisions, and effortlessly carrying the heavy cardboard boxes on their heads, had immediately set off at a fast trot up the long rough track that I was now having so much trouble negotiating.

I was with a group of Indonesian artists and a television film crew. We were guests of the residents of a remote mountain community, eleven hundred and fifty metres above sea level on the slopes of Mt Agung in East Bali. The volunteer artists were there to share some of their own knowledge with the youngsters by teaching them how to draw and paint. It was an opportunity to open the minds of these previously illiterate children and to bring out potential talents that had never before been unleashed due to the extreme isolation of their village, where some of the families live as far as two kilometres away from their nearest neighbours.

The seventy youngsters listened and watched intently as one of the artists explained some of the basic techniques of drawing, encouraging them to interpret the nature and scenery around them in their own personal styles. Possessed with the natural creative ability of the Balinese and stimulated by their environment, they were eager to pursue their potential talents. Witnessing the event was a joy, these kids were magnets for information and soon it was their turn to put into practice what they had been taught. Squatting together and holding their brushes, with their papers resting on the dry stony ground, these zealous young people tested their skills, drawing strong bold lines in black Indian ink, painting pictures of mountains, trees, birds, animals, and flowers. The broad canopy of the tallest tree was forming beautiful shapes against the bright blue sky, while Mt Agung, towering over the little village, was at its clearest, parading its magnificence and challenging all to reproduce its image on paper. I drank from a freshly picked coconut and watched as the children assimilated the advice of the artists as they examined and judged their artwork, some of which was a release of genuine locked-up talent.

After the children had finished their art lesson, they disappeared into the forest with large panniers strapped to their backs to collect food for the livestock. I joined some of the parents. I felt that as a guest of the villagers, I should mingle with them and show my appreciation of their hospitality. Several of the women were sitting on their doorsteps making baskets out of bamboo strips to sell at the traditional markets for a few cents each. One woman asked me if the baskets in Java were of the same size and shape. At first, I was puzzled, I had already told her that I was from England, but I realised that because of her lack of education and minimal contact with the outside world, her understanding was that anywhere outside of Bali must be Java. An open fire was burning inside her little windowless bamboo house, and chickens were running in and out of the front door; I asked if I could take a look at her home. As my eyes grew accustomed to the dark, I noticed three tiny puppies were sleeping on the dirt floor in front of the fire, their skinny trusting mother was watching me from the wall outside. Two single wooden beds were positioned against the far wall, each supporting a thin and tattered mattress, and the rattan ceiling was black with deposits of thick soot from the fire. Bamboo shelves housed a few metal pots, a packet of sugar and a bottle of coconut oil, some plastic bags, and five old tin plates. A pile of firewood was stuffed underneath one of the beds, together with a pair of rubber boots and a blanket; there were two basins of washing on the floor next to a small table and a broken chair in the corner. I felt intrusive as my eyes absorbed the worldly possessions of this family of five. A rudimentary concrete structure straddled the fireplace and water was boiling in a black cauldron on the top. The woman asked me if I would like to try some coffee, the produce of the trees in the valley. I joined her on the doorstep, next to a few old clothes hanging over a bamboo pole and watched her young daughter peel and chop up cassava roots into finger-food-sized pieces. My glass of sweet Bali *kopi* was delicious. I smiled at the friendly faces of my host and her family as they chatted together in Balinese; I tried to imagine what life must be like for these people.

Later, I watched the last shafts of sunshine fade on the steep western slopes of Mt Agung. I had been feeling hot all day but as the village was abruptly deprived of its natural source of warmth, the temperature suddenly dropped, and I began to feel quite chilly and pulled on a woollen sweater.

The men were smoking hand-rolled cigarettes made from locally grown tobacco. I was profoundly aware that everything I was eating, and drinking had been harvested within a few kilometres of where I was sitting. There was an appetising smell of fried rice, which I knew was to be our meal for tonight. We had brought our own provisions and food but our hosts in the village had insisted on cooking it for us. One of the men offered me a cigarette. I was curious and thought it might be rude to refuse, so I accepted graciously and watched the swift action of his fingers as one-handedly, he rolled it in a dried corn leaf, tying it with a narrow band across the centre. The tobacco was strong and rough; I nearly choked.

I had been expecting to sleep on the floor in the schoolroom with the artists and the film crew, but I had been offered a room in Pak Wayan's house. His sister, Ketut, had insisted on giving up her narrow bed with its thin hard mattress. Wayan reckoned he had been born into this illiterate farming community about twenty-three years earlier. He'd had a brief education, along with eleven other children from the village, when the government opened a school in the hamlet of Daya, further down the mountain. However, with an almost two-hour walk each day along slippery tracks and the teachers rarely turning up to take the classes, most of the kids had dropped out. Nevertheless, this fleeting education had impacted the lives of Wayan and his two sisters. One of the sisters left Cegi and found herself a job. She got married and was living in Bali's capital city, Denpasar, regularly bringing money back for her family; she was unusual because only five percent of these mountain people ever leave their villages. Ketut also left to look for work, but she found it almost impossible to adjust to life outside and returned home.

As with every community everywhere, there was an uneven division of wealth. Nearly all of Wayan's neighbours lived in windowless, single-roomed bamboo huts with dirt floors. Wayan's house, which he shared with his parents, as well as Ketut, and his brother, wife and child, was more comfortable; it had two rooms, glass windows, a concrete floor and was immaculately clean. Yet there was very little furniture, no electricity, no running water, sanitation, or bathroom, and the kitchen consisted of an open fire, a wok, a cauldron, and a plastic bowl outside the back door. Wayan's comparatively high standard of living was due to the money that his sister had brought into the family.

Darkness had fallen and with no electricity, the villagers lit some kerosene lamps and on this special occasion, a bonfire. We wrapped ourselves in blankets and sat around the flames. The artists entertained us, playing their guitars and singing songs, and the kids joined in. Later, we baked cassava roots in the glowing embers, and sprinkled them with salt and a few drops of coconut oil. They tasted superb. I walked to the boundary of the houses to look at the stars, which appeared to be brighter, bigger, closer, and clearer, enhanced by the soft black velvet sky.

At sunrise the following morning, I gazed out of my bedroom window at the spellbinding view of Mt Agung and contemplated the amount of money that some people might pay for a luxury property with an outlook like this.

31
THE PROMISED LAND
2004

In my early days as a journalist, I got work writing articles for a Lombok-based tourism magazine. Every couple of months, I would be invited on an all-expenses-paid trip to Lombok, during which I would stay in a comfortable hotel, explore the sights, interview the movers and shakers, participate in some of the island's tourist activities, eat in the restaurants and be pampered in the spas. All of which I would then review and write about for the magazine. Some of my trips were a week-long, and although the money was crap, it was worth it for the fun experiences and the knowledge that I gained about Lombok, which later qualified me to write for several international guidebooks to both Bali and Lombok.

Although there are only thirty-five kilometres of sea at the shortest stretch between Bali and Lombok, the physical and cultural distinctions are considerable. Towering mountains, mighty waterfalls, magnificent coral reefs, a colourful Sasak culture, ethnic markets, and tranquillity are among Lombok's many charms, yet this beautiful island has rarely received the exposure, attention, and visitor numbers it deserves. It was my job to promote it as an up-and-coming adventure and tourism destination. The magazine was a small one, produced on a tight budget, and at the time, it was Lombok's only home-based

English-language publication. The editor and I were the only contributors.

I'd been writing for the magazine for just over a year, when I received the owner's usual phone call offering me my next assignment.

'The people from the tourism board have got a new product,' she informed me, 'and they'd like you to write about it. Can you fly over on Tuesday? It'll just be for two nights, and you'll be met at the airport.'

She didn't give me any information about the product, and she didn't tell me what to bring. I should have asked, but I just assumed it would be the usual sort of assignment in which I would stay in a posh hotel, eat in a couple of fancy restaurants, and meet some interesting people. I assumed the new product would be something material, a boat perhaps, or a museum, shopping mall or a swish newly-opened beachside resort.

Dressing for the journey in a T-shirt, cargo pants and a pair of flat sandals, I took with me a small overnight bag containing a dress, some high-heeled sandals, make-up bag, undies, a cotton shirt, swimmers, and a sarong. I didn't pack soap, shampoo or a towel because I knew those items would be provided by the hotel.

A local man was waiting for me at Lombok's tiny airport, holding up a sign with my name on it. Introducing himself as Armasih, he ushered me into a small café, where his two male colleagues were waiting. One of them worked for the Rinjani Trek Ecotourism Programme, and the other was a representative of the tourism board, I was never introduced to him, and I never learnt his name, so I'll call him Nameless-Man.

Rinjani Trek? My heart lurched painfully in my chest. Surely, they weren't expecting me to climb Lombok's famous volcano. Mt Rinjani is Indonesia's second highest volcano, and one of the country's toughest and most challenging to climb. Trekking to the summit and/or the crater lake takes between two and four days. I was ill-equipped and physically and mentally unprepared.

'What's the programme?' I asked in a small quavering voice.

The boss man revealed, 'We've developed a new product called the Sembalun Wildflowers Walk and we'd like you to experience it.'

Armasih would be our driver and guide, and our accommodation would be a homestay at the village of Sembalun Lawang, which is the eastern gateway to the national park. Without giving me any more information, he led the way out of the café.

A wildflower walk sounded considerably gentler and tamer than a gruelling hike to Rinjani's summit. I experienced a surge of relief, but this was combined with feelings of anger at not having been given this information in advance and concern at not being properly kitted out. I prayed that I wouldn't need a warm jacket or indeed wet weather clothing or hiking boots. I wondered if my sensible sandals would be sufficient for my needs.

We all got into the car for the two-and-a-half-hour drive east to Sembalun Lawang.

'Do you like Indonesian food?' Maruf, the boss man, asked me.

'Yes, I love it,' I replied, adding, 'I'm a vegetarian although I do eat fish.'

Some discussion followed between the three men and then Maruf announced, 'We'll take you to a fresh fish restaurant for lunch.'

I wondered at the logistics of finding fresh fish in inland Lombok, as far as I knew all the fish restaurants were on the coast.

We stopped an hour later beside a series of boardwalks and pavilions on stilts above a large and murky pond full of goldfish, and for the second time that day, my heart lurched before sinking to the mucky depths of the pond. Damn! I should have said *sea*-food, not fish.

Please don't let this be a catch 'n cook restaurant, I begged silently.

I was relieved that we didn't have to catch our own fish, but the thought of eating muddy-tasting carp full of small bones did not appeal. I would have been perfectly happy eating rice, chilli sambal and water spinach. However, my hosts had brought me here to please me, they were expecting me to enjoy this, so I had to pretend that it was delicious.

Two hours later, after turning north and skirting the eastern side of the majestic Mt Rinjani, we reached our homestay.

Even though the term 'homestay' originates from a guestroom in someone's home, in my experience in Bali, it is most commonly a collection of standalone bungalows, each housing a bedroom, ensuite bathroom and a veranda, and positioned on the homeowner's land. Oftentimes, there will be a small restaurant on site as well. I had assumed that our homestay in Lombok would be along the same lines but instead, we had arrived at a very simple little house.

A middle-aged couple came out to greet us and welcomed us indoors; the wife disappeared out the back, returning a few minutes later with a tray of chipped cups filled with very sweet strong black coffee. We all sat down on the floor and, again, the wife retreated out the back. The house was tiny and very basic, where the hell were we all going to sleep? *Where was the bathroom?* The men were conversing in *Sasak*, the Lombok language, I couldn't understand a word of what they were saying.

Armasih moved around to sit beside me and explained that we'd be going out for a short hike that afternoon with our host, Heri, to 'get a feel for the area.'

No mention was made of the sleeping arrangements, and I was beginning to feel uneasy.

'Where's the bathroom?' I asked.

Heri pointed me in the direction of the garden, where I found a squat toilet and a *mandi* – a tank of cold water for washing – behind a corrugated iron screen. Back in the house, he led me to a tiny room containing two wooden cot-like beds with wafer thin mattresses each topped with a single grubby sheet and a hard pillow. Surely, he wasn't expecting me to share a room with one of the men? These people were devout Muslims, it was grossly inappropriate. What were they thinking? It was as if they were dismissing the fact that I was a woman and had slotted me into a different category altogether. They would have been familiar with the behaviour of the foreign backpackers, who bunk up with each other, sharing rooms in hostels with fellow travellers of the opposite sex. In my hosts' eyes, I was just another *bule* – a westerner – and all westerners had alien habits and loose morals. On the one hand, my hosts and companions were treating me like an honoured guest, they wanted me to enjoy the experience and they wanted to do everything they possibly could to please me, but on the other hand they were treating me like one of the boys.

The sun sets early in Sembalun, it disappears behind Mt Rinjani long before it drops below the horizon off Lombok's west coast. At about five o'clock, Heri led us all out to a river at the edge of the village, from where we hiked up the hill known as Bukit Selong, a practise run perhaps for our Wildflower Walk the next day. Heri's wife stayed at home. I tried to engage Nameless-Man in a conversation, but he seemed very shy.

It only took us about ten minutes to reach the top of the hill, from where we were rewarded with incredible views of a patchwork of rice fields on the valley floor below. On the other side, we were treated to a wider view of Sembalun Village. As we listened to the muezzin's call to prayer from the mosque, echoing around the mountain landscape, I prayed that my sandals would hold up for the walk tomorrow.

When we got back to our homestay, delectable aromas were wafting from out the back. Once again, we all sat on the floor, and Heri's wife – no one ever told me her name, I'll call her Ibu Heri – served us with plates filled with a fragrant bamboo shoot curry, it was exceptional. To my dismay, however, she didn't eat with us, returning instead to the room at the back to eat alone. After dinner, Maruf bid us goodnight, and went home to his own house in the village. I hadn't been included in the conversations, so I took this as my cue to escape, go to bed and read my book. I remained fully dressed on top of the sheet, the light was too dim to read by, and the room was too hot; I opened the window and was attacked by an army of mosquitoes. I wondered who my roommate would be.

After a while, the door opened and in came Nameless-Man. I pretended to be asleep and later heard him snoring in the other bed. Urghhh. The mosquitoes, the heat, the hard bed, and the bizarre situation kept me awake for hours. I lay there not only physically uncomfortable but also mentally and emotionally ill-at-ease about having a strange man in my room, as well as being seriously concerned that my sandals might not endure the next day's hike.

I eventually got off to sleep and when I woke up at six a.m., Nameless-Man was gone. He'd moved his bag out of the room too, so I think he was equally uncomfortable about the sleeping arrangement. I got up without changing my clothes, pulled on my inadequate sandals, and then washed my hands and face in the outdoor corrugated iron shack. I couldn't meet the challenge of having a strip wash and ladling cold water over my body with a plastic ladle.

Ibu Heri served up the leftovers of her yummy bamboo curry for breakfast, Maruf arrived, and all of us apart from Ibu Heri, set out on what I was only now told would be 'a nine-hour soft trek' that would take us through the Rinjani National Park to a height of about two thousand metres above sea level.

The heat of the early morning sun had not yet warmed the rugged mountain terrain as I scrambled up the stony track towards the ridge that marked the top of the first steep hill. Ahead of us, Mt Rinjani dominated the skyline. Behind us, grooved mountains towered around a fertile plateau. I realised we were perched upon the lip of a prehistoric caldera; it reminded me of a giant mixing bowl filled with an abundance of rice and vegetables. Below us, the nearest segment of the valley was a collage of bluish green cabbage fields embroidered with feathery carrot tops and garnished with lettuce. Still rainy season, the landscape looked lush.

We stopped for a breather and were passed by a group of women carrying huge piles of firewood on their heads; it was hard to imagine what it must be like to do this for a daily occupation. Clambering over a rustic stile of knotted tree trunks, we could hear the sound of brass bells jingling as a small herd of graceful, musical cows trotted towards a local farmer, enticed by the assurance of a saltlick. In the distance we could see a group of rare ebony leaf monkeys playing on a rocky prominence. We were still climbing slowly, but the ground underfoot became easier to negotiate as we entered the grassland area of Dandaun. It was here that Armasih, pointed out rough patches of bare, disturbed earth where wild black pigs had been foraging for food. It looked as if they'd been having a party. Spiky yellow flowers carpeted our path; butterflies fluttered in front of my face and dragonflies danced in thermal pockets. We rested in the shade of a tree in a scenic meadow. Our drinking water was still cool, and the sweet potatoes that had been baked in their skins by Ibu Heri were still warm, and wonderful.

After nearly four hours of climbing steadily uphill, we reached the top of a long narrow ridge to be rewarded with the most magnificent view of Propok. Filled with wildflowers, this was the beautiful destination that had been promised to us by Armasih. We spent nearly an hour on our high vantage point overlooking our 'Promised Land' – a dramatic flat valley filled with wildflowers and surrounded by mountainous hills and tropical forest. All we could hear was the sound of birdsong, the buzzing of bees and the rustle of the wind.

The sight of this secret land boosted my spirit for the return journey, which was not without incident. Much to everyone's merriment, I skidded on a cowpat and the sole of one of my sandals peeled off in the confusion. Someone wrapped a dirty old hand towel around my foot and the soleless sandal, and I limped the last two kilometres back to our homestay.

The sun had disappeared behind Rinjani, and the temperature had dropped. I was feeling cold, my legs were aching, and I was covered in cowshit, it had even got into my hair. There was nothing I would have loved more than a steaming hot bubble bath and a glass of red wine. I decided to bite the bullet and have a cold mandi. I had not been given a towel and I realised that my hosts probably didn't have one to spare. I didn't want to embarrass them, so I decided not to ask. I was glad I'd brought a sarong. There was no shampoo in the mandi shack, just a couple of tiny, dry, cracked scraps of some almost unlatherable soap. I scooped up the chilly mountain water and tipped it over my head and body and attempted to wash my skin and hair with the ineffectual soap. I was shivering with cold. I then patted myself dry with my rayon sarong, put on my clean shirt and slipped back into my smelly, shitty cargo pants.

Returning indoors, I joined the men sitting on the floor for a marvellous meal of young jackfruit stew, mountain fern tips and corn on the cob. I was so tired that I headed off to bed at the first opportunity. Thankfully, Nameless-Man spent the night in the living room.

32
LEAP OF FAITH
2003

I am perched on the edge of a wooden precipice, suspended forty-eight metres above the ground, level with Bali's carefree kites. My ankles are shackled, my heart is pounding, and every adrenaline-packed nerve in my body is screaming 'NO…!'

I'd watched scores of madcap individuals make this death-defying dive off AJ Hackett's bungy tower at Double Six, especially on Friday and Saturday nights when the nightclub was in full swing. On a few occasions I had even assumed the role of official photographer, reserved poolside seats, and rented a crowd to pay homage to some reckless visiting friend who wanted to do something wild to make Bali a holiday to remember. There was another instance when I'd been escorted up to the top of the tower; it was just to have a look at the view, that's all. It was three o'clock in the morning, the nightclub was packed and pulsating; the music was sensuous, provocative, and taunting. The bottle that I was clutching was temporarily confiscated for safety reasons and I felt privileged to have the opportunity to walk around the jump deck and peer over the railing. The view was bewitching; the deep swimming pool below me looked like a postage stamp. Not surprisingly, I wasn't going to jump on that occasion, I was wearing a long dress and skimpy underwear; but that was also the juncture when I decided that there was no way I would *ever* jump. I mean, why on earth would anyone want to leap into oblivion with an oversized rubber band tied around their ankles? I resolved that I would leave it to the adrenaline junkies.

So, what the hell am I doing, four years on, hovering on the brink, on a bright sunshiny day with my own little band of loyal supporters looking no bigger than soldier ants, forty-eight terrifying metres below me?

It was all my friend Christine's fault, 'I met AJ Hackett last night, he's in Bali for a few days, he's an interesting guy; I told him I'd got a journalist-friend and he wants to meet you.'

It was a Friday afternoon, and I was going away for the weekend. I reluctantly made an appointment to meet AJ at the tower the following Monday morning. I knew for sure that he was going to be a remarkable man, but an appointment at the tower? I felt like I had just sentenced myself to death at The Tower of London because, quite simply, I knew that my magazine story would be a whole lot better if I threw myself off the battlements. Every chef must taste his own cooking, and I had the whole weekend to stew on it.

Bungy jumping first started hundreds of years ago in Vanuatu in the South Pacific. Legend has it that a young woman leapt, apparently to her death, from a tall tree while being pursued by her jealous husband. In despair, and in the knowledge that he couldn't live without her, the man also threw himself from the tree. The woman, however, had cleverly cheated by tying forest vines to her ankles; her husband's jump was fatal, but she survived unscathed. The legend is still kept alive today by the young native tribesmen of the same village, who use tree vines to leap from man-made towers in a unique manhood-initiation rite.

English thrill seekers, calling themselves 'The Oxford University Dangerous Sports Club', were so inspired by the Vanuatu ritual that they went about replacing vines with rubber bands and did a series of spectacular and highly publicised jumps off the UK's Clifton Suspension Bridge in Bristol in the late 1970s.

In 1986, New Zealander AJ Hackett, together with an old friend Chris Sigglekow, decided to further the concept of jumping with elastic ropes. They contracted a professor at Auckland University to assist in the initial laboratory testing of rubber. The aim was to establish a predictable formula that would enable them to manufacture the first bungy cord, but AJ decided he would only continue to pursue his goal if he could devise a method that proved to be consistently workable. Having developed a special cord made up entirely of individual rubber strands, Hackett used local bridges in the North Island of New Zealand as testing platforms. To establish the predictability of the jump, he had to calculate the height of the bridge, the size of the cord and the weight of the person. He finally tested the outer limits of the system – the effect of extreme cold on bungy cords – by successfully jumping ninety-one metres in a temperature of minus-twenty degrees from a cable car at the French ski resort of Tignes. Totally satisfied with his system, AJ decided to go public, and in the early hours of a Paris morning in June 1987, he made a daring illegal leap from the Eiffel Tower. With this single jump, AJ gave the world a taste of what was to come.

The following year, AJ chose the historic Kawarau Bridge, forty-three metres above the river, on the outskirts of Queenstown, New Zealand, as the location for the world's first-ever commercial bungy jumping site. He has since gone on to develop a phenomenal global bungy jumping industry, and at the time of our meeting back in 2003, his international team had safely facilitated well over one million public jumps.

Originally built in Cairns, in Australia, and then shipped to Bali to be manually erected on site at Double Six Nightclub, AJ Hackett's bungy jump tower was in a fantastic location, overlooking the magnificent sands of Kuta Beach and the rolling surf of the Indian Ocean. It opened for business in 1995, and for more than sixteen years, until the closure of the nightclub in 2011, it stood as a local landmark and looked particularly dramatic at night with its alluring flashing lights.

When I arrived at the tower on that bright and breezy Monday morning, my palms were sweating, and I was feeling sick. Christine had organised the support committee. I didn't want too many of my friends to be there in case I couldn't go through with it – oh the humiliation. On the other hand, my greatest dread was that of personal failure and I knew that I'd be more likely to do the jump if at least one of my buddies had made the effort to turn up. It was also about not wanting to let my mates down. However, I warned them not to be late, I was certain that if I went, I would go quickly and I told them I would be waiting for no one. Meanwhile, I was hoping, desperately, that AJ would not be there to keep our appointment, but needless to say, he was there. I should have known better than to question the potential reliability of a man who has built an industry dependent on trust and predictability.

Like a prisoner being led to the gallows, I stepped on to the weighing-scales, emptied my pockets and entered the elevator with AJ. It was a long, slow ride up to the top, but the very modest Mr. AJ Hackett was both encouraging and reassuring. I asked him about going off backwards – a leap known as the *Elevator to Hell* – but he recommended the face-first *Swan Dive* – as if I could possibly be that graceful – and told me to fix my eyes on the horizon and not look down when I was preparing to jump.

Zombie-like, I stepped into a harness, a comforting back-up system, a bit like an emergency parachute. I then allowed my ankles to be bound by the jumpmaster and I hobbled to the edge of the jump deck.

So here I am, probably more physically frightened than I have ever been in my life, walking the plank at a height the equivalent of a sixteen-storey building. This is the point where I have to forget all the laws of common sense, which have taught me not to play with fire or jump out of trees. Numb with fear, I just know that I have to get this over with. I don't even wait for the countdown; I simply hurl myself over the perimeter, launching my trembling body into space before I have time to change my mind. My stomach plummets into my mouth and I find myself falling at an ever-increasing rate, powerless to stop. And so, I wait for it to end...

Then incredibly, I feel the gentle pull of the cord, and my body slows as if saved by some gravity-defiant miracle. An intense rush of adrenaline surges into my brain like instant morphine, and I open my lungs and scream with the pure euphoria of having overcome my terror. At this glorious moment in my life, I realise that I am capable of achieving absolutely anything. Suddenly I am catapulted skywards again, but this time I relish the ride. My spirit soars, I have survived.

34
GILI WIZARDRY
2008

I met Michael in October 2006, he had landed in Bali three months earlier en route back to his New Zealand homeland after six years of living in Tokyo, where he'd worked as a magazine editor. He'd only planned to spend a couple of weeks in Bali, visiting a friend, but captivated by the holiday island lifestyle, he decided to stay longer and scored a job as editor of a new tourist magazine called *Sweet Life*. The owner of the magazine offered me a gig writing stories for her publication and introduced me to Michael. I never imagined that fourteen-and-a-bit years later, we would get married. In New Zealand. In the middle of a global pandemic.

The first edition of the colourful Sweet Life magazine looked great, and its future looked promising, but it went belly up, flopping and failing cheerlessly after just one issue. The owner and her partner left the country to escape their creditors and Michael and I were left high, dry and unpaid. United in our displeasure, we became firm friends. Fortunately, more work came along for both of us; it always does.

Fast forward two years to October 2008. By now, Michael was working as editor of a magazine called *Tropiq*, and had met a potential advertiser, a man called Blake who'd sold a dotcom domain before the bubble burst. He had bought a pirate ship with the proceeds. While discussing life on the ocean waves, Blake invited us to join him on his boat for a voyage from Bali to Sumbawa – the island lying east of Lombok – and back. We arranged to meet him early the following Sunday morning at Bali's Serangan Harbour, where his boat was moored. Blake, however, proved to be a bit of a flake; he kept us waiting all day before telling us that he'd changed his mind about going to Sumbawa and would, instead, be mooring the boat for a few weeks in Lombok while he did some maintenance work. Nevertheless, he still offered us a 'lift' to Lombok, and we eventually set off at midnight.

On deck, under the stars, having been lulled to sleep by the purr of the engine and the rhythmic splashing of the waves against the bow, Michael and I were abruptly and simultaneously awakened by a deafening crash of thunder and a sudden cloudburst of torrential, tropical rain of biblical proportions. We quickly took cover but remained on deck. The sky was filled with dramatic flashes and forks of lightning from seemingly every direction. We were unsure of our whereabouts until the silhouette of Bali's mighty volcano, Gunung Agung, was suddenly illuminated in all its towering magnificence. The rain stopped but the dry lightning storm continued, rendering the mountain visible every fifteen seconds. We sat back and relished the show.

Blake-the-flake dropped us off on Gili Trawangan, one of a trio of tiny white-sand holiday islands off Lombok's northwest coast. Within minutes of our arrival, we bumped into the owner of a groovy new resort, which she was hoping to promote in a Bali magazine. I was writing for nearly every tourist magazine in Bali at the time, so I called one of my editors and secured an assignment, and the owner was very happy to comp us a night's accommodation in exchange for a story in the next issue.

While we were enjoying a sunset Bintang, a beach hawker approached us with three bags full of Lombok pearls. Strings and strings of them in a whole range of shapes, sizes and delicate colours. I've always loved our local sea-and-freshwater cultured pearls, I love to wear them, and they make great presents; I bought five strings for the equivalent of about twenty dollars each.

Gili Trawangan is the busiest of the three islands, so the next day, we swapped the bustling vibe for the much slower pace of Gili Meno, arriving by local ferry in the afternoon. We decided to stay a few nights on Meno, our accommodation was simple, cheap and cheerful. We snorkelled off the beach and then walked barefoot around the island, ending up as darkness fell with bleeding feet, at the edge of a boggy lake, getting bitten by mosquitoes, but we didn't care, we were having fun.

'How much cash have you got on you?' Michael asked me a couple of hours later, while we were sitting in a beachside cafe enjoying a *nasi goreng*.

'Hmm, not much,' I replied, 'I spent all my money on pearls. What about you?'

'I've only got four hundred thou' (forty dollars), he replied. We pooled our cash and found that we just had enough to cover our food and accommodation for two more nights. Not that anything was expensive on Gili Meno, we just hadn't brought very much cash with us because we'd been expecting to stay on Blake's boat.

Michael summoned our waiter, 'Is there an ATM machine on this island? Do you take credit cards?'

'No,' replied the waiter, looking concerned.

This was in the days when cash was the only currency.

He added, 'The only ATM machine is on Gili Trawangan.'

'That's okay,' we reassured him, 'We've got enough cash to pay for our meal.'

Over breakfast the next morning, we reviewed our situation. We weren't ready to leave the peaceful Gili Meno, and neither of us fancied getting the public ferry back to Gili Trawangan merely to visit the ATM and then wait for another ferry back to Meno. We figured we could manage on the little bit of cash we had in hand, but more importantly, we had to book a fastboat back to Bali; the cost of which would be the equivalent of fifty dollars each.

I had a potential solution. Only two months earlier I'd celebrated my birthday with a party on Gili Trawangan, which had attracted a few gate crashers – Gili regulars and residents. I had welcomed them graciously. One of them was a man called Dean, who owned one of the fastboat services between Bali and the islands. He had been an apologetic gate crasher and had promised me the birthday present of a free one-way trip on his boat. It was most fortuitous. Hoping that he was still in the country and that I'd be able to get hold of him, I sent Dean an SMS message:

Hi Dean, this is Rachel, remember me? We met at my birthday party, and I was wondering if I could claim my birthday present of a free trip on your boat?

Certainly, was Dean's response, *when do you want to travel and in which direction?*

Tomorrow from Gili T to Bali if that's okay? Also, I'm with my friend Michael, you haven't met him but he's the editor of Tropiq magazine. Would you be prepared to give him a free ticket as well, in exchange for a free ad for your boat services in next month's edition of the mag?

Absolutely, replied Dean, *thank you very much and I'll tell my sales manager to book you both a passage on the boat tomorrow. It leaves at midday.*

It was as simple as that.

We then counted up how much money we still had between us, putting aside the small amount that we needed to pay for one more night at our little hotel. We were left with the equivalent of just twenty dollars between us. We'd have to forgo lunch, but there was enough to pay for a simple meal that evening, *fried noodles, perhaps,* and the nominal cost of the next day's eight-a.m. public ferry from Meno back to Gili T.

We spent the day on the beach, reading, enjoying the sunshine, and swimming in the clear turquoise sea. We were on the quietest side of the island and there was nobody around.

In fact, we didn't see anyone until the late afternoon, when a young local guy approached us. 'Have you got a plan for dinner tonight? Would you like to come to my restaurant?' He indicated the direction. 'It's just over there on the beach.'

We'd already explored the length of the beach and we hadn't seen any restaurants, only a tumbledown building.

'What's on the menu?' I asked.

'There's no menu,' the boy replied, 'but if you'd like some fresh fish, I can prepare a romantic dinner for you both.'

He was really keen to have our custom, but I felt bad because I knew I was about to burst his bubble.

'We haven't got any money,' I announced, knowing that he wouldn't believe me because undoubtedly, anyone who looks like a tourist is bound to have money, right!

He must have thought I was trying to negotiate a price, 'How much do you want to pay?'

I was now in danger of offending, or even worse, insulting him. 'Look, we've almost run out of money, I explained, 'we've only got Rp 100,000 (ten dollars) between us.'

We actually had Rp 160,000 but I didn't want to tell him that, because I'd mentally set aside Rp 60,000 to cover the cost of a couple of Bintangs each.

'I can do it for that,' he replied eagerly, and pointing to a dilapidated open-sided structure with the fractured remains of a thatched roof, he added, 'I want to give you a really special experience so that you'll tell all of your friends to come to my restaurant when it opens.'

Introducing himself as Irfan, he then went on to tell us that his family owned the piece of land adjacent to the beach which had once been home to 'The Beach Café' but no one had had the skill or the ambition to put in the hard graft to make a success of it. He said he'd learnt to speak English from talking to visitors and watching subtitled Hollywood movies, he loved to cook, and he had a dream of someday opening a seafood restaurant and a bar, and maybe even a small hotel.

'But you've still got to rebuild your restaurant,' I mentioned casually.

'I've already got a kitchen,' he replied, 'my plan is to start by just setting up some tables and chairs on the beach, and when I have enough money, I'll build a terrace and make a new roof.'

He couldn't have been more than about eighteen years old; he was opening his heart to us, and I was already loving his sense of purpose and ambition.

Irfan asked if he could have a deposit in advance so that he could go and buy the ingredients. I didn't doubt his sincerity for one moment, so I handed over a fifty percent deposit plus an extra sixty thousand and sheepishly asked him if he could buy us four bottles of cold beer as well. His face lit up with a beautiful smile, 'I'll be back soon,' he said. He then jumped on a bicycle and was gone.

Fifteen minutes later, Irfan returned with a huge snapper and our cold Bintangs. He told us to stay where we were, while he prepared our table. *Table?* we wondered; we hadn't seen any tables or chairs.

On clear days, folks on the Gili Islands are treated to glorious west-facing views of the sun dropping behind Gunung Agung, way across the Lombok Strait in Bali's Karangasem Regency. And this was the scene when Irfan summoned us to our table. A tatty old bamboo coffee table, positioned between a pair of sun-bleached driftwood tree trunks – our seats. The table was covered with a plastic cloth and adorned with a jam jar of red hibiscus flowers and another jar containing a candle. Our cold beer had been poured into two glasses and the two remaining unopened bottles were sitting in a plastic bucket of ice. More driftwood had been hastily gathered and Irfan was in the process of lighting a bonfire right next to us on the beach.

'I'm going to start cooking now,' he announced, leaving us to enjoy the deepening red and orange hues of the sunset sky.

When the food arrived, Michael and I looked at each other, astonished. Irfan delivered an oval plate containing the whole grilled snapper, served with a fresh barbecue sauce filled with sliced onions and slivers of red capsicum, along with two plates of mixed salad and fried potatoes. We dined by candle-light and told stories beside the dancing warmth of the fire. It was exceptionally romantic.

Bali's most exclusive boutique hotels offer some extraordinarily romantic toes-in-the-sand dining packages to couples and honeymooners at mega dollar prices – which we've since been fortunate enough to experience on occasions when we've been writing stories or reviews for magazines. Yet, to this day, this young man's random, uncontrived, spontaneous act of open heartedness continues to exceed them all.

When we paid the measly balance of Rp 50,000, we apologised for our lack of funds. I so wished we had enough money to give Irfan a big tip. Yet the whole encounter had gone way beyond that.

'Please,' he said smiling and shaking his head, 'it's okay, we negotiated the price in advance. I've still made a profit and most of all I just wanted to show you what's possible. I hope you'll come back when my restaurant is fully open, and please bring your friends.'

We left Gili Meno on the eight o'clock public ferry the next morning, and fifteen minutes later we disembarked on the sands of Gili T. We had nearly four hours to wait for our fast boat. 'Let's go to the ATM,' suggested Michael, 'get some cash and then have a slap-up breakfast somewhere.' It was a great idea until we got to the island's one and only ATM to find that it, too, was out of cash.

'Let's go to the Compass Club,' I indicated towards the restaurant-venue of my birthday party. 'Hopefully Mia (the owner) will be there and will agree to let us pay later.'

Mia was away, in Bali, but her staff remembered me. Her restaurant manager made a quick call, our request for credit was approved, and Michael ordered two cooked breakfasts and a couple of Bloody Marys. A few more Bloody Marys later, with full stomachs, we boarded Dean's fast boat back to Bali, marvelling at how good it was to have friends.

We reimbursed Mia the next day as well as sending a generous tip to Irfan via the captain of the returning fastboat. The sealed envelope containing the money had to pass through three sets of hands and cross over to Gili Meno on the public ferry, but I received a grateful text message from Irfan, confirming he had received it.

Fifteen years on, the Gili Islands are much more developed; there are now lots of restaurants on Gili Meno's west-facing beach and it's hard to discern the little spot on the sand where Irfan created our romantic feast. Nevertheless, I'm prepared to make a bet that he realised his dream.

34
BEWARE OF THE BOGEYMAN

At the end of 2008, during the short window of time between Christmas and the New Year, Michael and I went on a trip to Sulawesi, that large spider shaped island, which straddles the Equator, northeast of Bali. We flew to Makassar, capital of the South Sulawesi province, with a plan to visit the villages of Bira and Tana Beru, located at the fingertip of the island's southwestern arm. South Sulawesi is home to the bogeyman, that shapeless mythical monster, which jumps out of the wardrobe at night to frighten little children. In other cultures, the allusion to the bogeyman is used by parents to scare their children into good behaviour, but in Indonesia, the bogeyman or *Bugis* man is real.

The seafaring Bugis tribes are the master shipbuilders and seafarers of South Sulawesi, and in particular, Tana Beru, where they handcraft exceptionally strong *phinisi* schooners, using the robust timbers of the islands, age-old techniques and a skillset passed down through the generations. These boats are capable of sailing vast distances and coping with the heavy seas of the region. Long before the European explorers and traders arrived in what is now called Indonesia in search of spice, the hardy Bugis people had gained prominence as one of the greatest seafaring ethnic groups in the world. In fact, they had been constructing and commanding fleets of sailing ships to support Asia's thriving spice and cargo trade for hundreds of years before the Europeans ever arrived. These Bugis traders, travellers, pirates, and sea warriors controlled the major trade routes, and were known for their fighting prowess. They would raid foreign trade ships and were so greatly feared that the British, Dutch and Portuguese sailors took terrifying tales of these pirates back home.

Telling their children, 'Beware of the Bugis men.'

Meanwhile, there was something else we needed to beware of in Sulawesi, but it wouldn't become apparent until after we got home.

Our first priority was to find somewhere to stay in Makassar and then establish the best way to get to Bira and Tana Beru. After checking in to a hotel, we got a *bemo* – an open-sided public minibus – to the Mallengkeri Bus Terminal to learn that alas, all the buses to Bira were fully booked for the next two days. A nice man standing behind us, registered our disappointment and told us he had a friend who could take us there in his shared car. He duly called the friend and asked him to come and meet us. While we were waiting for this prospective driver to arrive, Michael asked the nice man where we could buy some beer. His request was misplaced. We were in a strict Muslim area, where beer was not readily available; the consumption of alcohol was frowned upon and the selling of it was considered illegal, apart from in the tourist hotels and at a few licenced restaurants. The nice man informed us that he had another friend who could help us, and we were ushered into the back room of a small convenience store. Soon, four bottles of warm beer arrived wrapped in plain brown paper, money changed hands, and we were instructed to stay indoors and drink it out of sight of the beer police. Our gracious hosts provided us with glasses and ice. The beer was so warm that the ice melted very quickly.

We were soon alerted by the arrival of our driver, Zainal, who told us he'd be happy to take us to Bira the next day for a fair price. The journey would take between five and six hours; Zainal would meet us at the bus station at nine o'clock the following morning.

That evening, we walked alongside the seafront, where we found a Chinese restaurant and karaoke bar. Fuelled by chow mein and Dutch courage, we sang karaoke until two a.m., and struggled to get up for breakfast in the morning. We checked out and leapt into a bemo. Michael had recently started his new job as editor/creator of Tropiq magazine, the first issue of which had just been 'wrapped up and put to bed' or so he thought until his phone rang in the bemo. The call was from the printer who had a problem, some photos hadn't translated properly, and he needed to get some new copies. Solving this glitch was a little bit stressful, especially back then when documents and emails couldn't be transmitted by phone, and phone signals were often weak and unreliable. Fortunately, Michael was able to contact his designer and we learnt from the experience that it really is possible to work remotely, even while crossing Makassar in a bouncy old bemo.

As soon as we got in the back of the elderly eight-seater Toyota Kijang, Zainal asked us to squeeze up a little bit more so that some other passengers could sit with us. The final seating arrangement was outlandish: Zainal, an adult and two small kids in the front seats, four adults and a child in the middle seat, and four adults in the back seat. In total, we had thirteen people cramped into the SUV. It was pretty confined, but the journey took us down the coast, the scenery was lovely, and the five-and-a-bit hours passed surprisingly quickly. Zainal dropped us off in Bira and told us he was staying locally with his brother for a few days; he gave us his number so we could contact him if we needed a lift back.

We checked into a guesthouse beside the beach and rented a motorcycle to get us to Tana Beru, where we were greeted by the whine of chainsaws and the percussive tapping of hammers. All along the high tide mark, sawdust mingled with sand, and we could see a line of boats in various stages of construction. We had found the Bugis men.

Each colossal ship takes a year, or more, to build, and is put together using little more than experience, an unspoken synergy between the boatbuilders, and a literal rule of thumb. The finished ships are sailed and sold all over the world; many carry cargoes of spice, rice and building materials, while many more are sold to small cruise operators who take divers and adventure tourists all around eastern Indonesia.

~*~

Apart from watching the boatbuilders and swimming and snorkelling on the beach, there wasn't a great deal to do in Bira and Tana Beru, but Michael had noticed a small harbour from where public ferries were departing twice daily to an island known as Pulau Selayar. The name was familiar. 'Selayar,' I gasped, and excitedly told Michael I'd been there before. It had been on my very first voyage on a phinisi boat, way back in 2001 on my first trip to Komodo, when a group of us had cruised from Bali to Komodo to South Sulawesi and stopped at Selayar en route.

'We spent the afternoon on a golden sand beach,' I remembered it had been completely deserted and peppered with large and gorgeous seashells. At the time, I'd decided it was the most beautiful beach I had ever seen.

We consulted our Lonely Planet and learnt that the island was long and skinny, measuring about eighty kilometres from north to south, and the main town was a place of 'little distinction' called Benteng with no tourist facilities. We read that myths and ghost stories had been kept alive on this island, which lay on what had once been the Chinese trade route. 'The west side of the island is mainly inhabited by fishermen, who live in small villages and continue to follow their traditions largely unaffected by Western influences.'

There was a car ferry leaving at two p.m., and it would take about two hours to get there, but when the ferryboat arrived, it took a long time to unload the buses and vehicles, and in the end, we didn't leave the harbour until nearly four p.m., arriving at Pamatata Port in the northern part of Selayar Island just after sunset.

'Are there any hotels around here?' we asked a local woman.

'No, you'll have to go to Benteng, hurry, this is the last bus.'

'How long does it take?' we asked the driver as we climbed aboard.

'One hour,' he informed us.

The fare was ludicrously low, which was rather concerning because it implied that very few tourists came this way, which in turn meant there would be very few hotels and facilities.

It was almost dark when the bus set off, which denied us the opportunity to enjoy the scenery. Peering out of the grimy windows, all I could see was a landscape of stunted bush and strange shadowy apparitions that darted, twisted, floated, and rolled beside the road, defying my conventional understanding. Maybe I was just imagining it, but the place felt mysterious, ominous, and foreboding.

We arrived at the bus terminal, more of a wasteland really, which seemed to be in the middle of nowhere, rather than in the town centre.

Dozens of local men were there to greet the bus, *ojek* drivers who were offering motorcycle-taxi transport into the town. Our white faces represented baksheesh, and suddenly we were surrounded by a circle of unruly men battling for our business. Everyone was vying for our attention, shouting, pushing us, pulling us, trying to grab our backpacks in the belief that this would guarantee them a fare. Michael had already started to negotiate a fare with one of the drivers but kept getting interrupted by others claiming they were first in line, while three more were trying to engage *me*.

'Will you all just SHUT UP,' yelled Michael in English, and to my great surprise everyone went quiet.

Michael selected the two men directly in front of him and asked them to take us to a hotel. We were tired, hungry, and dirty after our long wait at the ferry port, a hard-seated boat crossing, and a bumpy bus ride; all we wanted was a comfortable hotel room, a hot shower, a decent meal and a bottle or two of Bintang.

Michael got on the back of one bike, and I got on the back of the other. There were no helmets of course; we had no choice. My driver wasn't very friendly. Holding onto the back of my seat, I was putting my life in his hands and worried I'd get separated from Michael. Happily, that didn't happen, and we arrived at a building that could have been a hotel but looked more like a *kos-kosan*, a residence with basic rooms that are usually rented by the month. People were leaning out of the upper windows, staring at us, and once again a crowd gathered. Having established that this wasn't a hotel, our drivers were directed somewhere else. The next place was indeed a hotel of sorts, it looked pretty quiet, but the manager took one look at us and told us it was full. I began to feel quite concerned, *where were we going to sleep that night?* According to one of the inquisitive locals, there was another hotel – the only other hotel – and it was on the beach road, which sounded a bit more promising.

The hotel looked rough but there was a room available.

'Up the stairs on the left at the front,' instructed the owner.

It was a shithole; at least the door had a lock. The shower discharged only a dribble of cold water, so we didn't bother, we just dropped our backpacks in the room, and headed down to the dining room.

'Our kitchen is closed,' said the owner.

'Is there a warung near here?' I asked, 'somewhere we can get something to eat?'

'No, everywhere is closed,' was the response.

It was only eight o'clock. 'We're hungry, explained Michael, 'any chance you could cook us a mie goreng?'

The man kindly obliged with two small bowls of unappetising fried noodles, which we hastily consumed before heading back upstairs. We looked out of our window but there were no streetlights, and it was way too dark to see anything. We'd established that there was a morning bus back to the ferry port, leaving from the terminal at nine o'clock.

'We'll get up at seven,' declared Michael, 'and if we don't like what we see outside of this window, then we're getting the hell out of here.'

The new day dawned, and filled with dread, we opened the curtains and looked out of the window. It was even worse than we had anticipated. We had a river view and appallingly, just metres from its entry point into the sea, the surface of the river was entirely covered by an unimaginable amount of waste, completely choked with garbage.

Living in Indonesia, the world's fourth most populous country, we understand there simply isn't a proper system in place to handle the massive amounts of waste. Even if the locals were able to confine it into one space, there is no system to move it to a processing plant. With more than 280 million people in Indonesia, and some 17,500 islands – actually more than the government has ever been able to fully count or name – of which about six thousand are inhabited, the logistics are mind-boggling. Sadly, the country is not sufficiently eco-focused, and nobody wants to take responsibility for it. Yet the sight of this trash-filled river was shocking even to us, clearly there was no programme in place to attract visitors to this town.

We decided to have a look at the beach but what we had assumed would be a beachfront promenade was just the end of the road, with some ugly unfinished concrete structures. The beach was stony, grey, and dirty.

What had happened to the paradise I'd visited seven years earlier? Neither of us felt inclined to look for it. We returned to the hotel and checked out, noticing that we'd been grossly overcharged for our meagre meal of fried noodles the night before. We no longer cared, we just wanted to get away from the place. The owner ordered a couple of ojek drivers to transport us to the bus pickup point, and once again I experienced the discomfort and fear of being at the mercy of a stranger and getting separated from Michael.

We were delivered to the terminal where the bus was waiting. Getting on board, we handed over the equivalent of three dollars each, the same amount that we'd been charged on the journey from the port. The driver spoke to us in the local dialect, we didn't understand his language, but we understood his hostility.

'He says you must pay him Rp 300,000 each,' said a woman sitting in the front seat.'

'But we only paid Rp 30,000 to get here,' protested Michael.

A heated conversation ensued between the woman and the driver. I think she was trying to negotiate on our behalf, but the driver looked angry.

'He says he doesn't like you,' said the woman, 'and he says if you don't pay Rp 300,000 each, you can get off his bus.'

'Tell him I don't like him either,' countered Michael, begrudgingly handing over the fare.

In our since-extensive travels around Indonesia, we have only ever been met with smiles and curiosity, we have never visited a place where the locals have been so unfriendly. We've always taken great care to be considerate and respectful. There are few places in Indonesia that I've visited and not found something to like. At that moment, as far as I was concerned, Selayar was the cesspit of the country.

Later, we referred back to our map and identified the paradise beach. Accessible only by boat, it was quite some way from Benteng on the almost uninhabited, south-eastern side of the island, which is still covered with original rainforest. The beach was the site of Selayar's first eco-dive resort, and a marine park has been founded there. In fact, on my first and only visit to the beach in 2001, I remember meeting a man who told me that he was building a dive resort in the vicinity. He was carrying a satellite phone because there was no mobile phone signal.

After having felt so saddened by the sight of the polluted and plastic-choked river mouth from our hotel room window, Michael and I were pleased to learn that there was at least one example of conservation and environmental responsibility on this uninviting island.

En route to the ferry port, the bus stopped at a small traditional market where I purchased a fresh coconut from a courteous woman who was fascinated by my hair, which was blond at the time. Perhaps there were some friendly people on Selayar after all.

Meanwhile, Michael and I were both suffering from Bali belly, or perhaps I should call it the *Sulawesi shits*. It wasn't too bad, but we'd had it since the day after we'd arrived, and we couldn't work out what had caused it. Could it have been from our Chinese meal on our first night in Makassar? Or was it from the ice in our warm beer at Mallengkeri Bus Terminal?

We made it safely back to Bira, checked into a small homestay and called Zainal, who told us he was planning to return to Makassar the following day, and yes, there was room in his car. 'How many other passengers will there be?' enquired Michael.

'I don't know yet,' said Zainal, but if you want a more comfortable journey and don't mind paying a bit more money, you can charter the back seat just for yourselves.'

We weren't keen on this class distinction and wondered if the other passengers would resent us for the social privilege that enabled us to fork out extra money for extra space. However, we elected to do it anyway and it turned out to be a wise decision because later that evening, Michael started suffering with stomach cramps and his diarrhoea moved to the next level.

'How the hell am I going to survive a five-hour car journey?' he wailed, he'd been running to the bathroom all night. He took an Imodium; we feared the unthinkable and we hoped for the best. Fortunately, Michael's gut-brain axis worked in reverse, in his favour, with his brain kicking in to control his bowels until we reached a place of safety. Furthermore, he was able to stretch out within the limits of our private back seat and make up for his lost sleep from the night before. Rather than showing any signs of resentment, our fellow passengers viewed us with fascination and amusement.

We had planned to stay longer in Makassar but by the next morning I had also developed stomach cramps, and Michael was not much better either, so we decided to head home. This was before the days of booking online via a

Smartphone, so we found a travel agent and secured a flight for the following day.

Michael made a good recovery over the next few days, but my loss of appetite, shits and cramps continued. Or maybe I should say, 'shits and giggles' because I was delighted to find that I was losing weight.

'Maybe you've got a parasite,' suggested Michael.

'You've probably got giardia,' advocated Kristen, who not only lived in Indonesia but also worked in the public health sector.

I did some research and learnt that giardia infection is caused by a microscopic parasite that is found in areas with poor sanitation and unsafe water. I blamed it on the ice in our warm beer at the bus station. Although ice-making in Indonesia is government controlled, and ice is safe in Bali, its purity may be questionable in the less touristy regions. I decided to give the infection another couple of weeks to clear up. After all, Michael must have been suffering from the same thing, and his condition had cleared up on its own.

I was loving the weight loss and didn't feel ill, so I think I waited about two months before visiting the doctor. ~ *Please don't try this at home* ~ A lab test confirmed that it was indeed giardia, and the doctor prescribed a ten-day course of a nasty antibiotic called Flagyl (metronidazole).

'Do not drink alcohol during the course,' she warned, 'and you need to rid your body of alcohol before you start, and then stay off it for at least three days afterwards.'

Well, that put the cat among the pigeons. At the time, I was writing food reviews for two or three different magazines, and I had a date booked ten days later for a review of the wonderful KO Japanese Restaurant at Bali's InterContinental Resort. I'd invited Michael to join me, and it promised to be a fun, boozy night. As far as I was concerned there was no option but to delay my course of Flagyl for a further twelve days.

By the time I started the course, I'd happily lost a total of eleven kilos, which stayed off effortlessly for the next two years.

35
ALL IN A NUTSHELL
2009, 2014

When I was a little girl, my mother used to make this old-fashioned yogurt-like dessert called junket. She would liberally sprinkle the top with ground nutmeg, claiming it was a good remedy for an upset stomach. My mother also used nutmeg whenever she baked apple-pie or potato gratin, and she'd sometimes add it to soups and sauces. I remember her telling me that wrapped around each nutmeg was another spice, called mace, which she would use in biscuits, cakes, and her home-baked breads. With its distinctive, pungent, and musty fragrance, and its warm, slightly sweet taste, the nutmeg flavour is almost too powerful for everyday use.

Yet Mum maintained it was her favourite spice because of its extraordinary history, assuring me, 'It was once more valuable than gold,' and 'it was believed to have been a cure for the bubonic plague.'

She told me that it came from some obscure tropical islands on the other side of the world.

Nutmeg is indigenous to the volcanic soils of the Indonesian Banda Islands, and in the fifteenth and sixteenth centuries, this aromatic spice spurred exploration and shaped colonial empires with European traders selling it at a six thousand percent markup. People wore bags of the spice around their necks as a protection against the Great Plague of London, and it's plausible that it actually repelled the fleas that carried the plague-causing bacteria.

It's not surprising, therefore, that colonial powers vied bitterly for control of the only place on Earth where this spice could be found. In the early seventeenth century, the Dutch were so ruthless about getting the nutmeg trade for themselves that they massacred most of the native population of the Banda Islands. Land parcels known as *perken* were then handed to Dutch planters, *perkeniers,* to manage, and the nutmegs were coated with lime before export, preventing enterprising farmers from sprouting the seeds. To curb the black-market trade, sailors on the nutmeg ships were required to strip naked and be searched before being allowed to disembark at the destination port. At that time, three nutmegs provided sufficient wealth for the purchase of a small tract of land near London.

Dutch attempts to maintain a total monopoly on the nutmeg trade were thwarted by the British, who controlled Run, one of the tiny islands in the Banda chain. It turned out, however, that another island, 9,500 miles away, would be the key to securing Dutch control of the nutmeg trade. New Amsterdam was Holland's strategic colonial outpost in the New World, and in 1667 under the Treaty of Breda, the English traded Run for New Amsterdam, which later became Manhattan. That deal seems ridiculous to us today. Manhattan turned into the world's financial capital, while Run is a rocky backwater covered with nutmeg trees and simple village houses. Nutmeg and mace can be seen drying in the sun outside nearly every home on Run, but the locals aren't getting rich from their cherished spice.

An early European report described the Banda Islands as: 'A jewel-like cluster surrounded by crystal waters and brilliant coral reefs, containing hills lined with aromatic spice trees on which perched flocks of green and red parrots.' This description can still be applied today.

Despite their illustrious history, the Banda Islands are a destination that time seems to have forgotten. A destination that is so far off the tourism map that few people know of either the islands' existence or their major historical importance. These days, intrepid visitors go not to trade for spice – although there is plenty to be found at the market in Banda Neira – but to absorb the historic atmosphere, visit the old forts and the ruins of the perkeniers' houses, climb Gunung Api – 'Fire Mountain', dive, snorkel, and marvel at the dolphins that cavort alongside the local boats.

Many decades after watching my mother sprinkle nutmeg on her junket, I came to live in Indonesia and decided to follow the spice trail for myself. However, it was to be ten years before I finally made the journey, in 2009, along with my fellow adventurers, Michael and Scott. We'd been told that the Banda Islands see fewer than thirty visitors a month and getting there would be like falling off the edge of the acknowledged world. The trade winds would favour an October visit, and our voyage would lead us east, to Maluku Province. We would have to fly to Ambon and from there get the Pelni ferry, which ran every two weeks. There was also a supposedly-twice-weekly ten-seater plane from Ambon to Banda Neira but more often than not it didn't fly because the runway is very short, and at the end of the runway lies the *Sonnegat* – a deep and narrow sea channel, and directly beyond that is the volcano. So, if the wind is blowing from the wrong direction on the plane's approach, it must return to Ambon, and wait another week before attempting the landing again.

We needed some advice. So, before we set off, Michael and I met up with Mira, the Bali-based daughter of Des Alwi, the self-appointed King of Banda, a renaissance man and a cult figure in Indonesian history. He'd been an Independence fighter, and a diplomat; and was a driving force behind the preservation and restoration of the islands' heritage. Mira proved to be delightful, she'd grown up on the islands, and was able to give us loads of information and advice, while offering us a generous discount at the family-owned Hotel Maulana on Banda Neira.

The following week, we were on a flight to Ambon, timing our arrival with the departure of the next Pelni ferry, but upon landing, we discovered to our horror that the date and time of the ferry had somehow got lost in translation. We'd missed it by a week.

Michael was gutted, snarling at me when I suggested we explored Ambon instead, 'We're here to see the Banda Islands, stop trying to appease me. Leave me alone, I need to think.'

I was glad Scott remained calm.

Michael called Mira for help, and she suggested we contact Johnny, a faithful old retainer who lived in Ambon and had worked for Mira's family for decades. She told Michael that Johnny could arrange for a speedboat to take us to Banda Neira, it would be a six-hour journey and we'd have to pay for the petrol which, she warned, would unfortunately be pretty expensive.

It was not an ideal solution, but Michael phoned Johnny, who said, 'I'll see what I can do, and I'll get back to you.'

Fifteen minutes later, Johnny was on the phone instructing us to meet him at the port at nine p.m., 'Bring your bags,' he said.

The man was clearly a magician. Incredibly, he had conjured up three first-class tickets for an old wooden passenger ferry, called the Gravila, which just happened to be departing for the Banda Islands that evening.

Jam packed with passengers, the hull of the boat was equipped with 270 narrow plastic mattresses, resting side by side on a series of platforms, beneath which was a jumble of luggage, plastic carrier bags, building materials, cardboard boxes of provisions, a pile of ten-kilo bags of rice, some caged birds, and several live chickens. A door swung open to reveal a shockingly primitive bathroom. Yet despite the cramped conditions, everyone seemed to be smiling and laughing in true Indonesian style.

We were directed to the upper deck, which was reserved for the first-class passengers; we were the only ones. Again, the hierarchal system didn't sit well with us, but we were grateful that a few extra dollars had bought us some fresh air and privacy. We had two tiny cabins, with doors that didn't lock. Each cabin contained two wooden child-size bunks and a dusty old electric fan.

Amid the creaking timbers of the boat, within the swell of the Banda Sea, we managed to grab a few hours of uncomfortable sleep. Michael and I woke at five, and Scott who'd been awake most of the night brought us each a cup of sweet steaming *Kopiko* made from a three-in-one instant coffee mix. I shivered in the cold pre-dawn air and a kindly member of the crew appeared with some blankets; we wrapped ourselves up and moved to the stern of the boat, watching traces of grey, pale purple and pink tinge the eastern sky, followed by a blaze of red and gold, mirrored in the waters of the vast and lonely ocean.

As the brightness and warmth of the day rose above the horizon, we discarded our blankets and climbed up onto the roof of the boat, which became our private headquarters and viewing deck for the remaining six hours of our fifteen-hour voyage. To our delight, we found ourselves alongside a pod of migrating sperm whales with their calves. Distinguished by their square heads, they were fluking together just metres away from the boat. In the distance, we could see the fountain-like waterspouts of another pod, and we were privileged to see some of the whales breaching. It was amazing to witness the elegance and smooth control with which they were dropping their huge masses while barely rippling the water.

Sitting on the roof of this old wooden boat, I felt a connection with the pioneering adventurers, especially when we spotted land on the horizon. It was Banda Run, a tiny speck of an island less than two miles long and just over half a mile wide. This was the fabled island that the English had traded for Manhattan. As we got closer, tinny *dangdut* music crackled through a megaphone loudhailer, the boat's captain clearly wanted to announce our arrival. Run is bordered by a shallow reef and although a jetty extends to deeper waters, large boats can't reach the jetty at low tide.

However, the residents of Run know exactly what to do when a ferry arrives, and very soon a taskforce of canoes was paddling towards us. With the help of gangplanks and ladders, a few dozen passengers disembarked from the ferry and scrambled into the canoes along with their chickens, rice and luggage.

The next island we passed was the beautiful Banda Ai. Looking across an expanse of white sand beach, I spotted a wooden homestay with arched windows and a green-painted balcony peeking through the shady fig trees. 'Let's come back and spend a couple of days here,' I suggested.

Ahead of us, we could see the active volcano, Api, rising a foreboding 666 metres from the sea. Soon, heralded by much noise and excitement, our ferry was gliding through the Sonnegat – the Sun's Gap – the deep trench of water that separates Gunung Api from the island of Banda Neira, and there was the Hotel Maulana, its faded 1960s' faux-colonial grandeur beckoning us from the wharf. To our astonishment, our ferry had delivered us to the very doorstep of our accommodation. A man approached us on our upper-class deck, introducing himself as Yosef, the hotel manager.

'How did you find us?' I asked.

'It wasn't too hard,' he smiled, 'Johnny assured me that you were the only bule onboard.'

The hotel staff greeted us like honoured guests, eagerly sitting us down at a table on the terrace before serving us with tea and homemade bread, spread with nutmeg jam, which is made from the apricot-sized yellow fruit that envelops the nut; it was unbelievably good. The hotel was run-down but had retained its charm. During its glory years in the 1990s, it had been a secret jet set destination. At the invitation of its socialite owner, it had attracted celebrities, royalty and rockstars, including Jacques Cousteau, the Rolling Stones, Princess Diana, Sarah Ferguson, and numerous Asian and European nobles. We were offered the upper floor, which opened out onto a huge balcony with a stone balustrade. Michael and I chose the room where Mick Jagger had once stayed, while Scott opted for Princess Di's room, later assuring us that he was visited by her ghost during the night. I was more interested in the resident Eclectus parrot, a red female – the males are green. Her name was Karma, and she listened to me intently as I complimented her with platitudes,

'Hello, pretty Polly.'

To which she replied in perfect Bahasa, 'Apa kabar?' meaning, 'How are you?'

Scott, Michael and I then changed into our swimmers and spent the afternoon with the local kids, jumping and somersaulting off the wharf into the deep blue water below. Dinner that night at the Hotel Maulana was a real treat: fresh fish and a local Banda delicacy called *Terong Kenari* – fried eggplant with kenari nut sauce. The towering kenari trees provide essential shade for the nutmeg trees within the plantations. Later, from our balcony, we gazed at Gunung Api silhouetted against the magnificent night sky.

Maybe one day we'll come back again and climb it, I mused.

~*~

In the morning, we asked Yosef about chartering a small boat because we wanted to visit Run and go snorkelling. He suggested we wait until the following day, which was when the residents of Run would be inaugurating their newly built mosque amid much pomp, ceremony, and celebration.

So instead, on our first morning, we made the short crossing to the island of Lonthor, also known as Banda Besar, the biggest of the eleven Banda Islands, and there we wandered through the dappled nutmeg plantations. I was awestruck. The evergreen nutmeg trees – identifiable by the hundreds of ripening fruits that hang from their branches – grow randomly among the kenari trees, which themselves yield an almond-like nut locally used in confectionary and in the sauce we'd tasted the night before. Kenari is what keeps the nutmeg trees growing; towering trees – tall like the buildings in Manhattan, planted to protect the nutmeg from the sun. The fruit is a pendulous drupe, and when it's ripe it splits in two, exposing a crimson-coloured, lacy or filigree-like aril – the mace, surrounding a single, shiny brown seed – the nutmeg. The locals use the pulp of the fruit to make their delicious jam, as well as syrup and candy; the mace is removed, flattened out and dried in the sun, and the nut is also sun-dried for up to two months until the inner nut rattles inside the shell. The shell is then broken to reveal the valuable, edible nutmeat. Second-rate nuts are pressed for the oil, which is used as condiments and carminatives, and also to scent soaps and perfumes. In the courtyards of the pastel-coloured houses, we saw nutmeg and mace laid out to dry.

Back on Banda Neira, we explored the town on foot, beginning at the majestic Fort Belgica, built by the Dutch in 1611. Presiding over the island from its lofty perch, the ramparts of the fort offered us a spectacular view of Gunung Api. Evidence that Banda Neira was once a great trading centre was everywhere. The little streets were lined with crumbling colonial houses. One had been the residence of a British sea-captain who captured Fort Belgica from the Dutch; another was once the home of Hatta, an exiled independence hero and Indonesia's first vice president. We stopped at the bustling market, where we found ourselves captivated by the vibrancy and colour as we sought shade from the sun and bartered for cloves, tamarind, cinnamon and, of course, nutmeg. The former palace of the Governor of the Dutch East Indies appeared to be closed but we managed to find an unlocked side-door and ventured inside, wandering through the empty-yet-once-opulent rooms. In the overgrown garden, I stubbed my toe on a rusty cannon barrel abandoned in the grass. These ancient cannons can be found all over Banda Neira – on the ramparts of the fort or just lying around, too heavy to move, while others have been mounted on concrete blocks, to serve as a reminder of the days when the islands' produce was worth fighting for.

The next morning, our boatman, Manasseh, picked us up at seven o'clock and we set out for Run. Scott, who's a filmmaker, was carrying his bulky video equipment, and we had dressed respectfully because we were attending a religious ceremony, and because the Governor of Ambon would be in attendance. Ninety minutes later, as we were approaching Run, we heard loud music, and what sounded like a commentary being delivered through a loudspeaker. We were surprised to see a flotilla of canoes and small motorised boats decorated in coloured bunting and Indonesian flags, coming directly towards us. There was even a *kora-kora* – a traditional Malukan war canoe. It was being paddled by a crew of twenty-four shirtless men, with red and white bandanas tied around their heads; they were singing loudly in unison.

Manasseh looked decidedly alarmed and said something that I guess meant 'Arghhh shit' in the local dialect, adding in English, 'they've mistaken us for the Governor.'

I've never seen anyone turn a boat around so quickly. The music stopped, along with the singing, and confusion reigned on everyone's faces until they spotted the real Governor's boat behind us. Manasseh pulled into the miniscule islet of Nailaka, and we graciously waved to the Governor as he chugged on ahead. The music and song recommenced, and the welcome party continued as planned. Meanwhile, we nonchalantly looked for shells in Nailaka's powdery white sand while waiting a respectable ten minutes.

About two thousand people live on Run, and they had all turned out in their best clothes for the occasion. Approaching the jetty, we could see about thirty Indonesian naval personnel, immaculately attired in white and lined up precisely two metres apart, saluting the governor, his wife, and their entourage.

Manasseh hung back but within seconds, friendly hands were securing our boat to a post and helping us disembark. Waiting at the far end of the jetty was the *kepala desa* – the head of the village – along with the committee of elders of this island-community, and a troupe of *Cakalele* war dancers. The sailors saluted and piped us ashore, while ahead of us, the important people were exchanging pleasantries.

All smiles, the elders gestured us to come forward, and one by one they solemnly shook our hands. I guess when they saw Scott's video camera and wide-angle lenses, they assumed that we belonged to the Governor's party… or the BBC. Backed by the rhythm of a drum and a gong, five men began to dance. They looked magnificent, dressed in full ceremonial warrior costumes featuring red and yellow satin jackets and three-quarter-length baggy pants. They carried spears and long knives and wore antique Portuguese helmets, one of which was topped with a stuffed bird of paradise.

When the welcome ritual was over, we were swept away with the crowd through the streets of the village for the inauguration of the new mosque. Everyone gathered outside, posing for Michael's photos, and claiming parts as extras in Scott's movie. Amid the celebrations, the crescent was carried up a rickety, temporary ramp and positioned in its final place atop the yellow dome.

Loaves and fishes, or rather cardboard lunchboxes, were distributed to the two thousand, including us, each one carefully packed with a bottle of water and a *nasi campur* of rice, chicken, and veggies along with a piece of fruit. Enticed by the pink, yellow and blue houses that were cascading down the hill towards the beach, we asked our hosts for permission to explore their island. A guide was instantly appointed, and he proudly led us on a walk through Run's nutmeg plantations.

We finally found Manasseh waiting for us at the jetty, bid farewell to the folks we had befriended, and Michael promised to send them prints of our photos in the post. It had been an extraordinary day but unbeknown to us, the best was yet to come.

~*~

We were hot and sweaty and ready for a swim, so Manasseh took us to a shallow spot off Banda Ai, where we were lucky enough to snorkel with a small school of Bumphead parrotfish, which are decidedly prehistoric in appearance. Some of them were nearly a metre in length. Interestingly, they live in groups consisting of one male and many females. If the male dies, the dominant female will undergo a sex change to become the new dominant male.

Ten minutes later, as we were chugging through the deep channel between Banda Ai and Gunung Api, our little boat was suddenly surrounded by dolphins. Michael and I quickly grabbed our masks and leapt into the water to join them, Michael off the starboard side of the boat, and I off the port side. Immediately I hit the water, two dolphins swam right up to my face. Were they merely inquisitive or were they communicating with me? I reckon it was a bit of both.

Hello! Hello!

I certainly had no problem understanding them.

Look at us, look at us, they grinned, as they pirouetted in front of me, performing a series of twirls and whirls. They're not called spinner dolphins for nothing.

Treading water, I was spellbound as they gazed directly into my eyes, *Come with us, come with us...* they beckoned, tilting their heads like sirens luring me into their lair.

Then, with a final acrobatic flourish they pointed their beaks into the deep and I watched them dive in unison, spiralling down and down until I could see them no longer.

For an instant, there was nothing I wanted more than the ability to follow them.

Back on the boat, reunited with Michael, I learnt that he had enjoyed exactly the same experience as me, except he'd been approached by five, equally playful, curious, alluring dolphins. When they, too, had invited him to dive with them, he'd followed them trancelike for about thirty seconds until he reached the limit of his freediving capability. It was one of those magical encounters that we both rate as being among the best moments of our lives.

Maybe it was the dolphins that drew us back to Ai a couple of days later, or maybe it was the serenity and natural beauty of the island. This time, instead of chartering a boat, we boarded one of the small public ferries, known as *pok-poks*, which unite the eleven islands in the Banda chain. Once again, the local people were travelling with crates of provisions and live chickens. We watched anxiously as more and more passengers scrambled aboard, and the boat dropped lower and lower into the water. When there was no more standing room available, the punters climbed onto the roof and perched on the gunwales clinging onto whatever cleats or grab handles they could reach.

The vessel was seriously overloaded, and the engine was labouring but no one, least of all the captain, seemed to be concerned.

'It's always like this,' said the man next to me.

'Do they ever sink?' I asked.

'Of course,' he replied.

Scott was worried about losing his camera equipment, I was worried for my life. I closed my eyes and wished I could swim like a dolphin. We were on the choppy sea for well over an hour before we alighted safely at Ai.

After spending a couple of blissful nights at the green-painted homestay, swimming, snorkelling, exploring, and enjoying a fresh fish barbecue with the owner, we got ready to return to Banda Neira.

Again, we watched in dismay as the boat rocked precariously on the water under the weight of double the legal capacity of passengers.

'We're not getting on that,' declared Michael, 'let's see if we can charter a boat.'

Keen to earn some commission, a local man procured us a boat; we negotiated a price with the captain and paid him up front. Our own private transport. We climbed aboard, only to be followed by about twenty of the locals, all of them jumping at the opportunity to get a free ride and a seat.

Banda is a hard place to get to and an even harder place to leave, and that's without factoring in any of the sketchy ferry and plane schedules. We weren't ready to leave but the Pelni ferry that we'd missed a week earlier, which had continued on to Tual in the Kei Islands and Fakfak in West Papua, was now on its return journey to Ambon and ultimately Jakarta, stopping to offload passengers and provisions and pick up more at Banda Neira. If we didn't board it, we would have to stay another two weeks and we had neither the time nor the wherewithal.

Under the gaze of Gunung Api, Michael and I sat upon a four-hundred-year-old Dutch cannon and promised to return at some point in the future.

The ferry terminal was a hive of activity and excitement as the population of Banda Neira eagerly awaited the arrival of the Nggapulu, an old German cruise ship that has been plying this fortnightly circuit since 2001. Watching from the balcony at the Maulana, we heard the blast of her horn before we saw her, slowly emerging from behind Gunung Api and cruising across the Sonnegat; her eight decks towering above us as she pulled into the wharf just metres from the hotel.

In a supremely chaotic scurry of porters, luggage, crates and personal belongings, the throngs of passengers waiting at the terminal rushed towards the ferry. Where was the turnstile? Where were the ticket collectors? Where was the crowd control? Where were the health and safety measures? Before anyone had a chance to disembark, the urgent mobs on the shore hastened aboard to occupy the limited facilities. Instead of embarking in a civilised manner, dozens – possibly hundreds – of people were clambering up the sides of the vessel, tossing and lugging crates, baggage, and babies from ground level up through the open sides of the lower decks. Scuffles took place as disembarking passengers wrestled to get out. Peering over railings of the upper decks, were Javanese, Bugis, Papuans and Ambonese, family groups, newlyweds, students, and the ubiquitous traders from the eastern half of the archipelago.

Mesmerised, fascinated and a little bit terrified, I suggested we waited until everyone else was on board before we even left the safety of our hotel, but then Yosef arrived with our 'first-class' tickets and offered to escort us to our cabin. Travelling first class didn't include a streamlined check-in procedure but I stayed close to Yosef who was carrying my luggage. Within seconds I had lost sight of Michael and Scott in the crush, however, I appreciated Yosef's ever watchful eye as my feet were literally lifted off the ground. Implausibly, I managed to keep my head and remain in an upright position, as I was forcibly *walked*, buoyed up by the people around me, and transported midship by the surging crowd like a piece of meat being forced through a hand-cranked mincer. Yosef told me the ferry was designed to accommodate 2130 passengers, but it generally transported closer to three thousand. Indeed, passengers had bedded down and made camp everywhere, from the decks to the corridors to the stairwells. Somehow, we all found our way safely to our four-berth air-conditioned cabin, bid farewell to Yosef and settled down for the thirteen-hour voyage to Ambon. At one point, I wandered up onto the top deck, but it was too cold to lean on the rails and too crowded to move around. I saw group after group of people blatantly throwing their garbage overboard, neither knowing nor caring about the need to protect our fragile world, and I felt a sharp jolt of despair for the future of humanity.

When we arrived in Ambon at about ten o'clock that evening, we waited for as long as we could before leaving our cabin and, happily, we were able to disembark the ferry in an orderly fashion. Regrettably, the downside of this was that the one-or-two-thousand passengers who had disembarked ahead of us had nabbed all of the city's hotel rooms. The city's taxis had all been taken too, so Scott, Michael and I loaded ourselves and our luggage onto a pair of *becak* bicycle rickshaws and with much merriment and laughter, our drivers pedalled us from full hotel to full hotel trying to find one that still had a couple of available rooms. Eventually, the three of us were offered the last remaining room in an overpriced hotel. We would just have to make do and share the king-size bed. It wouldn't be for long; it was already eleven-thirty p.m., and we had booked a wake-up call at five and a taxi at five-thirty to drive us to the airport for our seven-thirty a.m. flight.

Scott, however, had other ideas.

After dropping his luggage, including his expensive video camera equipment and his unwrapped speargun on the floor of our room, he looked out of the window and said, 'Hey guys, there's a karaoke bar across the road, let's go...'

With a sinking heart I reminded him that we had to be up in five hours' time, and that he still had to find some large pieces of cardboard and masking tape to securely pack up his speargun before heading off to the airport and checking in.

'It'll be fine,' assured Scott, opening the door and leaving the room with Michael in tow as I declined the offer to join them.

I should have just settled down and gone to sleep, trusting them to return soon, but instead anxiety set in. What if they ended up going on a pub crawl around the city? Did they even know the name and address of the hotel? What if they got drunk and got lost and didn't get back in time to get to the airport in time for our flight back home to Bali? An hour later, I looked out of the window and noticed that the lights of the karaoke bar had gone out, the place was closed. I decided to call Michael but in doing so I heard his phone ringing on the other side of the room. I then tried calling Scott but heard his phone playing a tune from somewhere deep inside his backpack. I paced back and forth on the tiled floor, chewed the skin around my fingernails, leaned out of the window, and peered up and down the street, which was surprisingly empty for a Saturday night in the centre of a city into which an ocean liner had just discarded two thousand passengers.

The hours ticked by, I lay down on the bed, but I couldn't sleep for fear of Scott and Michael not returning. Suddenly, at four a.m., the bedroom door burst open. It was a very merry Michael.

'I've just come to get my camera,' he explained.

'Where have you been all this time?' I demanded.

'Oh, the karaoke bar was closed so we've been hanging out with the hotel staff, drinking Indonesian whisky. We just want to take some photos of our new friends. We'll be back in an hour.'

Sleep came easily once I knew they were safe, but it was only an hour before I was woken by my phone alarm. Seconds later, a very drunken Scott burst into the room and rushed over to the window, throwing it open before throwing up in a bizarrely silent manner; all I could hear was the splitter-splatter of his vomit as it landed upon the flat roof below.

'I'm fucked,' he announced, 'you two get the plane without me, I'll fly back to Bali tomorrow.'

'Absolutely not,' retorted Michael, ushering Scott into the bathroom for a shower, 'we three are a team.'

'But I haven't even wrapped up my speargun,' whimpered Scott.

'I'm sure we can do it at the airport,' I told him.

Ten minutes later, there was a knock at the door. 'Your taxi is here…'

With the help of the staff, who Michael and Scott had befriended, we brought our gear downstairs, loaded up the taxi and said our goodbyes, before setting off on the one-hour drive to the airport, which was punctuated by the occasional too-loud drunken comment and a couple of urgent toilet stops.

~*~

Arriving at Ambon Airport, we unloaded the boot of the taxi.

'Where's my camera tripod?' asked Scott.

We checked the backseat and then rechecked the boot, but there was no tripod in sight.

'Where's my camera bag? Where's my video camera?' screeched Scott, in panic.

'Oh shit, we must have left it at the hotel,' exclaimed Michael as the horrible realisation dawned that we had just lost six thousand dollars' worth of uninsured camera equipment, as well as the precious photos and video footage of our trip.

I've never seen two drunken men sober up so quickly.

'It may not be too late,' said Scott in an unaccountably calm voice, 'I'll call the hotel.'

None of us could even remember the name of the hotel but thankfully our taxi driver was able to give us the phone number. A quick conversation with one of the friendly fellow whisky-drinkers ensued, and Scott waited anxiously while someone went to check the room.

'He's got it,' he shouted joyfully, 'he's got it all and he's going to dispatch someone to drive to the airport to deliver it to us.'

'But our flight is due to depart in one hour, and the drive from the hotel to the airport will take an hour, and it's a snaking, winding road, how will it be possible?' I stated to no one in particular.

Nevertheless, we checked in, while Scott explained the situation to the airport staff. His speargun was check-in luggage, obviously, and they kindly offered to wrap it for him.

Surely, they're not going to hold the flight for us? I thought.

It was a fearful wait, but just forty-five minutes after the phone call ended between Scott and the hotel staff member, our dispatch rider pulled up on a large motorbike with the camera gear on his back. Everything was going to be alright after all. Scott tipped his saviour well, and then he and Michael immediately reverted back to being drunken fools, but happily we made it back to Bali safely and intact.

~*~

Our next trip to Banda was in 2014. Michael was still working as editor of Tropiq magazine, and because of his fascination for phinisi boats and the exploration of the remotest reaches of Indonesia, he was trying to persuade the manager of a company called 'SeaTrek Sailing Adventures' to advertise in the mag.

The company had two phinisi boats, offering cruises through the waters of the Komodo National Park and beyond, including Flores, the Banda Islands, Raja Ampat and Sulawesi. Michael even offered SeaTrek a reduction in the cost of the ad in exchange for a free cruise and a story in the magazine. The manager agreed, and in October of that year, we found ourselves bound for Banda, once again. We were joined by a couple of friends who couldn't resist the opportunity of a discounted twelve-day trip from Flores to Wakatobi to Banda Neira on a beautiful boat called the Ombak Putih.

After notching up what was my fourth visit to Komodo, our boat sailed north to a group of remote islands off South Sulawesi, the largest of which is Selayar Island. Yes, *that* Selayar, the island with the elusive paradise beach, the river full of garbage, the apathetic hotel owner, and the obnoxious bus driver. In fact, this group of islands is collectively known as the Selayar Islands, and there are seventy-three of them in total, spread far apart. The Ombak Putih took us to four of the tiniest, most isolated of these islands, including the miniscule, completely-off-the-grid island of Karompa-lompa – such a cool name – giving us and the other guests the opportunity to step ashore and meet the local residents. An island-village with a population of about three hundred, most of whom, the children at least, had never seen a white-faced bule. We were transferred ashore in one of the speedboats, and as always, we were in the company of about four members of the crew. On this occasion, we were with Hatta, the Ombak Putih's second engineer, who hails from East Flores, and totally by chance, we witnessed a remarkable, beautiful, and joyful reunion between Hatta and his long-lost brother; the two men hadn't seen each other for fifteen years. Hatta believed that his brother might be living on one of the Selayar Islands, but they had lost touch from the get-go, and with no telephone lines, no mobile phone signal, no internet connection, and an unreliable postal delivery service, they had been unable to re-establish any form of contact. Incredibly, Hatta found his brother, together with his wife and children, by complete chance, on Karompa-lompa. Without knowing the backstory, we observed the two men emotionally greeting each other in absolute disbelief, and we watched as Hatta was introduced for the first time to his sister-in-law and two nephews. Interestingly, Karompa-lompa is almost directly north of Hatta's hometown, probably no more than two hundred kilometres as the seabird flies. For his brother, however, fifteen years earlier, it would have been a long, slow, potentially dangerous journey in a small boat across the wide and lonely Flores Sea with no land in sight all along the way.

Now that there is a cell phone tower on the island, Hatta has been able to keep in touch with his brother – he probably bought him a cell phone. He has revisited him three times that I know of, and enabled WhatsApp video calls between his brother, their parents and other family members.

The group of islands that we were most excited to revisit was the Banda Islands, aka the Spice Islands. The first island we landed on was Run, coincidently, it was exactly five years and one day since our previous visit on the occasion of the inauguration of the new mosque. Five years earlier, Michael had kept his promise and had snail-mailed the printed photos, which he'd taken of the event, to the head of the village. We assumed they would have arrived but no one we spoke to was able to confirm it for us. Nevertheless, we talked to some of the villagers and showed them some more photos of the event on my laptop, which brought some big smiles to their faces.

On Banda Neira, the Ombak Putih moored alongside the wharf outside the Maulana Hotel, where we treated our friends to a dinner of fresh fish, served with our favourite side of aubergine doused in kenari nut sauce. On our last day, we employed some *ojek* (motorcycle taxi) drivers to take us on a tour of the parts of Banda Neira, we'd not yet explored. This included the tiny airport, where we found the gates to be wide open because there were no flights coming in that day. Some young skateboarders were playing on the runway, so just for the hell of it, we joined them, cruising up and down on the bikes.

Ten months after our first SeaTrek sailing adventure, Tropiq magazine was sadly deemed no longer profitable enough to continue publishing, but when one door closes another one opens. Michael was headhunted by SeaTrek and offered a job as the company's Sales & Communications Manager. This has led to numerous more adventures for us together with various friends and family members aboard the Ombak Putih and her sister ship, the Katharina.

36
A HUMBLING THERAPY
2007

A would-be rock star was playing a guitar and singing a Javanese folk song, a man was vending canned drinks, a woman was waving a bunch of fresh grapes and a young boy was trying to convince me that I needed a pair of pink plastic sunglasses. My rumbling stomach, meanwhile, had just done a deal with a sweet talker who was selling *tahu isi* – chilli-and-beansprout-stuffed tofu, wrapped in cones of brown paper.

I was alone on a public bus travelling from Denpasar in Bali to Ketapang, Banyuwangi, the portal to East Java. Having just arrived at Gilimanuk, the bus was preparing to drive onto the ferry when it was suddenly boarded by a miscellany of hawkers and buskers. Being the only white face, I was a sitting target; but I smiled and went with the flow. This was the beginning of an eight-day journey that would take me through the rice fields, rainforests, plantations, national parks and cultural heritage of Java's most easterly region. My modes of transport would include buses, ferries, the cycle-rickshaw known as a *becak*, a vintage Land Rover, a bamboo raft, a traditional *jukung* fishing boat and the third-class carriage of an Indonesian train.

My first assignment, however, was much more glamorous. I had been invited to judge a beauty contest in Banyuwangi. Backstage, they dressed me in a bright orange, beaded kebaya, sarong and a flowing headdress, and made me up like a Javanese *Ibu* (the Indonesian word for Madam, Mrs or Mother). It was a two-hour process; I didn't even recognise myself in the mirror. My hair was backcombed to within an inch of its life before being set with half a can of hairspray. Never again will I travel without conditioner.

~*~

One week later, I'm naked, hot and bothered in a tiny plywood cubical, my body is covered in a layer of grit, I have no towel, and I'm sweating profusely. I open the door and hurriedly push my arms into the sleeves of my cotton robe, which like my skin, is still covered with the grainy remnants of my body scrub. The robe sticks to my sweaty body, barely concealing my nudity, and I notice that a gap has appeared in the curtain of my scant changing space.

As I try to protect my modesty from prying eyes, I hear the voice of my therapist, 'Kembali masuk.' I am being ordered to go back into the stifling cubicle.

Inside, a bamboo pipe is merrily pumping out hot steam; the floor is carpeted with a sheet of shiny brown paper and just four little holes are serving as a drain for the excess water.

'You've got to stay in there for at least fifteen minutes.'

Obediently, I peel off the damp robe and trot back into my steaming cell to sweat out the remainder of my fifteen-minute sentence.

I'm still in East Java, and I'm experiencing the dubious delights of a traditional spa.

~*~

But let's go back to the beginning...

After the beauty contest, I'd spent a day and a night at the peaceful plantation resort of Margo Utomo in Kalibaru, built during the Dutch colonial era, and home to a herd of forty, black & white Friesian cows. I'd jumped at the chance to milk a cow in a country where dairy produce is not a feature of the cuisine. My charge proved to be gentle and friendly, patiently indulging me with all the milk she could muster, until my aching fingers had had enough.

Next, my Javanese companions and I found ourselves journeying across extensive rubber, teak and mahogany plantations, passing through *pos pemeriksaan* checkpoints, set up to control the movement of the highly prized timber. We had frolicked on the pristine Rajegwesi Beach before traversing the mountain range that borders the phenomenal Meru Betiri National Park. Located on the southeast coast, this 580-square-kilometre park is one of the most important and least accessible nature reserves in Java, with bridgeless rivers, impenetrable bamboo thickets, and rainforest hills rising steeply to over one thousand metres.

Down in the valley, we had ridden on the roof of the Land Rover, fording a river and catching a glimpse of an iridescent blue Java kingfisher with its distinctive red beak. At sunset, a loud rhythmic thrumming had drawn our attention to the splendid sight and sounds of a family of hornbills passing overhead.

At our simple homestay, I'd found a leech on my damp bathroom wall, but it didn't dampen my enthusiasm for a dinner of nasi campur followed by a walk to the protected Sukamade 'Turtle Beach', a wild, three-kilometre crescent of sand beside the Indian Ocean. We were hoping to witness a sea turtle laying her eggs. We were in luck.

A full moon had guided us through what I perceived to be an enchanted forest, past the dunes, to a torchlight signal from the beach guards who had found a deep nesting pit containing a huge turtle. This matron of the sea had lumbered up the beach to drop her clutch of 160 ping-pong-ball eggs, which she had then buried about sixty centimetres under the sand. It had taken her about two hours to recover from her labour and I felt an intense tug of emotion as I watched this beautiful creature propel herself resolutely into the pounding moonlit surf, before gradually disappearing into the darkness beneath the waves. A conservation effort has been underway for many years at Sukamade Beach, which is the most important nesting site in Java. Stability of the turtle population has been helped by a careful system of tagging and monitoring, as well as the use of special hatcheries.

The next day, driving through neatly planted avenues of coffee and cacao plants, I had suddenly been struck by the distant memory of a school project. Aged eleven, I had been tasked with writing "The Story of Chocolate" – from the fluted, yellow and red pods in the distant tropical rainforests to the foil-wrapped bars of 'Cadbury's Dairy Milk'.

Crawling back up the mountain, our vehicle had bounced and cavorted along a tortuously rough and rocky track. The dust had penetrated our pores, and the uneven motion had jolted our spines and left our jaws vibrating.

My male travel buddies had decided to treat my aching limbs and polluted skin to a royal pampering.

'We're going to take you to our local sauna,' they announced proudly.

~*~

I speculated on what a sauna in Islamic East Java might entail. *Would I have to share my space with other women?* In a town where a *bule* – a foreigner – was such a rarity, I was bound to be an object of curiosity. *Would I have to take off all my clothes in front of strangers?*

Arriving at our destination, I noted the name on the dilapidated board at the entrance, *Yuli Sauna & Spa.* We were greeted at the door by the manageress and led to a waiting area. The staff clearly weren't ready for us; I could hear frenzied activity behind the flimsy, makeshift partitions. Our hosts brought us each a 'welcome drink' of strong black Java coffee loaded with sugar; this was most certainly a departure from the customary healthy ginger tea. The plastic cups were scratched and stained with caffeine and the sugar set my teeth on edge. After about twenty minutes, we were invited behind the screen into the spa reception, where I was politely welcomed before being asked to sit down and complete the consultation form. I expected the usual questions:

'Do you have any allergies? Are there any problem areas on your body? Are you pregnant?' In fact, some of the fancy spas even ask about your music preference.

No such questions on this form, all that was required was my name, home address and date of birth. All eyes were watching as I jotted down my age, knocking twelve years off in the process.

I was shown the spa menu and asked to select a treatment. My three comrades were so eager to please me that they chose on my behalf. My indulgence was to include a massage, a Javanese *mandi lulur*, a sauna and a facial. It all sounded very agreeable to me. The eldest and portliest of the trio then requested a massage for himself, while the youngest and vainest member of our group opted for a facial and a body bleach. The third guy only wanted to hang around and observe. I noticed that none of *them* were asked to fill out a consultation form.

Aware that a spa experience should be delivered through 'the vehicle of the five senses,' I allowed myself several minutes to observe my surroundings and absorb the ambience. The interior walls were painted in a bold orange, Elton John's *Crocodile Rock* was blaring out of a portable cassette player, and I could detect the smell of fried chicken mingled with hairspray and essential oils. To my left was a small salon with two tattered posters displaying the latest hairstyles; I suppressed a smile because here we were in darkest Asia, yet all of the models were blond, brunette and red-headed western women. I peered around the corner, expecting to see doors leading to male and female changing rooms, treatment rooms and presumably, in Islamic Java, separate areas for men and women. Instead, I saw six plywood cubicles, each one screened by a curtain. There was also a lazy chair and an unidentified standalone cubicle, while a partially open door revealed a scruffy bathroom. A rat scuttled along one of the roof beams; there was no evidence of a sauna and not a locker room in sight.

A young therapist led me towards one of the curtained cubicles. Inside was a massage bed. I was given a sarong and instructed to remove all of my clothes. *Where were the paper panties?* I momentarily panicked. *Where was the locker for my handbag, my jewellery? Where were the slippers? Where was the hanger for my clothes?* The men were milling around outside my ill-fitting curtain, I hastily undressed while trying to hold the curtain closed with one hand. I lay face down on the treatment couch and waited for my massage to begin.

To my surprise, the mandi lulur was administered first. Alas, here I was in Java, the island of palaces from where this exotic exfoliation and body-polishing treatment originates, yet this was nothing like the royal lulur elixirs I had enjoyed in the sumptuous spas of Bali. I was expecting a fragrant paste blended from natural yogurt, sandalwood, turmeric, ground nuts, rice powder, herbs and jasmine flowers. I was anticipating that it would be massaged into my skin with gentle circular movements performed by healing hands. Instead, I was rapidly rubbed with a granular white substance scooped out of a plastic jar. The therapist then endeavoured to remove it with a damp towel, but much of it lingered on my skin. After informing me that my mandi lulur was over, she vanished through the curtain, leaving the jar behind. I sneaked a look at the ingredients and discovered to my dismay that it contained skin whitener – *surely my Caucasian skin didn't need this*. The curtain parted abruptly and a wizened old *Ibu*, a petite Javanese woman in her sixties wearing a woolly hat, marched in and began to massage me, rhythmically propelling her fingertips and the heels of her hands in strong-pressured strokes all over my body. Although I was already familiar with Javanese massage, I had never experienced one as powerful and as intense as this. It continued for ninety minutes and my masseuse asked me, several times, if it was good.

When she had finished, she held out her hand and urgently whispered, 'Uang, uang.'

I couldn't believe that she was so blatantly asking me for a tip. Nevertheless, I gave her some money; the massage had been well worth it.

It was at this stage, while still covered in oil and particles of skin-whitening grit, that I was told to put on the thin cotton gown before being directed to the 'sauna', the mystery cubicle, which turned out to be a very basic, dark and claustrophobic steam room. I emerged red-faced and dehydrated, streaming with sweat, my hair plastered to my head and my wet robe glued to my gritty body. My male companions were laughing at me, I felt exposed and vulnerable in my nearly nude state. I was told to sit down on the lazy chair and wait. Elton John had handed the mic to Julio Iglesias, who was now crooning majestically. A glass of water was proffered, and a new flurry of activity was taking place behind the closed door of the bathroom.

Presently, I was escorted to a small pink bathtub that had been filled with hot water and garnished with aromatic roots and seed pods. I was then left alone to inhale and soak up the healing properties of the plants.

Positioned on the side of the bath was a *jamu* drink – a Javanese medicinal tonic, sold daily on the streets of Indonesia by ladies on bicycles, clad in sarongs and conical hats, with huge baskets strapped to their backs. The secret recipes, dating from the ninth century and passed down from mothers to daughters, comprise a concoction of herbs and natural ingredients. The drinks claim to increase stamina, rejuvenate the skin, cure numerous ailments and – miraculously – restore virginity.

It felt so good to rinse the grit off my skin, but when I came to wash my hair, I realised that the single tap emitted only cold water. No wonder it had taken the staff so long to prepare my bath; they must have been filling it with pan after pan of boiled water. I immediately felt sorrowful for my silent critique; they were obviously going to a lot of trouble to ensure that my spa ritual was as soothing and as pleasurable as possible.

Ten minutes later, I was reclining on the lazy chair in my clammy, itchy cotton robe undergoing a facial. I relished the rehydration, the deep cleansing, and the refining scrub. My only disappointment was that once again, the scrub was laced with skin whitener, probably eliminating the light suntan I'd acquired during the last few days. Interestingly enough, it was this same golden glow that the vain member of our group was now trying to eradicate from his Asian skin through the body bleaching procedure.

Suddenly Julio Iglesias stopped singing and all the lights went out. It was already dark outside and now we had a power cut to enhance the atmospheric experience. The electricity returned within a few minutes, illuminating the portly member of our group as he scurried out of his massage cubicle, attempting to take advantage of the cover of darkness to retrieve his clothes.

Facial complete, I was also ready to retrieve my clothes, but the thoughtful spa manageress had a tail-end treat up her sleeve. I was hustled into yet another cubicle by two therapists and instructed to take off my gown and don a tent-like garment over my naked body. The girls then jostled me onto what appeared to be a commode, telling me to splay my legs as they carefully arranged the tent over the sides of the 'hotseat'. Beneath me, inside the commode, an urn was releasing fragrant smoke.

I was grateful that this wasn't my first encounter with the renowned *ken dedes*, I already knew the objective of this seemingly bizarre therapy. I therefore relaxed and went with the flow of the special herbal smoke treatment, which was originally developed to cleanse and firm the most intimate parts of a woman's body in preparation for her wedding night. I idly wondered if, in conjunction with a few jamu drinks, it might restore my virginity.

Feeling clean and serene, I was finally allowed to get dressed. My Javanese indulgence had given me a true insight into the evolution of the spa industry; it was humble sanctuaries like this that were the forerunners of the opulent spas and wellness retreats that can be found all over Asia today.

37
LOVELY, LAZY, LUANG PRABANG
2011

'There are Visa-on-Arrival facilities at the international airports in Vientiane, Luang Prabang and Pakse, and at all border crossings. The payment must be made in cash, and the cost is US$25 if paid with US dollar notes; paying with Thai baht will cost considerably more and border officials will not accept Lao kip at all. A passport-style photo is required.'

I stared at the paragraph in the Laos guidebook, which I'd purchased only ten minutes earlier, and chided myself for not having done my research in advance. I was in the departure lounge at Bangkok Airport waiting to board a plane to Luang Prabang and I had no US dollars and no passport-style photo.

I asked an airport official who told me there was a photo-kiosk situated air-side in the Departure Terminal; it was not too late, I still had time. I sprinted back the way I'd come, but looking for this distant machine, and hoping to hell that it would be working, was stressful to say the least. At last, I found it, and its working order was confirmed when four, identical, passport-style colour photographs of me, looking red-faced and sweaty, emerged from a slot in the side. Now all I had to do was find a money changer where I could purchase some US dollars, or alternatively an ATM to acquire 'considerably more' Thai baht. Ten minutes later, after yet more running around like a headless chicken, I could only conclude that all the money dispensing facilities were in the Arrivals Terminal. By now, my heart was racing and I needed to use the toilet. *It's okay, I still have time.*

Heading back to the departure gate, I heard my mispronounced name being called over the tannoy, 'Passenger Raheel Loverlork, Raheel Loverlork please proceed to Gate 8 immediately.'

A woman in uniform was waiting for me, 'Hurry,' she said, leading me away from the gate, into a lift, and down to a corridor on the ground level, where a group of about ten other passengers were likewise waiting for me.

'Surely boarding time isn't for another forty minutes?'

'Everyone is here, we've got an earlier departure slot.'

We were flying out of a major international airport and this woman's explanation sounded a bit suspect to me.

A minibus pulled up outside of the automatic glass door. *A plain white minibus? Why aren't they using the normal airport buses?*

'Perhaps we're being kidnapped,' muttered another passenger.

Trying to appear blasé, I followed the herd and boarded the bus. Happily, all fears of abduction receded as soon as I saw the frangipani flower logo of the Lao Airlines plane – a small, twin-engine turboprop. I slipped into my window seat and straightaway checked my wallet to see how much Thai currency I had left after my two-day stay in Bangkok. It was roughly the equivalent of twenty-five US dollars. *Maybe that would be enough.*

I'd been visiting Bangkok on my own for a routine medical check and had decided to take an extra few days and fly to Laos, a country that had been on my wish-list for quite some time. Everyone I spoke to recommended I visit the city of Luang Prabang, 'Go now,' they urged, 'before it's too late.'

I was writing for a travel magazine at the time, and my editor had already contacted one of Luang Prabang's boutique hotels and got the go-ahead for me to enjoy a complimentary stay in exchange for writing and publishing a couple of stories.

The two-hour flight was delightful. Our small prop plane was cruising at a lower altitude than a typical commercial aircraft, which meant that the view of the Mekong River snaking through the Luang Prabang Mountain Range was wide, open and spectacular.

In contrast, Luang Prabang Airport was tiny, archaic and exceedingly bureaucratic. Formerly part of French Indochina, Laos is one of the few remaining communist regimes in the world, for centuries this landlocked territory was isolated from the rest of Southeast Asia by its mountainous territory. It was only as recently as 1989 that it opened up to tourism. I'd not yet entered the country – and this is a well-worn travel cliché – but it already felt like I was stepping way back in time.

Waiting in the immigration line, I was relieved that I'd got the mandatory passport photos but worried about my lack of US dollars. I looked around for an ATM but there wasn't one. *Would I need to bribe the immigration officer? And if so, what with?*

Remarkably, the Thai baht in my wallet amounted to the exact cost of my visa. The immigration officer counted the cash, examined my red-faced photo, gave me a nod, and filled a full page of my passport with a quaint, old-fashioned visa sticker, followed by a half-page entry stamp.

The next challenge was to find an ATM; I doubted that anyone would know what to do with a credit card in this sweetly-backward country. I breezed through customs and found a vintage free-standing machine on the other side, it was red in colour, the metal surfaces were flecked with rust and the screen was almost too scratched to render it useable. *Was it in working order?* I inserted my card and hoped for the best. The machine wanted to know how much money I would like to withdraw. I had no idea. I had forgotten to check the exchange rate. I opted for one hundred thousand kip. *But maybe that was too much? What if the taxi driver didn't have any change?* The notes were, you've guessed it, quaint and old-fashioned, and in much smaller denominations. I had no idea of their value. I kicked myself again for not having done my research. There were no taxis waiting outside the airport, but very soon a *tuk-tuk* pulled up; I gave the driver the address of my hotel. The fare, he told me, was twenty thousand kip and the ride was ten minutes. I handed over thirty grand, hoping it wasn't worth a hundred dollars; this may have been a huge tip. I soon learnt that the Laotian kip was worth about the same as the Indonesian rupiah. At that time, ten thousand was the equivalent of an American dollar.

Lovely, lazy Luang Prabang, the former royal capital of Laos, is an enchantingly mellow town, which neither teems with excitement nor seethes with intrigue. Life was flowing slowly here, like the Mekong. This tiny city with its mix of gleaming temple roofs, crumbling French colonial architecture and stunning scenery, dozes in ancient splendour. For me, it proved to be one of those rare destinations, which I felt was the genuine article. In the evenings, I'd see numerous vendors peddling the flavours of the province – bright-red curries, grilled river-fish, local vegetables, and steaming pots of rice. French cuisine was also abundant; I loved the charming riverside cafes, where I'd indulge daily in a Beer Lao and a croissant, or a cheese baguette.

Luang Prabang is so small that just about everywhere can be reached on foot or by bicycle. One morning at dawn, I watched the monks padding barefoot through the streets, while the pious townsfolk, me included, placed balls of sticky rice in their begging bowls. I explored the temple architecture and the markets, and I took a two-hour cruise on the Mekong. At sunset, I climbed the grand stairway to Wat Chomis, a little temple at the top of a sacred rock hill, called Phousi, which rises up abruptly in the middle of town, looking directly down upon the elegant Royal Palace and out over the mountains in all directions.

On my final afternoon, I decided to visit an elephant sanctuary, where, freed from brutal logging work, the elephants have been provided with a comfortable retirement. Wearing shorts, T-shirt and sneakers, with my bikini underneath in anticipation of perhaps finding a waterfall and swimming hole along the way, I borrowed a bicycle from my hotel and set off on a solo adventure. The sanctuary was fifteen kilometres away and the road was direct; it all looked very straightforward on the map and I foolishly assumed the terrain would be flat and the road smooth. However, on this sweltering hot afternoon, my journey took nearly two hours because after about fifteen minutes the road turned into a yellow-ochre dirt track, heading down a winding hill that became progressively steeper. In fact, it was so steep that I had to keep my hands on the brakes all the way, while often having to dismount. Did I mention that the bike was gearless? I was scared that I might meet a vehicle coming towards me on one of the sharp bends, so my progress was slow. The steeper the gradient, the more concerned I was about getting back, my return journey would be uphill all the way. It became increasingly obvious that I was heading down to a river, the track got rougher, I was nervous about skidding on the loose gravelly sand, and after more and more twists and turns, I was worried I might be on the wrong road.

Eventually the milky-brown waters of the Nam Khan River came into sight, and a sign portraying an elephant pointed inland. I dismounted again and pushed my bike along a rutted jungle track, and by the time I reached the entrance to the elephant community, my legs had turned to jelly and I was drenched in sweat.

A staff member came out to greet me, 'I'm so sorry, we've already closed for the day.'

I looked at my watch, it was two o'clock. 'Am I too late? I thought you were open until five? I've just cycled all the way from Luang Prabang.'

'You look really hot. Why don't you walk down to the river and cool off, we're about to take some of the elephants down there to bathe; you should join them.'

After being introduced to the gentle giant beasts and their mahouts, I strode with them back through the jungle, and watched as they walked into the river, cavorting and submerging themselves in the cool cloudy water. 'Come on in,' invited one of the mahouts.

I was longing for a swim but I felt that stripping down to my bikini was not the done thing, so I kept my clothes on and plunged in.

A storm was brewing, the sky had turned grey and I was aware that it would be a long, slow and miserable, uphill slog back to my hotel, but I didn't care. I already knew that my interaction with these divine creatures in a river in Laos with not another tourist in sight was an experience that I would never forget.

The elephants finished their bath, and after I'd donated to their upkeep, it was time to say goodbye. The sky was still looking angry but it hadn't started raining yet, *maybe it would hold off long enough for me to get back.* Who was I kidding? I made a quick calculation, there was no way I could cycle up that excessively steep twelve-kilometre-long hill, in the rain, on a single speed bike. I would have to push it all the way back to the top and then cycle the remaining three kilometres back to my swanky hotel in my waterlogged clothes and sodden, muddy shoes. I remembered Naismith's rule – Naismith was a nineteenth-century Scottish mountaineer – 'Allow one hour for every three miles forward, plus an additional hour for every two thousand feet of ascent.' In wet clothes, pushing a bike, I could probably only manage three or four kilometres an hour; this marathon was probably going to take three-and-a-half hours. *C'est la vie, what will be will be.* I set off bravely.

After about ten minutes, an upwards glance revealed that the sky had darkened to an indigo-black. A rapid gust of wind ripped across the road ahead. The thick, low clouds converged and the first plump drops of rain splashed to the ground. The pitter-patter on the huge leaves of the jungle trees became faster and faster, and within minutes the downpour was in full flow. An unending torrent of water sluicing from the sky like a biblical deluge and gushing down the track, which was rapidly turning into a braided river of mud. There was nowhere to take refuge from the storm, and then suddenly an electric flash ripped through the sky, followed by an almighty crack of thunder. I was in danger; *surely it would be foolhardy to continue?*

I stopped, wondering what the hell I was going to do. There was no signal on my phone and I hadn't seen a single vehicle since I had turned off the main road in Luang Prabang. The river of mud was now swirling around my ankles. I prayed to my friend Ganesha to make something happen.

And then something akin to a miracle happened...

A hazy outline materialised in front of me, it appeared to be stationary. I strained to identify it through the blinding rain; it had three wheels, it was a tuk-tuk. *Had I manifested it? Was it real or was it a cruel mirage?* My heart leapt and then quickly sank, it was coming towards me, there were three young kids onboard, the driver was not going in my direction. Nevertheless, he stopped.

'Where are you going?'

'Luang Prabang,' I gave him the name of my hotel.

'I'll take you there.'

'But you're heading in the opposite direction?'

'That's okay, I'll turn around.'

'How much for the ride?'

'Fifty thousand,' he shrugged.

'Can you take my bike as well?'

'Of course,' he replied, spinning his tuk-tuk around upon a sixpence.

He loaded the bicycle on board through the open side of the vehicle, and the kids moved over to make space for me. They were fascinated; they didn't speak any English but they asked plenty of questions, which my saviour, whose name was Dang, translated.

'What are you doing here? Where have you been? Where do you come from?'

Although Dang was essentially a taxi driver and I was his fare-paying passenger and, for him, a fortuitous opportunity; for me, his deed was a remarkable act of kindness. He had rescued me. It was as if he had saved me from drowning. *How much should you pay someone for such an action?*

I tipped him well; well enough to feed his kids for a week.

Undeniably, the memory of my last day in Laos is one that I cherish with gratitude, wonder and joy.

38
A ONE THOUSAND RUPIAH VIEW
2011

Explorer, sea captain, privateer and pirate, Sir Francis Drake was born to a peasant farmer in my old hometown of Tavistock – a Devonshire market town with a present-day population of only about twelve thousand. In 1577, Drake was secretly commissioned by Queen Elizabeth I to set off on an expedition against the Spanish colonies on the American Pacific coast. His travels took him onwards to parts of what is now the Indonesian archipelago, including Maluku (aka the Moluccas). Here, flush with victory and booty, Drake dropped anchor off the small, clove-perfumed, volcanic island of Ternate, where he was well received and lavishly entertained by the Sultan, who gifted him with six tonnes of cloves for English protection against the Portuguese. When he sailed out of Ternate, his ship, the Golden Hind was so weighed down with plundered Spanish-American gold that Drake had to jettison a cannon and two tonnes of cloves to lighten the load so that the vessel could clear the reef. He arrived back in England in 1580 with a rich cargo of spices and Spanish treasure and the distinction of being the first Englishman to circumnavigate the globe. Our morally dubious hero was knighted on board the Golden Hind a few months after his return.

In 2011, I visited the far-flung island of Ternate for the first time. More than a thousand miles, as the crow flies, northeast of Bali, and nearly eight thousand miles from Tavistock, Ternate is a hard place to get to, and therefore not visited by very many tourists. So, I couldn't help wondering if I had the distinction of being the first person from Tavistock, since Sir Francis himself, to have set foot on these distant shores.

I was travelling in a posse of five – Alain and Véronique, Rita, Michael and me. The first drama took place at Denpasar Airport, less than forty minutes after we'd left home, when our photographer friend, Rita, let out a great howl of dismay, having realised she'd left her camera behind, despite having placed it in a prominent position on her kitchen table. There wasn't time to go back for it.

'There's no point in me coming without it,' she wailed, 'I might as well just forget the whole trip now and go back home.'

'Don't be silly,' I snapped unkindly, feeling pissed off because I had brought my own SLR camera and I knew the only solution, the only way to keep our party together, would be to lend it to Rita for the duration of our trip. It's worth mentioning that this was before any of us were in possession of quality Smartphone cameras, so unfortunately I didn't have a backup, but at least Rita gratefully accepted my offer and once again we were a team.

We flew from Denpasar to Makassar and then on to Manado, which is the capital of North Sulawesi and the jumping off point for some of Indonesia's best dive sites and explorations into the wild. We could have flown to Ternate from there, but we were on a quest for adventure and a pilgrimage of history, following in the wake of those whose past adventures had brought us here. We stayed overnight in Manado, explored the city and purchased our ferry tickets to Ternate.

The next day, we were back at the dockside, dismissing the multiple offers of 'I carry your luggage' by the many porters, for fear of losing our bags, losing the porters, or boarding the wrong boat. We should have been more trusting; these professionals know what they're doing and in retrospect we could have used their help. We were directed towards an old wooden ferry, which was moored on the far side of six other similar vessels, each linked by nothing more than a narrow twelve-inch-wide, twelve-foot-long plank of wood. Our embarkation involved crossing six decks and literally walking the warped, wobbly planks between each boat, while precariously maintaining our balance by using both hands to equalise the weight of our luggage, until we reached the last boat, the MV Theodora. This 150-foot-long, Indonesian ferry was of the type that gets mentioned every so often in the world's daily newspapers, when they sink with all hands.

The uncomfortable voyage, in a tiny, hot, six-berth cabin, took nearly fourteen hours, during which the five of us played cards and consumed the first of the five bottles of Havana Club rum that we'd brought with us to see us through our five-day adventure.

Perched on the bow of the boat as the dawn broke on the eastern horizon, I marvelled at my first view of Ternate, it was the same first sight that Drake must have witnessed of the forest-clad slopes of Gunung Gamalama volcano. The pyramid-like volcanic cone dominates the entire island leaving only a narrow coastal strip, across which sprawls Kota Ternate, the biggest and most densely populated city in the North Maluku province, while the lower slopes of the mountain are dedicated to clove plantations. Drake wrote of the scent of cloves on the breeze while still many leagues out at sea. I could smell it too but actually it was the sweet smell of clove cigarette smoke, the Indonesian kretek, wafting across the foredeck and reminding me of why cloves are still very much in demand in Indonesia.

The spice trade made the ancient Islamic island sultanate of Ternate, and its nearby rival Tidore, the two most powerful territories in mediaeval Maluku. They were once the world's only source of cloves, through which their rulers became among the wealthiest and most powerful sultans in the region. Much of their wealth, however, was wasted on fighting each other. Indian, Arab, Chinese and Javanese merchants used to call on these islands to carry home this precious cargo. The land route to Europe was mainly under Muslim control. So, by the time the cloves, as well as the nutmeg and mace from Maluku's Banda Islands, reached Spain and Portugal, they had passed through many hands and become prohibitively expensive, selling at exorbitant prices in Europe and the Orient, where they were used as condiments and medicines. It's not surprising therefore, that the early explorers came to Ternate on a mission to corner the clove trade. The Portuguese were the first, building the first of several forts on the island in 1511.

As latter-day explorers, we had come to Ternate to delve into the forgotten history, the volcanic scenery, the beaches with black glittering sands, the turquoise waters and the swaying coconut trees.

Ternate is also the island that forever changed science because the British naturalist Alfred Russel Wallace made it his home for three years in the mid-nineteenth century. Wallace had come up with the basics of evolution, including natural selection, and it was from Ternate that he posted his famous letter and essay to Charles Darwin. Realising that he wasn't the only one working on the theory of evolution, was the catalyst for Darwin to publish his own writing. However, Wallace's *Malay Archipelago* is a much more engaging book of nineteenth century natural science than Darwin's *On the Origin of Species*.

We wanted to walk in the footsteps of Wallace, we wanted to look around the forts, filled with ghosts and untold stories, and the Sultan's palace, and we wanted to visit Tidore, which today slumbers in relative obscurity. Rita wanted to take photos for a story that Michael was writing for a magazine. Alain wanted to climb Mt Gamalama, which erupts with unsettling regularity, while Michael and I had been drawn by a photo of the view of Tidore and Maitara from Ternate, which was featured on Indonesia's Rp 1000 banknote; we wanted to find the spot and replicate the photo.

Our first objective was to find a comfortable hotel, and we quickly spotted one in a commanding hillside position with great views. It was a modern, soulless, business hotel, remarkably cheap, with a swimming pool and a restaurant. The staff were well meaning but incompetent; it took the receptionist two hours to check us in, she kept stalling the process without explaining why. Despite being only three years old, the property was already showing signs of neglect. There were holes in the carpet in the corridor outside our rooms, a cracked mirror and a faulty kettle in Rita's room, broken tiles around the pool, potholes in the driveway, and no international channels on the cable TV. But none of this bothered us too much, we were more than happy to have airconditioned rooms, comfy beds with deep mattresses, soft yielding pillows, and most importantly, in Islamic Ternate, a bar on the premises.

We spent the rest of the day exploring the town, later gazing down at the 'bottomless' Tolire Besar Lake from the hillside above. No one dares to fish in the lake because it is said to be protected by hundreds of white crocodiles that only a few can see. We didn't see any. Another bizarre local legend maintains that any rocks thrown into the lake will never touch the surface because of a mystical exception to the law of gravity. We tossed a few stones but we were too far away to see or hear any of them hit the water. That evening, we dined on fresh seafood and drank the hotel dry of Bintang. Ternate is girded by a well-paved coastal road, and the next day, we arranged for a car and driver to take us around the island, stopping at Fort Kastela, Fort Tolukko and Fort Oranje, a former bastion of the Dutch East India Company, along the way. He took us to *De View Cafe & Resto*, which marks the spot where the photo had been taken for the Rp 1000 banknote.

From here, we recreated the scenic picture of the neighbouring island of Maitara, sitting alongside the larger island of Tidore, which is shaped by the beautifully symmetrical Mt Kiemtabu volcano, emerging from the deep Maluku Sea.

While we were there, a local boy asked us if we'd like to buy some coconuts.

'Yes, please,' we responded, at which he shinned up the nearest coconut palm at lightning speed, dropping ten coconuts to the ground.

I asked him the price and he didn't seem to know what to say, and finally suggested Rp 20,000 for the lot. The going rate at the time was about Rp 10,000 apiece, so I gave him Rp 60,000, which delighted him, leaving me also thinking I'd scored them for a bargain price until it suddenly dawned on all of us that these hadn't been his coconuts to sell. The boy quickly disappeared, and we hastily bundled the coconuts into the back of the car.

Arriving back at the hotel, we were greeted by a porter pushing a luggage trolley with a brass birdcage frame and a burgundy carpet base. He probably thought our group was a new arrival and looked a bit surprised when we loaded up his grandiose trolley with our ten coconuts. We instructed him to take them down to the kitchen and ask the chef to crack them and extract the liquid – we'd pay for the service, of course. The chef filled a large glass jug with coconut water and flesh, added ice and a generous squeeze of fresh lime, and sent it up to the bar for us to consume with our Havana rum. No one in the hotel seemed to care that we'd brought our own spirit and mixer to the bar. We named our new cocktail, *Captain Ternate*, and each time we emptied the jug, the chef sent us up a replacement. Meanwhile, we enthusiastically made plans to explore Tidore the next day.

~*~

The yang to Ternate's ying, Tidore is her sleepy volcanic sister-island. The larger of the two, but with a population only one third of the size, she has no major urban centres, and in contrast, is dotted with small villages. We chartered a boat and sped across the strait to Tidore in fifteen minutes. We were met on the wharf with offers of taxis, but instead we rented motorcycles, which gave us the freedom to circle the island on the forty-eight-kilometre coast road at our own pace. Tidore's single-storey houses are rendered in every fruity flavoured milkshake colour from banana, lemon, strawberry and raspberry, to lime, peach, orange, blackberry and blueberry, with a few gem-like hues: turquoise, emerald and lapis, whisked in for good measure. This picture book island is completed with flowering roadside bougainvillaea, the Sultan's palace and a well-maintained Spanish fort, which we visited, as well as acres of clove trees under the peaceful gaze of the volcano, Mt Kiemtabu.

~*~

As I mentioned before, Alain wanted to climb Ternate's volcano, Mt Gamalama, which was fine except that he expected us all to join him on his expedition. None of us wanted to but we were all afraid to admit it, so it was now just a matter of who was going to crack first. Back on Ternate and pretending to be enthusiastic, we accompanied Alain in his search for a guide, and were directed to take some ojek taxis to the house of a man named Pak Habakkuk in the mountainside village of Moya. On the steep slopes we saw local men wielding machetes. They had been harvesting cloves, which were now spread across tarpaulins and left on the roadside to dry in the sun.

Happily, Habakkuk was at home and willing to guide us. He asked us to meet him at the Moya village trailhead at two a.m., assuring us that the early start was essential if we wished to see the sunrise from the top. However, he was concerned because there were five of us, an uneven number; a local superstition asserts that any team planning to climb Mount Gamalama must have an even number of members, excluding the guide. This gave one, or three, of us the perfect excuse to drop out, and led by Michael who had hurt his foot, three of us promptly announced our intentions not to tempt fate, leaving Véronique with no choice. She reluctantly agreed to accompany Alain. Habakkuk warned them that some high winds were coming, but said he'd meet them anyway at the appointed time just in case the storm failed to materialise.

Meanwhile, with our hotel still clean out of beer, and having established that the management didn't mind if we brought our own, we headed back to the town and tried to find a convenience store to buy a few bottles of Bintang. After visiting three shops without any luck, we finally understood that Ternate was a dry town. Michael and Alain approached a couple of cocky-looking characters on the street, and discreetly asked if they could help. Véronique, Rita and I then watched apprehensively as the two of them got whisked away on the back of motorbikes. They returned about half an hour later with ten overpriced bottles, but everyone was happy.

~*~

That night, Alain and Véronique retired early, hoping to get a few hours' sleep, or at least rest, before their two o'clock rendezvous with Habakkuk. At around midnight, Michael and I looked out of our window to see the coconut trees bending and swaying in the wind.

'I think Habakkuk might be right about a storm coming.'

Nevertheless, we were still surprised when Alain and Véronique rocked up to breakfast at eight o'clock. They told us they'd got dressed and ready for their hike and had met Habakkuk at the trailhead as planned. However, he'd regretfully informed them that when he'd been out earlier to check the mountain paths, he'd smelt rain in the air, seen two fallen trees and a lot of broken branches and debris, so he felt it was unsafe to head up the volcano that night. Alain was disappointed but suitably prepared to put his trust in the guide's judgment. Habakkuk was the expert after all, and his decision meant that he would miss out on the fee that he would have earned for his services. Véronique whispered to me that she was secretly delighted. Like the rest of us, she'd been dreading the hike.

It had indeed rained during the night, but now the wind had calmed, and the sun was shining again, such is the nature of a tropical storm.

We spent our last day playing cards and drinking Bintang beside the pool, where patches of parched grass were growing between the cracked paving stones. It was a Friday, and the sound of the *adzan*, the Islamic call to prayer, blared all day long from the loudspeakers of the mosques around the city and its surrounding villages. In the Muslim world, this ancient call is repeated for each of the five *salat*, prayers, during the day, with an extended salat on Fridays. The adzan will typically last about two to three minutes each time, although it can continue for as long as an hour, particularly in a compact city where it's not delivered in unison. On Ternate Island alone, there are well over a hundred mosques, and they don't all do it at the same time. For us, it was all part of the cultural exposure and adventure.

However, none of us could face the cultural adventure of another uncomfortable fourteen-hour ferry ride back to Manado, so we endured a bumpy flight instead.

39
MANDARIN MISSION
2018

Staring at the painting in my hands, I gasped at not only the quality of the artwork but also the significance of the subject. The painting was an early birthday present, six months early, from my dear friend Viv, who I only get to see about once a year. The birthday was a big one, one of those landmarks that you choose to either ignore or celebrate in style. I was planning on doing the latter.

The subject of this small and highly detailed watercolour was a mandarinfish – flamboyant yet elusive, arguably the most beautiful fish in the sea; each one a work of art in its own right. Even their scientific name, *Synchiropus splendidus*, acknowledges just how extravagant they are. The significance, unbeknown to Viv, was that on my actual birthday, I would be at one of those far-away destinations where these mandarin dragonets reside. You've guessed it, the Banda Islands.

Viv had never heard of a mandarinfish, let alone seen one, but she'd spotted the painting in a gallery and thought it was gorgeous. I'd also never seen a mandarinfish so I decided that come what may, I was going to find one on this forthcoming birthday trip, which would be our third visit to Banda.

Six months later, my mission began. Another sailing adventure on the Ombak Putih, along with Michael's parents.

The trip had been booked almost a year earlier. I'd done some research and established that these tiny fish – named for the colourful silk robes of the Imperial Chinese mandarins – dwell on the seabed at about eighteen metres deep. Yet, all-year-round, at dusk, they emerge from their hiding places and rise closer to the surface in search of potential mates. My persistent Googling had ascertained that to see them, I would have to don a wetsuit, a regulator, and a pressurised tank. Although I have dived many times in the past, snorkelling is my preference. Yet it wasn't until the dawning of my special day that my main concern arose because in another form of birthday observance, I had already risen at four a.m. and climbed Gunung Api volcano. A boatman had picked me up, along with two other guests on the Ombak Putih and crew-member Hatta, before chugging across the Sonnegat to begin our adventure. Michael didn't come with me, choosing instead to accompany his parents on a gentle stroll through the nutmeg plantations on Banda Besar.

The night before, we had read some TripAdvisor reviews of the climb, which were dominated by comments such as:

Hellish.

Horrible.

Challenging.

Much more difficult than expected.

An unforgiving path.

This is not a walk in the park.

You need an extra pair of lungs and mental determination to get to the top.

This climb is not for the unfit.

Indeed, the climb had been evil, six hundred and sixty-six metres doesn't sound like a big deal, except that it's the number of the beast, the devil, the antichrist.

The trail is steep, and more than three quarters of the track is slippery due to the loose volcanic scree. Our two guides accomplished it in bare feet, with one or other of them always providing a hand to pull me up over the toughest bits. After a two-hour sweaty slog, we reached the top and enjoyed a glorious vista of all the islands in the Banda archipelago. We even watched a tiny plane land on the tiny runway where we'd played four years earlier. I could see the Ombak Putih moored beside the wharf, and while eating his breakfast on the deck, Michael could see our team of six tiny figures moving around on the crater rim. We met some local, habitual hikers on the top; they'd climbed up the previous afternoon, reaching the peak in time to watch the sunset. They had then spent the night there, sleeping on the warm centrally heated ground of the active volcano, and waking up to watch the sunrise.

I'd climbed the volcano to prove that I was still capable of accomplishing such a vigorous feat at my new milestone age. I was thrilled at my successful achievement, but the descent was equally hellish. By the time I reached the comfort of the Ombak Putih, I was worn out, which didn't bode well for a scuba dive, so when Michael returned from his walk through the plantations, we went ashore to enquire if it was possible to see mandarins whilst snorkelling. I'd already noticed a colourful wall mural depicting our goal.

We stopped for a celebratory birthday beer at the Maulana Hotel. To our delight the owner came to join us. He introduced himself as Ramon Alwi; son of Des Alwi and brother of dear Mira.

'Where is the best place to see the mandarins?' I asked him, 'and can it be done with just a mask and snorkel?'

'Absolutely,' he replied with a grin, 'they'll be over there under the palm tree off the side of the wharf at a quarter to six.'

We couldn't believe how easy this was proving to be.

Returning to the hotel wharf just before sunset, we lowered ourselves into the cool still water below the palm tree, and within minutes, one of the legendary fish appeared. With his large, outward-set eyes, amphibian-shaped head, and wavy stripes of royal blue, bright yellow, neon green, turquoise and vivid mandarin-orange, he was just like the psychedelic little critter depicted in my painting at home. Watching the rapid pulse of his fins and his hovering movements, I likened him to a tiny underwater hummingbird. *Could this be his courtship dance?* Three more mandarins appeared on the scene, and in a flash of vibrant colour my little guy found his dance partner. The couple conjoined and rose up, cheek to cheek, for the briefest of passionate moments before releasing their spawn, instantly separating and darting away in opposite directions. Evidently, there was to be no parenting in this family.

Birthday quest accomplished, I couldn't stop grinning and I certainly couldn't wait to tell Viv.

40
A PARISIAN PARTY
2012

We first met Cyrille, the French friend of a French friend, when he came to Bali for a holiday. His visit coincided with the rugby world cup final – New Zealand versus France – and he joined us as a guest at our Kiwi dominated party. France lost the championship by a single point, but it didn't spoil the show for Cyrille; with a Gaelic shrug he continued to party with us 'til late into the night. He told us that if ever we came to Paris, he would return our hospitality by treating us to a barbecue on the balcony of his apartment, which overlooks the Moulin Rouge.

A few months later we decided to incorporate Paris into our Europe trip, so we Facebooked Cyrille and suggested a catch up. Cyrille replied with the affirmation of his promise to welcome us with a barbecue.

About a week before our arrival in France we received a Facebook invitation to an event – *Terrasse Barbecue Gambas à la Maison.* We noted that fifty-seven of the ninety-one invitees had already confirmed their attendance at Cyrille's 'Barbecue of prawns on the terrace at home.' What we thought was going to be an intimate gathering of about ten friends had escalated into a Parisian extravaganza.

We met up with Cyrille briefly on the night before the party and invited him to join us for dinner, but although happy to see us, he declined on the basis that he had to be up early to go to the market to buy king prawns and other fresh ingredients for the barbecue. The entry fee for each guest was a bottle of Champagne – there would be no other alcohol available. It was at this point that we learnt that Cyrille's parties were legendary.

On the evening of the party, our posse of four turned up at Cyrille's small-yet-chic apartment a little bit earlier than the official start time because we had been commandeered to lend a hand with the preparations. The furniture had been pushed back against the walls, the bathtub had been filled with ice, and already a table had been spread with canapés. We sank our bottles of Champagne into the tub of ice and helped load marshmallow mushrooms and candy fruits onto wooden satay sticks, which we then planted, in accordance with Cyrille's detailed pictorial diagram, amongst the geraniums and herbs in the terracotta pots that graced his fifth-floor balcony, just fifty metres from the red windmill of Le Moulin Rouge.

Gradually, the guests started to arrive, each depositing their Champagne offerings into the bathtub before greeting us, individually, with a kiss on both cheeks, 'Bonjour. Ça va?'

Gosh, these Parisians were so charming, so polite and yet so informal. With a French flourish, Cyrille popped the first magnum of Champagne, flûtes were filled and glasses clinked as expressions of 'Cheers,' 'Santé' and 'Tchin' were exchanged. More and more people came through the door, worked the small room and the breezy balcony where we were standing, some of them greeting us as if we were old friends, others inquiring if Michael and I were the Bali-dwelling journalists they'd been told about, on le grand tour d'Europe. The balcony became more and more crowded as more and more guests spilled out from the jam-packed room in search of fresh air. The music got louder, the barbecue was fired up and Cyrille's 850 previously-prepared satay sticks – containing prawns and courgette marinated in curry paste, and chicken marinated in Coca-Cola – were cooked, distributed and consumed, along with copious quantities of Champagne. Then, slowly, very slowly, the sun set, dusk fell, and the neon lights of the Moulin Rouge shone red in the darkness; what a shame about the broken lightbulbs in the first three letters, it seemed rather odd, and a tad tacky, that such an iconic sign had been so poorly maintained.

There was nothing tacky about the partygoers however, apart from a pair of Moroccan drug dealers who had managed to secure an invite from one of the attendees with the promise of an immediate and profitable business opportunity. The hashish, the Champagne and the conversations continued to flow; these charming, well-dressed French people, all of whom spoke excellent English, certainly knew how to enjoy themselves.

It was a weeknight. Shortly before midnight, just after the Champagne ran out, a significant number of guests departed, these were the folks who were aiming for the last Métro train – often called the *balai*, meaning the broom, because it sweeps up the remaining passengers – allowing them to grab a few hours' sleep before work in the morning. This partial exodus gave the rest of us some space to move around a bit more, converse with some of the people we had not yet had the chance to meet, dance, and search the apartment for more Champagne. We were gratified to find a secret stash of wine. The music changed with the mood and the party rocked on. Deliciously drunk and delightfully stoned, we finally left at four a.m. The party was by no means over, but we decided it was the right time to depart because the only people remaining were the remnants who had not yet found someone to go home with.

The streets outside the Moulin Rouge were empty apart from a few stationary taxis. We gratefully jumped into one and attempted to speak to the driver in French until after a few *pouvez-vous répéters*, he said to us in immaculate English, 'I'm sorry but I don't understand what you're saying?'

At that exact moment, we spotted the Arc de Triomphe looming ahead of us. 'Tourner à droite,' commanded Michael, 'turn right, take us down the Champs-Élysées.'

To which the driver replied, 'I can do better than that.'

With a flourish, he turned the wheel and proceeded to do a complete circuit around the arc, the plaza and the *étoile,* or star, of the juncture formed by its twelve radiating avenues, before driving down the famous, seventy-metre-wide, almost-two-kilometre-long, tree-lined avenue to the Place de la Concorde. It proved to be an expensive detour back to our hotel, which was near the Eiffel Tower. On the other hand, what price can you put on a private tour of some of the most iconic landmarks of the world's most romantic city, at a time when there are no other people in sight and no other vehicles on the road.

Thank you Cyrille, for inviting us to one of the best private parties we have ever had the privilege to attend. It's not often you get invited to a party where you know less than ten percent of the eighty guests, where everyone – apart from the Moroccan drug dealers – is French yet speaks superb English, where everyone has something fascinating to say, where the food is top notch and the only available beverage is Champagne... and there's plenty of it, and the location is a tiny balcony overlooking the Moulin Rouge.

~*~

41
FROM THE PALACE TO THE PRISON
2012

Strategically built on seven hills straddling Europe and Asia over the Bosphorus Strait, the achingly beautiful city of Istanbul is a place that every traveller should visit at least once in their lifetime.

In July 2012, I was visiting Istanbul for my second time, entrusted with an assignment to write a magazine article about two of the city's most luxurious, historic hotels.

Our first view of *Four Seasons Hotel Istanbul at Sultanahmet* was from the rooftop terrace of a neighbouring restaurant. From there, in between sipping a Turkish coffee and a cherry juice while marvelling at the astonishing views of the Blue Mosque and Hagia Sofia, the Bosphorus and the Marmara Sea, Michael and I gazed down into the hotel's manicured garden courtyard. It had once been the exercise yard of a Turkish prison. It was our first morning in Istanbul, we had an epic tour of Europe ahead of us – plenty to be excited about, but there was also a certain thrill in knowing that we would be returning to this city for the final two days of our trip and staying a night at each of Istanbul's stunningly different Four Seasons' properties.

The last time I had visited Istanbul was in the mid-eighties and being back there now released an assault of memories – tastes, landmarks, sights, sounds, words – that left me flummoxed. How could I have forgotten the cherry juice that I used to drink every day? How could I have not recalled the names of the bridges, the Galata Tower and Taksim Square? The toasted cheese sandwiches wrapped in paper. Each resurrected memory was like unexpectedly finding a wad of ten-pound notes in my back pocket, then pulling them out one after another after another and cashing them in for Turkish lira.

I took Michael to some of the places that I had *not* forgotten, such as the Blue Mosque and Hagia Sophia. I remembered Kapaliçarşi – the Grand Bazaar, which fulfilled my Arabian Nights' fantasies. Within this jumbled cluster of interconnected vaulted passageways capped with dozens of domes, I once haggled over a pair of lapis earrings, but now I found myself fascinated by the carpet shops – each one an art gallery. We didn't want to buy, and I explained this to a shop owner over a glass of apple tea. He didn't seem to mind. He was happy to chat, and proud to share his woven tales. Our next stop was the spice market, where everything was earthy and aromatic; it used to be the largest spice trading venue of the mediaeval world and business has been bustling there for the past three hundred and fifty years. I savoured the sight of the abundant stalls piled high with edible exotics, the bright colours, the cool pinks of the Turkish delight, the green pistachios, the red chillies hanging from the roofs, and all the time the shouts of the cheeky vendors.

As we passed one man, he cried out, 'Hello, let me take your money.'

It was the most honest and refreshing catchphrase we'd heard yet, so I stopped to buy some Iranian saffron.

One Turkish tradition I have always admired is the shoe-shiner. Sitting on the busy streets with their small stools and

Ottoman style boxes, shoeshine boys and men ply their trade to everyone who passes. Walking across the Galata Bridge on our first evening, we were overtaken by a shoeshine man. A brush fell off the top of his box; he was walking quite fast and didn't seem to notice. Michael picked up the brush and ran after him, and the guy was so appreciative that he insisted on shining Michael's shoes. He then charged him a grossly inflated price for a service that Michael hadn't even asked for but felt obliged to pay for. Years later, we saw this rip-off depicted in a Hollywood movie, and learnt that it's known as *the shoeshine scam of Istanbul.*

My good friend Barbara, who used to live in Portugal – yes, Barbara of the toenail saga – was living in Turkey at the time of our visit and on our second day, she flew down from Ankara to meet up with us in Istanbul. Knowing the city well, she became our guide for the next couple of days, allowing me to notch up some new experiences, such as ascending to the top of the Galata Tower and being blown away by an extraordinary view of the city skyline, the bridges, the boats, the Golden Horn, and the busy Bosphorus Strait.

We then dipped into a mezze feast in a street cafe, and in the confectionary shop next door, I greedily enjoyed an outrageous two-in-one sugar fix by sampling both the baklava and the Turkish delight. Later, at sunset, the three of us dined at one of the tourist-trap fish restaurants on the Galata Bridge. With much ado, we were ceremoniously served the delicacy of a fresh *palamut* (bonito) baked in a thick crust of salt, accompanied by the aniseed-flavoured firewater known as *raki*, Turkey's national drink. We had ordered three glasses and ended up with three bottles instead, an enormous bill and an inebriated walk back to our hotel.

The next day, we visited Istanbul's oldest and most famous hammam, Ağa Hamami, which was built in 1454 by the most important sultan of the ottoman empire. Michael disappeared into the men's section, while Barb and I entered the ladies' bathhouse. The experience is not for the prudish. I'd been told to leave my inhibitions at the door and had expected to be wearing nothing but a towel for the whole session, but we were each given a pair of black briefs to wear if we wanted to, so we did. I noted that all the other women, both the guests and the staff, were likewise half naked; I liked that element of equality. I was instructed to lie down on the heated marble slab while my body was soaped, scrubbed and rinsed by a smiling older woman with a round belly and huge breasts. Several times throughout the process, she proudly showed me how much dirt she had scraped off my skin. The service even included a comforting hair-wash as she pulled me towards her ample bosom; it was intensely nurturing, and I leaned into it. Michael and I had paid extra for a massage, which followed later in a separate room. We were both curious to see if it was as good as a Balinese massage, and although it was good, and highly professional, and although we might sound biased, both of us agreed that nobody does it better than the Balinese, with whom a massage truly comes from the heart.

On our last evening with Barbara, she took us on a ferry across the Bosphorus, re-entering Asia, to explore shadowy junkshops, a fruit and vegetable market displaying olives galore, and a couple of cheese shops, before dining amongst hundreds of locals within a street full of cafes.

One month later, after a wonderful trip through Europe, we flew back into Istanbul and checked into *Four Seasons at The Bosphorus*, which is a nineteenth-century Ottoman mansion. Situated waterfront, it was a palace in every sense of the word; glamorous, grand and gorgeous with marble inlays, geometric motifs and of course, Turkish carpets.

From the cushioned seat of the bay window of our exquisite room, we were treated to a mesmerising, moving picture of teak-decked fishing boats, huge oil tankers and cargo ships, pilot boats, tugs, ferries, cruise liners, schooners and super yachts, meandering towards the majestic Bosphorus Bridge.

The following day, we left the commanding beauty of the Bosphorus for the confines of a Turkish jail. Thankfully, instead of being a Midnight Express nightmare, this was another one of those worthy dreams, and the perfect place to recoup on the final night of our grand tour of Europe. Set smack-dab in the middle of the Old City, Four Seasons at Sultanahmet is a century-old revivalist-style building, complete with the original prison watchtowers, vaulted ceilings and pointed-arch portals, wrapped in mustard-coloured walls. Interestingly, the building can never be extended because the history beneath it goes much deeper and must not be disturbed. During the renovation process, excavations revealed the subterranean remains of a palace, which was the seat of government for the eastern Roman and Byzantine empires for more than a millennium.

How ironic that we should feel privileged to stay in an ex-jailhouse that had once been home to some of Turkey's most illustrious prisoners, including dissident poet Nazım Hikmet, although not – as I had mused – to Billy Hayes, the protagonist in Midnight Express. An inscription in the Ottoman language on the main gate of the building states the name of the facility as the *Capital City Murder Jail*, while inside, an inmate’s poignant graffiti-inscription is still visible upon an old marble pillar.

In reality, our feelings of gratitude had much to do with a longstanding friendship with a Four Seasons’ regional manager, which led to a lavish upgrade fit for a sultan, a complimentary bottle of wine and an eight-p.m.-checkout to seamlessly correspond with a nine-p.m. -check-in for our flight home. Positioned within a quadrilateral corner of the building, with views of the cobbled streets, the Sea of Marmara, and the rooftop terrace of the restaurant where we had breakfasted on our first morning, our splendid suite was a prisoner's fantasy. It was lavishly furnished with sofas and armchairs with damask upholstery, cosy kilims, and a big, yielding bed with a headboard and posts designed to resemble a mosque's dome and minarets.

As we had already spent several energetic days exploring the city at the beginning of our trip, we had decided that our final weekend in Istanbul would be all about relaxation. Our late checkout enabled us to while away some time with a few rounds of backgammon hushed by the call to prayer echoing from the famous Blue Mosque nearby. I couldn't help thinking that the former detainees may well have engaged in the same activity all those years ago.

On a final note, during my first visit to Istanbul in the 1980s, I remember being romanced by the call to prayer, but after years of living in Indonesia, the mystique of the microphones has long worn off. Yet, upon returning to this metropolis of minarets, and hearing the simultaneous summons echoing around Sultanhamet, I was surprised to find the hairs on my arms were standing up on end…

~*~

42
AIRPORT DASH
2012

Travelling is without question a joyful and thrilling experience. However, the journey to the airport can come with some insane anxiety-producing moments.

It was the twenty-seventh of December, the date is easy to remember, and Michael and I were on our way to New Zealand for our annual Christmas holiday. We would normally have arrived in time to celebrate Christmas Day with the family but on this occasion, we had chosen to economise by flying a few days later for a belated Christmas, while knocking a few hundred dollars off the cost of our flight. What's more, we had only booked a one-way flight at this stage, keeping our options open regarding the date of our return journey.

The ride to Bali's airport from our homebase in Seminyak usually takes about thirty minutes, but Christmas is normally a busy time on the roads because in addition to the foreign tourists, thousands of Jakartans descend upon the island for the holiday, flying in, while their cars and drivers make the eighteen-hour road trip. The logic of this is hard to understand. Surely, it would make more economic sense to hire a car and driver in Bali, thus bringing income to the local businesses and providing work for the Bali-based drivers. A local driver would know his way around Bali considerably better than an overworked Jakarta resident, especially one who had been tasked with driving twelve-hundred kilometres on his own before resuming his responsibility as the family chauffeur. Anyway, the consequence of this is that the roads in Bali during the window between Christmas and New Year are always jammed with Jakarta registered cars and a significant number of clueless drivers. In addition to this, we knew that there would be traffic jams on the bypass because the new Simpang Siur underpass was under construction. With this in mind, we allowed ourselves well over an hour to get to the airport and instructed our taxi driver to take the backroads instead of the bypass.

Within five minutes of getting into the taxi, we found ourselves gridlocked. Nothing was moving in any direction, and all I could see was brake lights, lots of them, ahead. I tried to relax. After all, we had plenty of time, I knew there was a bottleneck ahead but all we had to do was clear it and we'd then be on our way. Car horns started to honk. Once in a while, the cars in front of us moved forward a metre or so. Our taxi driver followed suit but for most of the time, we were motionless. My heart started to thump. To the left and to the right of us, impatient motorcyclists squeezed past, filling in the gaps, riding along the pavements, negotiating their way over the cracks and around the holes, almost touching the stationary vehicles. Suddenly we started moving, my anxiety eased, and I began to breathe more freely.

We drove for about a hundred metres before we came to a total stop. Behind us, cars, SUVs, minibuses, and small trucks quickly built up and soon we were boxed in, bumper to bumper and no one was moving. It didn't look like we'd be going anywhere anytime soon. I strained to see what was going on, by now a cacophony of horns was beeping incessantly, our driver was non communicative, he looked pissed off. He'd refused to use the meter, so we'd agreed a fare in advance, but clearly, he was wishing he'd asked for more.

My heart was pounding and I was aware my breathing had become rapid and shallow, as if something bad was about to happen. I checked my watch for the tenth time in ten minutes, I could barely trust myself to speak.

'D'ya think we're gonna make it?' I asked Michael in a small tense voice.

'There's nothing we can do,' he replied, 'we've just got to hope our flight has been delayed.'

We started moving again, nudging ahead slowly. As we rounded the corner into the beginning of Kuta's one-way system, with each vehicle tailgating the one in front, I realised we couldn't turn around even if we wanted to. Metre by metre we crawled along. Fifteen minutes later, we were still stuck in what seemed to be a snarling sea of cars and motorcycles, inching forward at a snail's pace. Twenty more minutes on and I realised we had hardly moved at all. Feeling sick, I looked at my watch again, it had taken us nearly an hour and a half to travel one kilometre.

Images of being too late to check-in were racing through my mind, images of us running panic-stricken through the airport terminal, items flying from our bags, people giving us funny looks, while we hoped desperately that our plane had been delayed.

I began to feel panicky; the traffic jam was triggering my brain's natural response system, I could feel my body preparing to do something, the fight or flight response. *Were we prepared to fight for our flight? Surely we'd need to run if we wanted to catch our plane?*

'We can't just sit here, if we miss this flight we won't get our money back, we've got to do something.'

The brain's response prompts a burst of energy, and it was Michael who made the next move.

'You're right,' he agreed, getting out of the taxi.

Our driver looked concerned.

My intense physical discomfort began to ease as I watched Michael navigate his way between the stationary vehicles and begin a conversation with a man who looked to be the owner of one of the small roadside shops.

Returning, he announced that he'd found a couple of guys who were willing to drive us to the airport on the back of their motorcycles. He asked our driver to open the boot so that we could get our luggage out.

Our driver looked angry, '*I'm* taking you to the airport.'

'You're not going to get us there in time,' I shouted, stating the obvious, handing him the agreed fare, and leaving him to find his own way out of the stalemate.

We dragged our luggage – two large and heavy hard-shell suitcases, a hard-sided cabin bag on wheels, my overstuffed handbag, and a backpack – to the side of the road, where our new drivers were waiting on their bikes.

These guys were not professional ojek drivers, they were just a couple of local boys who were pleased to help us and eager to make a quick buck, while revelling in the excitement of a challenge. Michael had offered them a fair payment to drive us quickly to the airport; they had demanded double; they knew we were desperate.

Michael balanced my suitcase upright on his knees and held my carry-on in one hand. I did the same with my suitcase, my arms fully extended, I put my handbag around my neck and shoulder, and I wore the backpack. Neither of us had any hands free to hold onto the driver or the bike, neither of us were given helmets to wear.

Michael's driver set off at speed and my driver followed, mounting the curbs, bumping along the pavements, skidding on the gravel, bouncing back down the curbs, and squeezing between the cars. I sat as still as I could manage, holding onto my suitcase for dear life, and wincing when my hand scraped against the side of a bus, in danger of getting crushed. Without warning, we turned a corner and there we were in the maze of skinny alleyways, or *gangs,* and shortcuts, which are too narrow for cars. These boys knew the backstreets of Kuta like the backs of their hands. My initial fears of having an accident suddenly soared into euphoria as the adrenaline kicked in. Eight minutes earlier, the prospect of getting to the airport had not looked good, now it was looking almost like a certainty.

As we emerged from the gangs, briefly joining the main road, I was unexpectedly brought back down from my euphoria by the waaaaaahhhhhhhing howl of police sirens. Coming towards us was a convoy of black BMWs with blacked out windows, escorted front and back by police cars and police motorcyclists. I was mindful that I wasn't wearing a helmet, but these cops were too busy getting high on the superpower of the ability to keep The President and his entourage moving through a deadlocked traffic jam. I shut my eyes, the VIPs were coming straight towards us, and we were blocking their way. And then they were gone, and once more we were zipping through the traffic towards the airport. We turned into another tangle of narrow backstreets and stopped with a jolt when our drivers saw that our route ahead was blocked. Turning around, we took a sharp left and continued on our way. The ring road around the airport was as close as they could deliver us to our terminal, but we'd made it. We offloaded our suitcases and got off the bikes.

'We need to pay these guys,' said Michael, 'I'm out of cash, can you give them two hundred thousand?'

'I've only got eighty,' I replied, looking through my wallet.

'What? Oh shit, the ATM is more than five minutes' walk away.'

We couldn't expect our drivers to walk over there with us, but we also knew that our check-in desk could close at any moment and if one of us ran over to the cash machine, drew out some money and then ran back, we'd be pushing our luck.

Michael searched his pockets and found some more notes, I rummaged around in the bottom of my handbag and pulled out some fluff-covered coins. Amazingly, we had two hundred and one thousand between us. We thanked our saviours and ran towards the international departure terminal. I spotted our Virgin Blue check-in desk, but as I approached it, my vision started to blur. *There was nobody there, was it still open?*

A man appeared from behind a screen, affirming that the desk was still open, 'Your passports and tickets please?'

'Where is everybody?' I asked, as we handed over our documents.

'A lot of people haven't checked in yet,' he replied. I hear the traffic's bad.' Looking at me, he added, 'You do realise you need a visa for New Zealand?'

'No, she doesn't, she's a British citizen,' interjected Michael.

'I can see that Sir, but she hasn't got an onward ticket, so she can't enter the country without a visa.'

'But we visit New Zealand every year and I've never once been asked to show my return ticket when I've entered the country.'

'They don't need to see it because they know the airline won't have allowed you onto the plane without one.'

I felt my temperature rise and I began to sweat. Our early-model Smartphones were not yet smart enough to access the internet and book tickets on-line. It was 8.30 p.m., we'd be lucky to find any airline offices still open at this time within the vicinity of the airport, and I needed to physically have an onward ticket in my hands before I would be allowed to board the plane. I looked around wildly and saw a tiny office window on the far side of the check-in area. Michael was already running towards it.

'Is that an airline office? Can I buy a ticket there?'

'I can give you five minutes,' said the annoyingly unruffled check-in man, 'and then we're closing the desk.'

For the umpteenth time, we thanked our lucky stars, the office was open. Yes, the nice lady was willing to sell me a ticket, the price was affordable, and I had just enough money on my debit card to pay for an onward flight from Auckland to Brisbane. We'd get a ticket for Michael and tickets for the second leg of the journey at a later date. The exasperatingly impassive check-in man gave us our boarding passes. We'd made it by the skin of our teeth, and we were on our way.

We really were among the fortunate ones that day, we later heard stories about frantic passengers jumping out of their gridlocked taxis and running the last two kilometres towards the airport dragging their suitcases behind them.

43
A NEW YEAR BREAK
2014

As Michael gently peeled back the sleeve of my orange hoodie to reveal what I already knew, we were both faced with the severity of our predicament. My rapidly swelling right hand had been immobilised into the shape of an excavator grapple, complete with a distinct bump in my wrist, similar to the neck of a downfacing fork.

'We need to get you to a hospital,' declared Michael.

'How will that even be possible?' I countered.

It was New Year's Day and we were on a rocky beach on a remote island in New Zealand, four-and-a-half-hours' ferry ride from the city of Auckland.

I had slipped on the rocks and had experienced an instant, searing pain, but the rush of adrenaline that accompanies shock had enabled me to stay calm for a few minutes at least, while I fumbled to remove the gold bangle from my wrist. *How the hell am I going to remove my rings?* I wondered.

We were with our friends, Jim, Janet and Chang, staying in a *bach*, a beachside holiday home, on Great Barrier Island. We had arrived the day before, and Michael's friend Jamie, who had not yet met the others, was joining us the following day.

'Let's go back to the bach, and I'll borrow Jim's car and drive you to the clinic.' Michael is always good in a crisis.

Great Barrier is off the grid and it's self-sufficient. Typified by native forest, mountains, valleys and beaches, and a population of not much more than a thousand residents, it is tranquil and unspoilt.

'Are you sure there's a clinic here?'

'Definitely,' reassured Michael, 'this is a holiday island, there *has* to be.'

We got back to the bach but there was no sign of the car.

'Jim and Janet have gone to the supermarket,' explained Chang as he opened the door. When he saw my wrist, he froze in horror.

He may not be as proactive as Michael in a crisis but if I tell him what to do he'll be keen to help, I reasoned. 'Chang, have you got any painkillers? And can you bring me some ice and some soap, I need to get my rings off.'

Michael had disappeared but returned a few minutes later with the key to the neighbours' car. We'd not even met the people next door but they hadn't hesitated to lend us their rented SUV. I'd meanwhile taken a painkiller, packed my wrist with ice, and managed to remove my rings, but by now, the adrenaline had worn off, the pain had become intense, a post-rush drop in my blood sugar had made my hands shake, and my legs had gone weak.

There was a map in the car, so we easily found the clinic, but it was closed for New Year's Day. However, there was a sign at the door with an emergency number. The problem was that neither of us had a phone, we'd only just landed in New Zealand and hadn't yet purchased local numbers, so we hadn't brought our phones with us to Great Barrier. We needed a pen. We searched the glove compartment and the door pockets of the car; there was no sign of a pen, but then Michael remembered the Swiss Army Knife that I'd given him for Christmas only a week earlier. The embodiment of multifunctionality, this one had thirty-three tools including a pen. Michael copied the phone number onto his hand. All we had to do now was to find a nice person who would kindly lend us their phone. It didn't take long. We called the emergency number and the doctor said she would meet us at the clinic in a few minutes.

The doctor arrived with a radiologist.

With the tedious paperwork completed and confirmation that I was entitled to ACC – an accident compensation scheme, which covers all residents and visitors injured in an accident in New Zealand, the radiologist was ready to start.

'I'd like to give you some morphine.'

'Yes please! Bring it on!'

He told me my injury was known as a 'F.O.O.S.H.' – a fall on out-stretched hand' and instructed me to flatten my dinner-fork deformity onto the table so that he could x-ray it.

'I can't even move it, let alone flatten it,' I exclaimed.

'Try.'

To my astonishment, I was able to push my hand flat onto the surface. This morphine was good stuff.

X-rays complete, and a fractured wrist confirmed, the doctor informed us that they didn't have the authority or facilities to reset the bones, so a helicopter would shortly come to pick me up and take me to Auckland Hospital.

'Can Michael come with me?'

'Yes, of course.'

'Will the helicopter bring us back?' enquired Michael.

'No, sorry.'

'But we're here on holiday, we've paid for our accommodation, and it will scupper our plans if we have to leave.'

The doctor called Auckland Hospital and explained the situation. 'The clinician says you need to get to the hospital as soon as possible.'

The offer of a helicopter ride was very tempting but I didn't want to let our friends down and spoil everyone's holiday.

'Can't you just put it in a cast and see how it goes?'

'Sorry but we can't do that here, the broken ends of the bone need to be manipulated back into their original position before being fixed in place with a cast.'

'Why don't I just go back on the ferry as planned at the end of the week, and save the cost of a helicopter trip?'

'We can put it in a splint for now and I'll give you some more morphine but you'll need to get back to Auckland within the next couple of days,' said the radiologist.'

Yay! He was giving me permission to stay on the island for a little bit longer.

Twenty-five minutes later, with my arm temporarily secured in a splint and a sling, we returned the car to our kind neighbours along with the gift of a bottle of wine.

Jim and Janet were back and had been updated by Chang regarding the details of the accident.

Apparently, Chang had met them at the door and proclaimed, 'Something terrible has happened!'

But in reality, it wasn't too terrible at all. Yes, I'd broken my wrist but I was covered by ACC, and I'd get it sorted as soon as we returned to Auckland. Despite the instruction from the hospital and the advice of the doctor, I had already decided to stay for the remaining five days of our holiday.

So, I proudly took one for the team. I tried not to complain too much about the throbbing pain, and as if to prove my point, I even attempted – and failed – to single-handedly shell half a kilo of fresh peas. Jamie arrived; he was happy to see us and grateful we hadn't taken the helicopter option.

Four days after being patched up by the doctor, two days after the day on which we had promised to leave, we attended a mussel festival on the island. It was a sunny day, there was live music, a couple of beer tents and some live cooking demonstrations. A number of canopied food stalls were serving copious quantities of New Zealand's native, green-lipped mussels, which had been creatively prepared in many different ways: deep-fried as fritters, steamed in wine and garlic, braised in a stew, or steamed and served in a paella. Wandering around with a mussel fritter in my good hand and a beer tucked under the same arm, everything was going really well until I saw the doctor, enjoying an afternoon off. I had disobeyed her orders, and now she was about to bust me. Did she see me? I will never know because I turned my back on her and got the hell out of dodge, dragging everyone else with me.

Michael and I departed on the slow ferry the next morning, and headed straight to Auckland Hospital, where I enjoyed some hysterically giggly laughing gas while the doctors examined my wrist. Next, according to Michael, who was holding my feet, I screamed my way through a painful manipulation, which I promptly forgot all about under the influence of the twilight anaesthesia drug, propofol.

I guess it's all about personal perception, but as New Year breaks go, this one was a cracker!

~*~

44
PULLING TOGETHER ... THE LAUNCH OF A PHINISI
2015

In May 2014, Indonesia's Sangeang Api volcano spectacularly erupted, discharging a mushroom-cloud of ash twenty kilometres high into the sky. Almost exactly one year later, I found myself desperately seeking shade from the sun on a black-sand beach within striking distance of the still-active volcano. Separated only by a narrow shipping channel, the island of Sangeang towers over the tiny shipbuilding village of Sangeang Wera – a Buginese settlement in northeast Sumbawa. Here the men build wooden boats along the scruffy shores, while the village women weave brightly coloured textiles. Today, something huge was happening in Sangeang Wera, and just for once, the nonchalant volcano was failing to dominate the scene.

On this auspicious day, when the king tide was expected to reach its peak at one o'clock in the afternoon, all eyes were on *Al Fatah*, an enormous phinisi boat, which from ground level, appeared to soar even higher than the volcano. After eighteen months of handcrafted labour by four master boatbuilders, Al Fatah was ready to be launched.

Michael and I had stopped off at the village a couple of months earlier on one of our many SeaTrek voyages to Komodo aboard the Ombak Putih. Along with Jen, who worked as a tour guide for SeaTrek, we had seen how close the vessel was to completion, and we had resolved to come back for the launch.

The boatbuilders had been very specific about the date, 'It will be on the May full moon when the tide is at its highest.'

We rallied together a party of six, including our filmmaker friend, Scott, who had just purchased his first drone. He hadn't yet learnt how to operate it, so he'd brought along his expert drone pilot friend, Wajid, who lives in Jakarta, and Wajid had brought his wife, Aesha.

Jen knew the head of the village and had arranged accommodation for us in a local house, along the lines of a simplistic Airbnb arrangement. The homeowner and his family would move out for the night so that we could stay there at the cost of about ten dollars each. The money would be enough to feed this family of five for a week.

Wajid and Aesha flew into Bali from Jakarta and met us at Denpasar Airport, and from there we flew together to Bima on the island of Sumbawa, where we had pre-organised transport in two vehicles to Sangeang Wera, which was two hours away; the drivers were waiting for us at Bima Airport.

Unfortunately, Wajid had omitted to tell Aesha that this was a work trip. He had presented her with an air-ticket to Bali but had forgotten to mention that the real destination was a remote and very poor Muslim village in Sumbawa where the local people scraped together a meagre living from fishing. Aesha was carrying a bulging suitcase.

Our thoughtful host was there to greet us when we arrived at the village, amid a mishmash of colours, bicycles, boats, masts, fishing nets and wrinkled old ladies carrying plastic buckets on their heads. The dirty beachfront was lined with typical Bugis-style houses with corrugated iron roofs and scrap-wood panels painted in the same strong colours as the fishing boats: blue, green, turquoise, aquamarine and terracotta, shades that harmonise with the sky, the sea and the earth. All were constructed on high stilts with wooden shutters instead of glass windows. He led us to his own house, which was likewise a traditional wooden dwelling, an elevated platform resting on stilts and accessed via a ladder-like stairway. Inside was just one room, divided into a living and a sleeping area by a curtain. It was spartan and grubby and there weren't enough beds for us all, but that was okay, we were there for the adventure and there were some cushions and mats on the floor. The 'kitchen' was at the back beside a glassless window. There was no sink or running water, merely a disconcerting arrangement – in this flimsy wooden house – of three blackened stones that formed a stand for a cooking pot, under which was a cast iron vessel filled with pieces of driftwood. There was no electricity, and the 'bathroom' was outside, positioned about ten metres from the house. This standalone facility was shared between four households and contained a squat toilet and a *mandi* – a tank of cold water with a scoop for washing and manual flushing.

We dropped our bags and belongings inside the house. There was no lock on the door, but our host assured us that our gear would be safe, and we headed outside to look at the phinisi boat. Aesha stayed indoors.

Fashioned from ironwood, thirty metres long with a twenty-two-metre keel, eleven metres wide and weighing around one-hundred-and-fifty tonnes, the bulk carrier, *Al Fatah*, was the biggest boat ever to have been built in the village. She had been commissioned by six wealthy brothers from Surabaya in Java, at the cost of a quarter of a million dollars. The brothers and the builders were highly respected in the community and every member of the village was involved in an extraordinary manual operation to get the boat into the water. Vertical supporting beams had been positioned on either side of the vessel, logs had been laid perpendicular to the keel and planks had been laid parallel to form a slipway, which had been liberally smeared with thick, heavy engine grease.

We spoke to one of the builders who informed us, 'We'll start at sunrise tomorrow, and it will take three hours from the first pull until the boat reaches the water.'

No one was getting paid, it was a collaboration, people were going to be literally pulling together to help each other. To show their appreciation, the brothers had arranged for the slaughter of a small menagerie of cows, goats and chickens; the women cooked, and that evening the whole village feasted and we were included in the celebration. As a vegetarian, I was left a bit high and dry, but I made do with the boiled rice and chilli sambal. There was only one shop in the village and all it sold in the way of food was sacks of rice, packets of dried noodles, and a few bananas and eggs. I was told that the fishermen of Wera sell their catch to the middlemen of Bima.

After dark, the men gathered on board, and we were invited to join them. Prayers were offered to Allah for a smooth launch and for the future safety of the vessel. In an earlier ceremony, a hole had been drilled at the midpoint of the keel, a crock of gold had been placed in the hole and the drillings were placed in a bottle of coconut oil. The gold is to protect the boat from harm, and the oil is used as a medicine to be rubbed on the keel should there ever be any trouble at sea.

We were up before sunrise the next morning, none of us had slept well and I'd had to get up twice in the night to use the bathroom, which had meant negotiating the ladder and a plastic scoop in the dark. Michael had procured some plastic cups of instant ready-sugared coffee and a banana each for breakfast. Aesha looked like she'd been crying; I asked her what was wrong. It turned out that Wajid had promised her a holiday in Bali. She had been expecting to drink cocktails at sleek beach clubs and had excitedly packed a teenie weenie bikini, two pairs of up-the-bum shorts, a miniskirt, a glamorous evening dress, a hairdryer and curling tongs, five kilos of makeup, and three pairs of high-heeled sandals. As an Indonesian Muslim, albeit not a devout one, Aesha was at risk of being scorned and treated with contempt by the villagers of Wera, who would have considered her to be a prostitute if they had seen her wearing the clothes she'd brought for Bali. She had nothing conservative to wear apart from the skinny jeans she had arrived in, and a rain jacket. We'd visited the village before, so we understood the need to dress respectfully. I lent Aesha a sarong and a pair of flipflops, and Jen lent her a T-shirt, I couldn't quite understand how there could have been such a gross miscommunication between a husband and wife.

I surveyed the scene on the beach. Old and young, men, women and children, it was a frenzy of activity. Aft of the keel, winches had been prepared and ten men on each side of the boat were tearing on the chains. A lengthy block of hardwood had been inserted under the base of the keel, with another line of men using it as a lever to rock the boat into position. A man on a megaphone, the 'director of operations,' was shouting orders. After a few minutes, the boat made its first move along the heavily greased slipway towards the sea; it was a tiny distance of less than a metre, but she was heading in the right direction. Out came a man with a chainsaw; a plank at the back end of the sled was cut away, and the procedure started again. Twenty minutes later, the boat moved another half-metre, and so it went on, slowly, slowly, each time to a resounding cheer.

Suddenly there was a loud bang, and a shout, and everyone leapt back. I could feel the communal dismay hanging heavily in the hot sultry air. The winch had broken and after a failed attempt to repair it, we were told that a new one must be brought over from the Island of Sangeang.

The women saw this as a cue to serve lunch. More rice, goat satay, beef stew and water was distributed to the residents and guests of the village, including some government officials who had driven over from Bima for a photo opportunity. Once again, I made do with plain rice and chilli sambal.

A new winch arrived, it was put into place and the process began again, the boat moved another metre. Peak tide was approaching, the sun was directly overhead, the heat was relentless, and everyone was seeking shade. Aesha was way too hot and uncomfortable in her skinny jeans and retreated back into the house. I needed to sit down, but there seemed to be no relief from the sun. A kindly, toothless old man in a checked *sarung* and a white crocheted prayer cap, guided me to a large stationary truck; it wasn't until I squatted down beside it that I realised it was full of blocks of ice. Here was my respite; the breeze was blowing across the ice blocks straight on to my shoulders and back. It felt deliciously cool against my hot sticky skin.

The boat shifted another metre then there was another alarming bang; the new winch had snapped in half. This time we were informed that a replacement would have to be flown all the way over from Surabaya, the sun was obscured by a cloud of disappointment, but – as if from nowhere – a welder appeared on the scene, and half an hour later, the winch had been repaired and the boat was on the move again.

By now, however, the window of high tide opportunity had gone, and the man on the megaphone announced, 'Enough for today.'

We were meant to be flying back to Bali that evening but having come this far and seen this much, we couldn't bear the thought of missing the launch, and it was vital that it should happen the next day while the moon was still full, and the beach still blessed by a king tide. We changed our flight and negotiated another night's accommodation at the house. Everyone was happy to stay except for poor Aesha who had no choice.

Phinisi vessels, a masterpiece of Bugis-Makassar design, are exceptionally strong and are famous for their ability to break through high waves and cover great distances. Some, such as SeaTrek's Ombak Putih, are built for the tourist industry and fitted out with luxury cabins and sundecks. Others, like Al Fatah, are built as freight carriers, with a capacity of eight hundred tonnes for transporting cargoes such as rice, timber or cement. Amazingly, they are still built the traditional way; the master boatbuilders do not have special engineering training. They don't need architectural drawings or complicated technical calculations to determine the quantity of materials needed. Using a method that would be unworkable in mainstream shipbuilding, the builders first lay the keel; the stem and stern post are erected, and then the side planks are assembled before the ribs without the need for a frame. Yet the builders can accurately establish the boat's balance so it will float perfectly when launched into the water.

'We just go with our instincts based on our vision and judgment,' the master builder told us, 'our eyes and our feelings guide us when we're building a boat.'

The next morning, everyone was back on the beach. Everyone, apart from me and the captain & crew of a tugboat that had been brought in to bring some engine power to the proceedings. I had boarded the tug to watch the launch from offshore – yes, everyone seemed confident it would happen that morning.

All the boat needed now was one major pull to give it the momentum to slide the last twenty metres into the sea.

A rope was attached.

The tug moved into position.

The engine strained.

The rope broke.

The exercise was repeated, while on either side of Al Fatah, a gang of men, women and kids were hauling on two parallel ropes; it was like a massive tug of war, except that everyone was pulling and pushing in the same direction, with one common goal.

Finally, after several more failed attempts, the behemoth vessel started to slide, picking up speed and suddenly unstoppable, upright and perfectly balanced, faster and faster until she hit the water with a colossal splash and a mighty wave of triumph before smoothly gliding to a buoyant halt.

One year earlier, Mount Sangeang may well have spectacularly erupted but that particular event had paled into insignificance compared to the triumphant eruption of joy from the elated villagers on the neighbouring shore.

45
AWESTRUCK IN BORNEO
2016

I remember standing in the school playground when I was ten years old watching a solar eclipse with my classmates under the supervision of our teacher. The world didn't go particularly dark but that's because it was only a partial eclipse. I'd never seen one since, until the ninth of March 2016, when I watched one in totality in the clear blue sky of Balikpapan, in East Kalimantan, Indonesian Borneo.

Five of us had been planning this trip for several months and had given a lot of thought as to where we wanted to watch it. The path of totality was due to start at sunrise in Sumatra, and arch through Kalimantan, Sulawesi, Ternate and the Moluccas, finishing at sunset to the north of Hawaii. We didn't have the luxury of time on our hands, so we chose the easiest place to reach from home, which was Balikpapan on the east coast of Kalimantan, and we booked a sea-view apartment in the modern Aston Hotel.

We have a statue of Ganesha in our garden in Bali and before we left home, I put a flower behind his ear and asked him for a clear sky. Ganesha is the god of making things happen, so I figured he was the right god to ask.

Although we were away from home for three days, we spent the best part of a day getting to our destination. It was only two short flights but there was rather a lot of waiting around between plane rides, so my four companions and I only had one full day in Balikpapan. Arriving at the oil-rich city, I was impressed by the modern airport, the efficiency of the taxi service, the wide roads, and the free-flowing traffic, and I decided it was more like a Malaysian city than a typical Indonesian city. More like Kota Kinabalu than Jakarta, for example, but this was Borneo after all.

Upon arrival, Michael and I were delighted to find that our hotel apartment was on the sixteenth floor with a balcony facing east over the ocean. The eclipse was due to start at seven-twenty-five a.m. and would last for two hours twenty-eight minutes with two minutes of totality at eight-thirty-four a.m., and of course it was going to happen bang on time.

We ascertained the height and position that the sun would be in the sky, and before we went to bed that night, I looked up at the stars – yes, the sky was clear – and whispered another silent prayer to Ganesha, who is also the remover of obstacles. *Please don't let there be any clouds.*

The Indonesians are great at turning any event – celestial or otherwise – into a celebration, and the Aston Hotel opened its doors to the public and came to the party with a *Jazzy Eclipse Breakfast*. After getting up early to witness an auspicious sunrise and an almost clear sky with scatterings of high cloud, we headed down to breakfast at seven o'clock and found the poolside area packed out with eclipse goers, clutching their specialist eclipse eyewear, and claiming their front row seats for what promised to be the most spectacular celestial event visible from Balikpapan in living memory. Lunar eclipses and partial solar eclipses come and go, they wax and wane, ebb and flow, but this was to be the first total solar eclipse to occur in this region since May 1901.

We saw TV cameras and professional eclipse chasers with their tripods, fancy camera equipment and huge telescopes set up along the waterfront. One man later told us it was his forty-third eclipse; his wife was on her eleventh. I figured these must be the sort of enthusiasts who sell their photos to NASA and National Geographic.

A live band was playing mellow jazz on the deck, cooking stations had been set up, and a grand breakfast buffet, including innovative delights such as crescent-shaped Eclipse Pizza along with black & yellow Eclipse Cakes, was spread out along the pool terraces. By the time we'd found a table and grabbed some breakfast, it was almost time for the show to begin. So, cafe lattés in hand, we retreated from the madding crowd and headed up to our private sixteenth floor 'royal box', which was possibly the best viewing station in the house. By now, the sky was completely clear, how lucky were we.

Up on the balcony we set the GoPro rolling on a time lapse, donned our blacker than black cardboard-framed eyewear, and stared up at the sun. All of us, that is, apart from one member of our intimate group of five, Kristen, who had loitered for just a few minutes longer over her breakfast with the words, 'I'll see you up there.'

The time was seven-thirty and already we could see a tiny nibble on the side of the sun. Gazing in awe, we were shaken from our state of wonderment by a phone ringing somewhere in the distance. After picking up the phone in the kitchenette and another receiver in the bedroom, I finally located the source of the ringing, which was my own mobile phone in a bag on the floor. I noted with confusion that the caller was Kristen.

'Hurry up and get your arse up here,' I shouted, 'it's already begun.'

Her voice when she replied, however, was strained and serious, ‘I've got a problem.’

‘Really?’ What could possibly have gone wrong between the pool deck and the sixteenth floor?

‘I'm stuck in the lift.’

She might as well have said, ‘Houston, we have a problem.’

I repeated her words back to her in disbelief.

‘Yes,’ she assured me, ‘too many people got in, it's overloaded, it suddenly jolted and dropped and now we're stuck between floors.’

Shit! The eclipse wasn't going to wait for anyone; after all our months of planning, the thought that Kris might miss the event was unbearable.

‘Hang on in there,’ I told her, ‘We're on our way, don't worry, we’ll get you out of there.’

All four of us ran to the three elevator doors on the corridor outside the room, where we noted in dismay that instead of indicating a number and a flashing arrow, one of the floor designators above the call button revealed two ominous parallel bars: a flat-line.

‘Stay on the phone,’ I told Kris, ‘We’re not going to leave you now.’

This was the material of disaster movies and I swelled with pride as Michael, our very own Bruce Willis, raced to the phone in our room to inform the staff at the reception desk.

By the time he returned, it was all over. A man on the inside with a walkie-talkie had informed an engineer on the outside and after establishing, with difficulty, which floor they were closest to, the doors had been forced by the engineer, and the shaken occupants of the lift had been rescued and our Kris was on her way up the stairs.

Thankfully, the eclipse was nowhere near over; the tiny nibble had become a bite-sized chunk, but we were still only fifteen minutes into the event. For the next forty-five minutes we watched enthralled as the moon passed between the Sun and the Earth, and the Sun slowly became a crescent.

We had been a tad sceptical about our eclipse eyewear, ordered in the mail from a distributor in Surabaya and emblazoned with the words *Souvenir Eyewear, Great American Eclipse, August twenty-first, 2017.* The manufactures obviously hadn't anticipated the demand for the total eclipse of March the ninth, 2016, and had had to break into the next year's supply. Upon testing our eyewear, the night before, by holding the black polymer filters – which are designed to transmit no more than 0.00032% of the Sun's light − right up close against lightbulbs and cigarette lighters, we couldn't see a damned thing. Had we been conned?

Staring through our filters at the Sun however, everything had become clear, or rather we could clearly see the sun as the black bite became bigger and the crescent of light became thinner.

Just before totality, a single point of glistening sunlight made the moon look like a diamond ring. Then the tiny points of light known as *Baily's Beads* appeared like a string of beads around the vanishing edge of the sun. We watched engrossed as the shadow of the moon swept across the sea and the shore, transforming daylight into twilight.

During the two minutes of totality, bright white streamers, the corona, which is the Sun's atmosphere, emanated around the dark disk, and in the eerie gloaming, the temperature dropped; the planet Venus and some stars appeared; and the birds stopped singing.

We, too, were awestruck into silence.

I whispered, *thank you,* to Ganesha; our mission had been a success.

46
THE PLANTING OF A SEED
2015

In this modern world of ours, where communication and planning between friends is accomplished via e-mails, mobile phone calls and text messages, impromptu home visits are rare. Stopping by without notice, which was at one time a routine way to visit a friend, is often frowned upon as being intrusive. Yet, despite today's cultural expectations, it's flattering to be the recipient of a surprise visit. Dropping in spontaneously can be a very authentic and intimate gesture, generating joy and excitement while reaffirming the strength of the friendship.

A few years ago, Michael was the recipient of one such delightful out-of-the-blue visit, when a knock on the front door signalled the arrival of our good friends, Stefano and Monique. They live in South Africa and we had no idea that they were holidaying in Bali at the time.

They were no strangers to Indonesia, we had met them a few years earlier when they'd been living in Bali, and we'd felt sad when the time had come for them to return to Cape Town. On this occasion, they were only in the hood for two days before heading off to surf the waves of Sumbawa. We quickly arranged to meet for dinner that evening in a nearby garden restaurant.

However, three hours spent around a dining table didn't give us enough time with these two lovely people, so we adjourned to our local watering hole, The Orchard, and continued drinking, catching up, reminiscing, telling stories, and making merry.

'You guys should come and visit us in South Africa,' proposed Stef.

'Yay! Let's! That would be awesome. Let's do that,' we drunkenly agreed, 'let's go to Soof Effrehca. What's the weather like in April?'

And just like that, the seed for an impulsive fanciful plan was sown.

Michael had suggested April because he'd already purchased a pair of bargain priced one-way tickets to visit Tokyo in the springtime. He wanted me to experience the centuries-old Hanami cherry blossom festival, which celebrates the traditional Japanese custom of enjoying the transient beauty of flowers. What did *that* have to do with South Africa, you may ask. Well, we'd not yet bought our return tickets, so this had sparked an idea to fly to Cape Town directly from Tokyo. It was a crazy itinerary for a two-centre holiday, which would require our suitcases to be packed with both cold- and warm-weather clothing, but hey, we had made a commitment; now all we had to do was book our onward flights.

Our surprise reunion with our South African buddies was about to become the most expensive night out that we'd ever had in a Bali pub.

My then-boyfriend-now-husband is nothing if not resourceful, he relishes the planning as much as the journey and the adventure, and he's always up for a challenge. He hopped on the Internet as soon as we got home to discover that flights from Japan to South Africa were ridiculously expensive, 'It's a preposterous idea, I think we've been a tad too hasty to agree to this,' he snorted.

But it was already well after midnight, so we decided to get some sleep and revisit the idea in the morning, and indeed, by the time I woke up, Michael was already on the phone to a man who was possibly in a position to help us.

Cousin Dan is a senior employee of a flag carrier airline, which offers each of its staff members the benefit of discounted flights for a limited number of relatives or friends, and he was happy to oblige us with return tickets from Tokyo to Johannesburg at a much more affordable price.

'What do you think?' Michael-the-facilitator turned to me with the phone still in his hand.

'Yes, let's go for it,' I eagerly replied.

'And there's more,' he grinned, 'we're gonna be travelling business class.'

Ten months later, we were on our way, heading first to Tokyo for twelve days, to be followed by sixteen days in South Africa.

47
THE HANAMI
2016

No one can guarantee the date that the cherry blossom trees will start blooming in Tokyo. The first flowering of this pink manifestation has been known to occur more than a week early or more than a week late, but it generally begins towards the end of March with the trees hitting full bloom about eight days later and continuing for another week. Naturally, it can be affected by heavy rains and strong winds, which knock the petals off. For the Japanese, the blossoms symbolise: 'A time of renewal, the fleeting nature of existence, the impermanence of beauty, and the essence of the moment.' During the Hanami, thousands of people flock to the parks, securing the best spots for picnics and parties.

I'd been to Tokyo a couple of times before but only for the briefest of brief stopovers; and I'd been overwhelmed. I couldn't quite get my head around *kawaii*, the Japanese culture of cuteness, Hello Kitty, cartoons everywhere, Disneyland-style love hotels, the vending machines that sell everything, and the musical toilets with heated seats. I didn't understand the obsession with photobooths, bizarre music videos, video game arcades, the eccentric Harajuku fashion, and Cosplay, which is the practice of dressing up as a character from a video game, a movie or a book. I just didn't get it.

I knew enough to understand that as an island nation with a long history of isolation, many aspects of the culture had developed completely unaffected by outside influences. This, understandably, made it very unique, but since my first visit, I'd been of the opinion that the place was downright weird.

Michael, however, had lived in Tokyo for six years before moving to Bali; he loved Japan and understood it, and he wanted me to love it too. You'll meet my friends; I'll show you around and I'll help you to make sense of it all.'

We flew into Tokyo on the last day of March, and luckily for us, our arrival coincided perfectly with the beginning of the cherry blossom fortnight. Wandering through the lovely Shinjuku Gyoen and picnicking under the flowering cherry trees on our first day, I began to see Japan with fresh eyes.

Everywhere was so clean. It felt safe, and I remembered that the Japanese are renowned for their honesty; a Bali friend had once told me how he'd accidentally left his cash-and-credit-card-filled wallet on the Tokyo Metro, but successfully recovered it by contacting the office of the lost and found.

A stranger approached us with two cans of Asahi beer; it was a gift. I observed that the local people were in a state of celebration at the arrival of spring, and I learnt that the spirit of valuing each distinct season is deeply rooted in the Japanese culture. They relish the flavours and freshness of their seasonal harvests and will often change the pictures on their walls in accordance with each season.

Near the Shinjuku train station, Michael took me to a hole-in-the-wall eatery in Yakitori Alley, where we drank beer and snacked on tasty grilled morsels under the railway arches.

At Omoide Yokochou – or Memory Lane, aka Piss Alley – we crossed the threshold into a different, darker Japanese world, which had once been the domain of post-war black-market traders. It was a dingy maze of crowded narrow alleyways filled with ramen shops, food stalls and a retro vibe. Yet the grit and the grime, the noise, and the smoke from the yakatori grills swirling out of open windows, was all part of the shabby charm.

At Nonbei Yokocho, or Drunkards Alley, close to the famous Shibuya Crossing, Michael introduced me to Tokyo's hidden nightlife, leading me into a series of tiny, very tiny, drinking bars, each measuring no more than ten feet by ten feet. Each one had a bartender and just five or six bar stools. Stacked above was another level, accessed by a tiny staircase and holding another tiny table or two. The narrow lanes outside were borderline creepy yet incredibly atmospheric, typified by barred windows, graffiti-covered walls, lamp posts plastered with stickers, and doors lit by neon signs and paper lanterns. I felt as if I had stepped onto the set of a movie. I was beginning to fall in love with this city.

In the ritzy Ginza shopping district, I was blown away by the shop window displays, each one an extraordinary work of art. And then there were the restaurant windows showcasing the world's most divine-looking plastic food, while serving exquisitely presented dishes of delicious-tasting *real* food where each edible item had been artistically shaped, coloured, and garnished. In fact, visual appeal was everywhere, ranging from the architecture to the cinematic tradition of Japanese anime. There is even a tradition called *kintsugi*, or golden joinery, the Japanese art of repairing broken pottery with pure gold.

Japanese people are extremely gracious hosts, and we became the beneficiaries of this generosity when we popped into a restaurant owned by one of Michael's old mates, a man called Michi. He was thrilled to reconnect with Michael for the first time in ten years and insisted on treating us to a marvellous four-course lunch. He mentioned that he would be going to the famous Tsukiji fish market early the next morning to buy more provisions for his restaurant and he invited us to join him.

I'd been to plenty of fish markets in Indonesia but nothing prepared me for the magnitude of Tsukiji.

We met Michi at six a.m. at the outer market and he led us into the inner wholesale market. 'Stick close to me,' he cautioned us, 'and don't take any photographs, the inner market is only open to traders at this time, and tourists are not allowed to enter until after nine o'clock, so don't expect welcoming faces. But don't worry,' he smiled, 'you'll be safe with me.' Walking through this colossal open-sided building, full of dedicated professionals with serious attitudes, we knew it would be highly uncool to draw attention to ourselves.

Seafood is one of Japan's biggest exports, and this was certainly the place to see it. Crammed with hundreds of vigorous wholesale operators in rubber boots selling every kind of seafood imaginable from sea urchin to deadly fugu pufferfish to whale meat, the energy was frenetic. Workers, transporting boxes of fish, glared at us as they haphazardly zoomed about in all directions on their electric turret trucks. Styrofoam containers, big blue buckets, hosepipes, plastic sheeting, blue nets, and boxes of ice were spread across tables and upon the shiny wet stone-tiled floors. We watched frozen tuna and swordfish being hacked with large band saws, and fresh tuna being carved with metre-long knives.

Here, in Japan's most iconic and historic marketplace, which had been operating since 1935, I was shocked and deeply saddened to see the vast quantities of the produce, including the giant Pacific bluefin tuna – the most expensive species in the world – as well as other near threatened and endangered species, which were being auctioned every day. Michi shared some of the statistics: three thousand tonnes of seafood, five hundred different species, valued at fourteen million dollars, sold daily.

After Michi had finished buying, he led us to a small eatery in the outer market where we joined some of the traders and breakfasted on the perfectly balanced texture and tenderness of some insanely fresh sashimi, served with a bottle of sake. This, evidently, was dinner, not breakfast, for the traders, who had been working through the night.

Two years later, in 2018, the Tsukiji inner market closed and relocated to a new site – the considerably less atmospheric Toyosu Market. We felt honoured to have been privy to such an authentic experience at Tsukiji, but this insight into the rape of the oceans and farcical notions of sustainability was the trigger for both of us to immediately stop eating tuna and to cut right back on our consumption of seafood.

~*~

I was stunned by how everything worked so smoothly in Japan, especially public transport. The average delay of the trains is less than one minute per year, which seemed like a very good reason to take the exciting high-speed bullet train to our next destination, the Hakuba Valley in the Japanese Alps. Here, we stayed with our friend Jen, who used to work for SeaTrek. She had just finished working at a ski resort.

Michael wanted me to experience an onsen. There are thousands of these public baths in Japan. Fed by hot springs, where the water has been heated naturally by geothermal energy, onsens offer plentiful health benefits due to the various minerals in the water. Most of the baths are segregated by gender, which meant I couldn't be accompanied by Michael. There are a number of rules and a definite onsen etiquette, and I was terrified at the thought of making an unforgiveable faux pas, so Jen agreed to accompany me.

The onsen she took us to in Hakuba was in a beautiful natural setting surrounded by snow-covered mountains; Jen assured me it would not be busy because the ski season was over. At least that meant there would be less people to witness my blunders.

Oh, and did I mention that the first rule of an onsen is that you have to get naked... fully naked.

Upon arrival, we were each given a modesty towel; it was very thin and about the size of a face cloth; not big enough to hide behind. Everyone is required to wash themselves thoroughly before entering the bath, and Jen instructed me to pull up a stool at one of the shower stations. I thought at first that I'd feel really uncomfortable walking out starkers into the open air, while being observed by a pool full of Japanese ladies. It was a daunting prospect. I tactically clutched my modesty towel close to my crotch, took a deep breath and entered the arena. Mercifully, there were only three other women there, and having overcome that first mental hurdle, I felt a certain kind of liberation.

'Now fold your towel and put it on top of your head,' whispered Jen.

And just like that, I entered the bath, immersed my body, soaked my skin and soothed my mind and bones in the hot healing waters, relishing yet another of Japan's ancient traditions.

I'd read that, 'In Japan, the old, the past, and the traditional coexist harmoniously with the modern and the futuristic.' After twelve days, I knew this to be true, and I was hooked.

48
THE LION, THE BAKKIE, AND THE BURNING TRAIN
2016

'Why didn't you just refuse to cooperate?' I demanded, angrily.

'That's not the way it works,' explained Michael, calmly.

'But we've paid for this.'

'Not really, we're flying on Dan's staff travel discount, remember?'

'But I thought our seats were guaranteed.'

'Our business class seats are on standby.'

'You didn't tell me that.'

'This is the way it works with staff travel.'

'How do you know?'

'Because my family used to fly on staff travel back in the days when Dad worked for Air New Zealand, remember?'

'But maybe there are other people here flying to Johannesburg on staff travel, why does it have to be us?'

'Because we're probably at the bottom of the pecking order, and anyway we have to be respectful and agree to cooperate, otherwise we'll be letting Dan down and he'll never give us a staff discount again.'

Bound for South Africa, we were at the business class check-in desk at Tokyo Airport; our wonderful holiday in Japan had come to an end, and part two of our trip was just about to begin. However, a courteous airline official had taken us to one side and sat us down, explaining that the business class section of our plane was overbooked by one seat. He had politely asked if one of us would consider flying in economy class.

I felt a bit let down but as Michael pointed out, there were two business class legs to this journey and it was only the first leg that was overbooked. I graciously agreed to the downgrade but only because I had travelled both business class and first class on some previous occasions and Michael had not yet experienced that pleasure. It was a night flight and the nice man had even said that he would block a row of four seats in economy so that I could stretch out and sleep. He added, 'There are still two business class passengers who haven't checked in yet, so there's still hope of a no show, I'll keep you posted.'

We moved into the departure lounge and kept our ears tuned in the hope of hearing our names being called over the tannoy. Eventually, the staff invited the business class passengers to start boarding the plane. 'Damn. Those no-shows must have shown up,' I said to Michael, 'Go on, join the line for business class, they're probably serving the Champagne already.'

'Nah, the least I can do is join your line and wait with you,' replied Michael chivalrously.

We reached the head of the queue and handed over our passports and boarding passes. A uniformed woman put my boarding pass into the scanner, which promptly emitted a loud bleeping sound. Simultaneously, as Michael's boarding pass was inserted into another machine, the same thing happened. Confusion reigned for a few seconds. 'It looks like your seat numbers have been changed,' the woman said, handing us both a new boarding pass each.

It was only then that I noticed our nice man standing to one side of the barrier. 'The other two passengers were a no-show,' he smiled, 'I decided to wait and surprise you.'

Both legs of our business class flight were a delight. Michael sipped Champagne and worked his way through the menu, while I slept like a log in my fully-flat bed, although at one point Michael insisted on waking me up to look out of the window for a magnificent aerial view of the Horn of Africa.

~*~

While planning our trip to South Africa, we had arranged to spend two nights with the good friend of a good friend who lives near Johannesburg. Then, instead of flying to Cape Town from there, we had booked tickets on the *Premier Classe* train because we'd been told that if we took a plane, we'd miss the most amazing change of scenery.

Even though we were going to be looked after by friends, I was still experiencing a certain amount of trepidation about visiting South Africa. Monique and Stef, as well as another South African friend, had often mentioned that people they knew well had experienced the terror and trauma of a 'home invasion.' I remembered that a famous South African reggae star, Lucky Dube, who also happened to be a friend of one of my friends, had been shot dead at a set of traffic lights. In fact, according to the British Government's foreign travel advice website, 'South Africa has a high rate of crime, including carjacking, house robbery, rape, and murder.' We'd heard that it was relatively safe in the tourist areas. We knew that we should be vigilant but we weren't going to let worry and dread ruin our holiday.

Willem, who was to be our host, has a water bottling business in a small rural settlement called Muldersdrift about sixty kilometres northwest of Johannesburg Airport. He was there to meet us at the international arrivals terminal when we landed; he told us he'd be wearing a red hat and we spotted him right away. As he led us into the carpark, he explained that he was driving a *bakkie*, which is the South African word for a pick-up truck. He apologised because there were only two seats in the front cabin instead of the conventional bench seat. As far as I could tell, the back end was open to the elements, theft, abuse, and potentially murder. Half of the back was filled with about a dozen one-gallon water bottles that Willem was delivering en route. My heart began to thump in my throat. It was six p.m., rush hour, and there was no way we could all squeeze into the front for a road journey that could take as long as two hours at this time of day. Michael said he was cool to travel in the back, along with our luggage – all our worldly goods at that moment. He climbed in and off we went, driving through the suburbs of Johannesburg at dusk.

There was a back windscreen between the cab and the pickup box, so at least I could see Michael. I kept turning around to make sure he was okay, but we could only communicate with waves, smiles and thumbs up. Scores of men were walking and running along both sides of the busy main road, nimbly dodging the traffic as they crossed from one side to the other.

'They're on their way home from work,' explained Willem.

Initially, we had to stop at red traffic lights every five or ten minutes, and my mind was filled with anxiety as I recalled the tragic story of the much-loved but inopportunely-named, Lucky Dube, who'd been shot dead in front of his children in a botched car-jacking. We passed gated communities enclosed by twelve-foot-high walls topped with barbed wire and electric fences. We'd only just arrived in the country and already I was living in fear. Michael, however, had blocked it all out; he'd put on his headphones and was singing along to Bowie.

As we left the suburbs behind and entered a more rural area, I began to relax, and we stopped at a hotel restaurant for a hearty feed, where Willem also dropped off his water bottles. Our journey continued for another twenty minutes although by now it was too dark to enjoy the scenery.

Eventually, Willem turned into a driveway. 'Welcome to my home.'

The house proved to be a classic South African farmhouse, single-storey with solid, white-painted stone walls and a red-tiled roof. The interior was simple and plain, with a basic kitchen, functional bathroom, very little furniture and bare walls; it was minimalistic but not in an intended, stylish way. Willem later told us that break-ins were so common that there was no point in keeping anything of any value in the house. He had no TV, no artwork; he played his music on an old tape recorder and wrote his emails on an ancient desktop computer.

Michael and I were both jetlagged so we bolted the doors and went to bed early and then woke with the birds at dawn. Curious to see the landscape in daylight, we quickly got dressed and ventured outside where we found a gorgeous little veranda with a half wall and three Tuscan-style stone pillars supporting a flat roof. The house was in the middle of nowhere, sitting on a block of land filled with trees and bordered by the Magaliesberg mountains.

As the sun rose behind the foothills, the hairs on my arms stood up on end and my spine tingled with the sudden deeply rooted awareness that I was in Africa. I mean, *of course* I was in Africa, we'd landed at O.R. Tambo Airport the previous day, but this was my moment of validation. Africa feels very different from Asia; it feels, smells, looks, sounds and tastes like only Africa can, and this was the same sensation I'd had upon landing in Tanzania twenty years before.

And then we heard it...

A resonating, low-pitched call, ringing out from across the wilderness. Followed immediately by another deep echoed grumble.

It was a lion's roar.

'Surely not? It couldn't be?'

'Definitely,' replied Michael, drawing on the same primal instinct that I'd experienced only a minute earlier.

We told Willem over breakfast.

'Ha, we have a game reserve next door,' he laughed, adding, 'Would you like me to take you there?'

An hour later we were back in the bakkie, enjoying an unexpected mini safari through the beautiful Bothongo Rhino and Lion Nature Reserve, where we saw four of the big five as well as African wild dogs, cheetahs, zebras, antelopes galore and plenty more. Michael and I both sat in the back until we entered the lion park, at which point we were instructed by a staff member to squeeze into the front.

Which was more dangerous? I pondered. *Riding the back of a bakkie through the suburbs of Jo'burg, or riding an open-backed bakkie into the lion's den?*

~*~

The next day, we set off for Johannesburg Railway Station. Willem was driving, and again Michael sat in the back with our luggage. The journey felt deceptively less scary this time because it was a much shorter distance undertaken in broad daylight and the first twenty kilometres was on the motorway. Everything was going well until Willem turned to me and said, 'I'm feeling very dizzy, would you mind driving?'

I decided I'd rather sit in the back than behind the wheel.

And I'd rather sit in the back than in the front with a vertiginous driver.

And we had to be at the railway station by ten a.m.

We stopped the car.

Michael agreed to drive but he needed Willem to sit in the front with him to navigate.

I climbed into the back.

Surprisingly the experience wasn't as nerve-wracking as I had imagined. It was probably foolish, but this was our only option and we had a train to catch.

Downtown Johannesburg was quieter than I would have expected for a Thursday morning. We arrived safely at the station, thanked Willem for his kind hospitality and advised him to take a rest and rehydrate before driving home.

Inside the station, we were shown to the Premier Classe lounge before boarding our train to Cape Town. An affordable alternative to the famous five-star Blue Train, the Premier Classe rail journeys were designed for tourists and marketed as South Africa's 'budget luxury.' We had a private four-berth sleeper compartment for the pair of us, which gave us the two lower berths, for the 1510-kilometre, twenty-six-hour trip through the heart of the country, with all of our meals included. In addition to the dining car, there was a lounge bar with armchairs and sofas where we hung out with our fellow passengers, about twenty of us altogether plus the crew. And with fine Cape wines at pleasingly low prices, it proved to be a jolly, social journey.

The motley assortment of passengers included a loud Australian bogan called Sheila (yes, really) who was travelling on her own, a young Filipino couple on their honeymoon, a pair of American thrill-seekers called Brandon and Troy, an opinionated English lush called Sally and her timid husband, and an Afrikaans couple, Frederich and Elna, who lived in Capetown and were on their way home after visiting their new granddaughter in Jo'Burg. The staff were fun and friendly, especially Theo, our exceptionally camp, chief steward.

The railway had been built in the late 1800s spurred by the discovery of diamonds in Kimberley, which determined the routes for the laying of the iron tracks, followed by the next bonanza – gold – when the lines were extended north to Johannesburg. We were now riding those historic tracks and after clearing the city suburbs, the scenery became increasingly spectacular.

We divided our journey time between our private compartment and, naturally, the lounge bar, where we mingled with the other guests and spoke of travel and adventure as the train climbed towards the Karoo Plateau. We all dressed for dinner that evening, just like they do on the cruise ships. We shared a table with the honeymooners, pretending to show an interest in the tedious particulars of their wedding day, when the train lurched just as I happened to be pouring some red wine into the groom's glass. Unfortunately, it splashed onto his pristine white shirt. I apologised profusely, he assured me it was okay, but his wife – I'll call her Precious – glared at me as if it was her wedding dress I'd wrecked. They both left the table and we didn't see them again until the next morning. Maybe they had more important things to do, it *was* their honeymoon after all.

Waking up in our sleeper beds to the sun rising while we trundled through the haunting barrenness of the Great Karoo is an experience I will never forget. Home to vast plains, wildlife, and high rocky escarpments, this ancient semi-desert is bigger than Germany. Surprisingly, there are towns out there too, steeped in history and intrigue. In 1867, Kimberley, the provincial capital of the Northern Cape, was the site of the biggest diamond rush ever seen.

Later, we stopped in Beaufort West to stretch our legs and befriended a dog on the station platform. We continued through a savannah-type landscape, and then watched as the grasslands became greener, giving way to lush arable land and fruit farms. Traversing the Hex River Pass, we entered the Cape wine region, where vineyards sprawl under towering mountains. On the approach to Cape Town, we went past shanty towns, until finally, the sight that we'd all been waiting for, the most iconic landmark of South Africa, Table Mountain, came into view.

Suddenly, our train screeched to a shuddering halt. The abruptness was alarming, an emergency perhaps. An accident? A train-jacking? Now that our journey was almost over, the edginess that had been defining South Africa in my mind had returned. Why had we stopped at this small station halt? I couldn't even read the name on the sign. It most certainly wasn't Cape Town Station.

'We must be on a red signal,' said Michael.

'We're only about a mile from the main station,' Frederich informed us knowledgably.

'There seems to be a problem,' announced Theo after about twenty minutes, 'our driver is on the phone to the stationmaster now.'

We had all moved into the bar by this stage but Theo then summoned his staff for a team meeting.

Precious looked scared.

Frederich looked angry.

Another fifteen minutes went by.

The crew returned but had notably all changed out of their uniforms.

'What's going on?' demanded Frederich.

'We don't want to draw attention to ourselves,' explained Theo. 'There have been some riots; local commuters are protesting about the illegal twenty percent hike in rail fares, and three trains have been set on fire. We're concerned that, as a tourist train, we might be a target. He noisily started dropping the blinds on the windows. 'May I suggest that you all go back to your compartments, close your blinds and hide from view.'

There was a tormented wail from behind me, Precious had collapsed into a flood of tears and wracking sobs, her new husband was trying to comfort her. 'She's a bit frightened.'

Frederich, meanwhile, was blasting Theo. 'You're supposed to be in charge here, you're meant to be protecting us yet you've changed out of your uniform like a coward. I will be making a formal complaint to Premier Classe trains and to PRASA' (the Passenger Rail Agency of South Africa).

'I think it's all rather exciting,' remarked Sally-the-lush.

We did as we were told and dropped the blinds in our sleeper compartments before returning to the bar, where Theo offered everyone a drink on the house.

I just wanted to get there; we'd been at a standstill for about forty-five minutes. Michael was trying to contact Monique on WhatsApp but the train's Wi-Fi signal had dropped.

Brandon and Troy, the two thrill seekers, had come up with a plan. With an open map spread over one of the tables in the lounge, they were calculating the distance and route from our current position to Cape Town Station. They were plotting their escape. Fascinated, we joined them around the table, but not because we wanted to go with them.

'If we can get over that bridge, we should be fine.'

'This is way too dangerous,' scoffed Sally's timid husband.

'So near and yet so far,' bemoaned Elna.

'I'd never be able to carry my luggage that distance,' observed Sheila.

'Look!'... screeched Sally, she'd raised the blind and was pointing out of the window, where we could see thick black smoke billowing up into the sky; we were even close enough to hear the electric overhead cables cracking and fizzling above the tracks.

Precious started crying again, snot pouring out of her nose. No longer looking like a beautiful bride, the poor girl was, indeed, terrified.

A decision had been made by the escape committee.

'We're going,' declared Brandon.

'I strongly advise you not to,' said Theo.

But the two American adventurers had already slung their bags over their shoulders. 'We're not waiting any longer, goodbye everyone.'

'Fools,' muttered Frederich.

Michael had finally got through to Monique, she knew exactly what was going on, and explained that there was a queue of trains waiting to get into the station and they just had to move two more out and then we would be head of the queue. She told us she was waiting in the station master's office; he was a friend of hers and had allowed her to park her car on the station platform inside the building. *A car on the platform*? I'd never heard of such a thing.

It was to be another hour before our train pulled into Cape Town Station. Monique was on the platform to meet us, along with the stationmaster. 'Welcome to Cape Town,' she looked remarkably calm, her only concern had been for us. 'I'm so sorry you had to wait so long,' she said, as she led us to her vehicle, which indeed was parked on the platform – a safety feature, accessed via a tunnel and perfect for a quick exit in times of peril.

'We've got an awesome holiday planned for you guys.'

And *awesome* was exactly how it turned out to be: from fine dining and wine tastings at the region's most prestigious vineyards, to swimming in the icy waters of the Atlantic at the famous Camps Bay, backed by the Twelve Apostles Mountain Range. We took a trip to the Cape of Good Hope, went cage diving with great white sharks, observed brown-striped Cape mountain zebras, and visited a colony of African penguins at Boulders Beach.

Finally, while revelling in the gift of a seafront apartment for our last few days, we took a cable car ride up Table Mountain, where, just for the hell of it, Michael and I joyfully danced upon the tabletop.

~*~

Since our trip in 2016, well over two hundred train carriages were set alight in South Africa in apparent arson attacks, with many of these incidents occurring in Cape Town and believed to be the result of a bitter dispute between PRASA and the two rail unions.

The Premier Classe trains stopped operating in 2020 due to Covid, and at the time of writing they no longer run. Two-thirds of the overhead cables that covered more than three thousand kilometres of track have been stripped by criminals looking to make money from scrap. We were very fortunate to have the opportunity to experience such an unforgettable train journey, but tragically the great South African Railways has since been brought to its knees by mismanagement, corruption, vandalism and theft.

49
RUMPY PUMPY IN THE RAINFOREST
2017

No other bird family is as beautiful or displays such a diversity of plumage, extravagant decoration, and courtship behaviour as the ostentatious birds of paradise, of which there are thirty-nine species. The male pole dancers strut and dazzle in costumes worthy of the stage, parading cropped capes and skirts, frills, ruffs and puffs, bonnets, neck wattles, expandable fan-like tails, streamers and twisted wiry feathers that curl like handlebar moustaches.

Back in 1988, I remember sitting down on four non-consecutive Monday evenings to watch the BBC TV series, *Ring of Fire*. This Indonesian odyssey documented the ten-year voyage of two English adventurers, Lawrence Blair and his late brother Lorne, through the world's largest and least-known archipelago. Travelling across uncharted lands, through islands where no white people had ever set foot, they explored places still blank and unknown on maps. The brothers sailed with pirates, got lost at sea, encountered primitive tribes and exotic creatures, lived with shamans and headhunters, and delved into the secrets surrounding the gods, demons and spirits of the oceans, jungles and mountains. Their extraordinary and captivating story had a powerful and lasting impact upon me. In truth, part of the reason why I had jumped at the opportunity to live in Bali was because I longed to explore these incredible places for myself.

I never imagined, all those years back that I would one day meet Lawrence Blair and hear some of those astonishing stories from the man himself. Yet, Bali is the place he calls home and I often see him around, or attend his occasional film screenings.

It was the Ring of Fire series that first introduced me to the fabled birds of paradise, and I finally got the opportunity to see some of these fantastical creatures in their natural habitat upon a tiny island in Raja Ampat.

Traversed by the Equator off the extreme north-western tip of Indonesia's Papua province, Raja Ampat is an archipelago of six hundred islands; a figure that can be boosted to more than fifteen hundred if you count the karst islets, which are so undercut by waves that they look like mushrooms, topped with rich jungle to create an astonishing, polka dot topography. The larger islands are distinguished by rugged coastlines covered with virgin rainforest extending right down to the water's edge, where nature has carved out a series of coves and lagoons, inlets, caves, and shaded, sandy beaches. If truth be told, the pure, unadulterated splendour of Raja Ampat astounds anyone who ventures the enormous distance to get there. In early 2017, Michael and I, and four of our friends – Kristen, Phil, Linda and Benita – ventured that enormous distance, but not without a little bit of drama along the way.

We flew from Bali to Makassar to Manado where we almost missed our connecting flight to Sorong because Michael was carrying a bottle of Johnny Walker. The rule on domestic flights in Indonesia is that alcohol must be carried in hand luggage, and we've done this, many times. On this occasion, Michael had cracked the seal on the bottle and had taken a sneaky sip. The broken seal was spotted by an eagle-eyed official – an arrogant, angry-looking man with a moustache – at the baggage scanner, who then informed Michael that he couldn't take it on board. Even worse was this man's self-satisfied glee at confiscating something that he clearly wanted for himself.

'Fuck!' said Michael to Phil, getting himself into even more trouble as the smug official turned on him, gesticulating wildly with his finger.

'You say fuck to me? You say fuck to me? No, you don't say fuck to *me*.'

At this point, our plane had already boarded, Phil and Michael's names were being called over the tannoy, and Linda and I were spanning the gate, begging the crew to hold the flight for a few more minutes.

'Our friends have been delayed at the security check.'

Unbeknown to us, Michael and Phil were in danger of being escorted to the 'little room' and detained for being rude to the airport security officials. There were only two flights per week.

'No, no,' said Michael, backpedalling, 'I didn't say fuck to you, not to you, never to you, I was saying fuck to the situasi… the situation.'

The smug moustached man let them go, keeping the bottle for himself, and they raced to the departure gate, feeling relieved yet pissed off at the same time. At least they made the flight and we all made it to Sorong, where we met up with Kristen and Benita, and boarded SeaTrek's Ombak Putih for yet another crazily wonderful adventure, this time through the waters of Raja Ampat.

~*~

While the predominant colour in the picture-postcard image of the tropics is blue, Raja Ampat is decidedly green. Here, translucent turquoise waters lap the scorching white sand beaches, coral reefs are identified by shining ribbons of aquamarine, and secret lagoons form the settings for emerald gems. The green theme persists in the deeper, distinctly jade-coloured channels that run between the many islands, morphing to milky mint in the narrow, river-like passages, all of which reflect the unrelenting verdure of the thickly forested hills.

On our first afternoon, about a minute before the Ombak Putih reached the Equator, the captain cut the engine, and the ship's GPS was displayed for us all to see on the big screen in the salon. As we counted down to zero degrees, we bore witness to the line-crossing ceremony, a centuries-old rite of passage to initiate Equator-crossing virgins into King Neptune's realm. According to the time-honoured custom, sailors who have never traversed the nautical line are forced to prove they are worthy to make the transition, often in a degrading, sometimes-brutal way, through a series of humiliating rituals. But, of course, that's not what happens to guests on civilian cruise ships.

Aboard the Ombak Putih, the ship's purser appeared in the guise of King Neptune, his trident in his hand and his crown upon his head, along with his representative, Davy Jones, and his royal court – a rowdy, colourful entourage. Amid the boisterous banging of old tin cans, the shaking of makeshift maracas, and the clashing of saucepan lids, we all jumped overboard, a drop of at least six metres, and triumphantly straddled the Equator with a leg in each hemisphere.

Each day, we donned fins, masks and snorkels and explored a below-surface world that was reminiscent of a living kaleidoscope. So beautiful was this underwater ecosystem that at times I felt like I was in a giant aquarium, expecting to swim up against a wall of glass at any moment, with onlookers regarding me from the other side.

Above the surface, Raja Ampat presents an exceptional wealth of exotic bird life, with hornbills, kingfishers, parrots, and five different bird of paradise species including the fabulous Red bird of paradise. Our voyage took us to the West Papuan island of Gam in the knowledge that every morning at dawn – during mating season – at the very top of the tallest tree, way up high on a forested ridge, the Red birds of paradise come out to perform their elaborate courtship dance.

I awoke at a ridiculously early hour, it was dark, wet and windy outside, and despite the fact that I'd been wanting to see these birds for almost as long as I could remember, I nearly changed my mind and very nearly stayed in my comfortable bunk.

'I don't think the birds come out in the rain.'

After a few minutes of indecision, my fear of missing out won the argument. I hauled myself out of bed and joined my companions, setting out in the inflatable tender and using a flashlight to identify the rendezvous spot on a nearby beach, where a local guide, Paulus, was waiting.

'Keep as quiet as you can,' he instructed, 'and you may spot a cuscus along the way.'

'What's a cuscus?' I enquired.

'You'll see,' he smiled, enigmatically, as he ushered us into the mist-shrouded forest for a slippery forty-minute hike up a steep, muddy track in the hope that the rain would stop in time for the birds to appear and do their thing.

Each male goes to the same tree every year to do it; some even use the same dancing trees generation after generation.

Luckily for us, the sky cleared, the sun came out and so did the birds. We heard them before we saw them, the males using clear, rising whistles and bell-like calls to broadcast their location and entice distant females, including me, to come and have a look. Then, silhouetted against the light of the new day, four males entered the canopied arena, their tail wires streaming behind them. Five minutes later, the arrival of two females, distinguished by their lack of ornamentation, sent the males into an ecstatic frenzy, each one lowering his head and erecting his plumes over his back.

What makes for such a sexy blend of attire and choreography is a mystery, but the more excessive the better, and all with the single purpose of attracting female attention. As the sky got brighter, their gorgeous colours came alive – the male's yellow beak, his iridescent emerald-green face, a pair of bottle green cushion-like feather pompoms above each eye and a train of glossy red plumes. What followed next was a shameless sex show, with one of the males posturing stiffly before hanging upside down from his branch. He then spread and fluttered his wings in a crimson fountain, claimed his prize and bowed to his voyeuristic audience below.

The sun was shining brightly when we emerged from the steamy jungle at the jetty from where we had begun our adventure three hours earlier, and we were able to see the enchanting little village of Saporkren, which we had bypassed in the dark. If the birds of paradise live in Paradise, then Saporkren must be the gateway. A big archway marked the entrance to the village, with a cheerful welcome message, and hand-painted images of the birds.

The place was idyllic, a quintessential paradise beach with soft white-gold sand, coconut palms, gaily-painted canoes, friendly families, happy smiling children, and pellucid luminous-turquoise waters. The final delight was when one of the villagers drew our attention to a cuscus – a marsupial, similar to a possum – eyeing us from the top of a fig tree. He was the size of a big pussycat with a pointy snout, ginger face, huge orange eyes and a gorgeous coat with caramel-on-white splotches arranged like dappled sunlight, camouflaging him within the leaves. His prehensile tail was long enough to wrap around a branch and strong enough to support his weight; the lower half covered in rough scales on the inside surface to give him grip. A local woman handed me a banana attached to the end of a long stick, the cuscus took the bait and obligingly posed for a photo.

The day had barely begun and yet I had already witnessed the dating dance of the rare Red birds of paradise and now I was feeding a banana to a spotted cuscus. Paradise indeed!

~*~

50
A MAGICAL WISHING LAKE
2001, 2015, 2017

Lying off the northern coast of Sumbawa is an ancient strato-volcano island called Satonda. This entire, small, circular island – just two kilometres in diameter – is the top of an emerging volcano, rising a thousand metres from the ocean floor with just three hundred metres exposed above sea level. In the centre, occupying the crater of the old volcano, is a mysterious salt-water lake that takes up about half of the island's surface.

Scientists have concluded that Satonda was thrust upwards by a volcanic eruption that took place on the sea floor some ten thousand years ago. Yet the salt lake was formed only two hundred years ago by the phenomenal eruption of the nearby Mount Tambora, which shook the world on the fifteenth of April 1815. This was the biggest volcanic explosion in the collective memory of mankind – spewing dust, polluting the Earth's atmosphere, and causing what became known as *the year without a summer* because of the effect on North American and European weather.

It is believed that the eruption of Mount Tambora also caused a tsunami, which filled Satonda's two nested calderas with saltwater.

This crater lake is much saltier than the sea and is surrounded by a ring of steeply forested land. Scientifically, it represents an ecosystem of global significance, unmatched by any other site currently known worldwide.

The local people believe that the lake is magical, and the residents of Nangamiro village in Sumbawa have long journeyed to Satonda to make a wish by tying a small stone or a piece of coral to one of the *wishing trees* at the edge of the lake. If a wish comes true, the wish maker is bound to return to the lake and give thanks in the form of an offering.

In April 2015, almost exactly two hundred years to the day since Tambora had erupted and caused the tsunami that had filled Satonda's crater with seawater, I was standing at the side of the lake, and I had a dilemma. In 2001, I had visited the lake for the first time. I had made a wish and it had come true. It was the type of wish that doesn't come true immediately – along the lines of *I wish I could still be living in Indonesia and still be living my dream many years from now* – and after fourteen years it was quite clear that my wish had been granted.

I made a new wish, and I gave thanks for the happy outcome of the original wish, but I didn't make an offering…

Four months later, chance, fate, luck, or that whole *living the dream* thing had brought me back to Satonda again, but my original wish and my new wish had both been weighing rather heavily on my mind, and here was my dilemma. My first wish had come true, but I hadn't made the required offering, did that mean that my equally important second wish might not come true?

Well, now I was being given the chance to rectify the situation. I would make an offering and I would reinforce my second wish. But what sort of offering? I couldn't possibly kill an animal, and while I was totally prepared to give thanks by offering up something of value, I would want someone else to appreciate it, I couldn't bear to waste something precious by tossing it to the bottom of the lake.

I then remembered that the animist element of any religion in Indonesia requires the ritualistic shedding of blood. In the Balinese village of Tenganan, for example, there is an annual theatrical fight known as *mekare-kare*, which takes place between the young men, utilising prickly pandanus leaf whips. Each dual lasts only a few seconds; as soon as blood is drawn, the game is over. There are no winners and no losers because the objective is to draw blood as an offering to the gods.

I made my decision; I would make a blood offering to the lake. A sterilised needle and a quick prick to the tip of my forefinger, and the job was done. I washed the tiny speck of blood off my finger in the salty, healing waters of the lake. I then tied a small piece of broken coral to one of the wishing trees and reiterated my second heartfelt wish.

Again, it was not the type of wish that comes true instantly, and it was not solely dependent upon luck...

Yet, as I write this, eight years later, having returned to Satonda on at least four more occasions, having made a third, highly significant wish and later another blood offering, I can confidently confirm that, in my experience, Satonda wishes really *do* come true.

These days when I visit the lake, I no longer make wishes, and if you're wondering why, it's because I decided it was now more important to count my blessings and give thanks.

I am so fortunate and so happy with my life and with the decisions I have made. I followed my heart and, of course, it hasn't all been easy, but I am truly living my dream.

And that, my friend, is more than enough.

~*~

To be continued...

Made in United States
North Haven, CT
29 August 2023

40889746R10243